Efficient Organization

Efficient Organization

A Governance Approach

MIKKO KETOKIVI AND JOSEPH T. MAHONEY

OXFORD
UNIVERSITY PRESS

OXFORD
UNIVERSITY PRESS

Oxford University Press is a department of the University of Oxford. It furthers
the University's objective of excellence in research, scholarship, and education
by publishing worldwide. Oxford is a registered trade mark of Oxford University
Press in the UK and certain other countries.

Published in the United States of America by Oxford University Press
198 Madison Avenue, New York, NY 10016, United States of America.

Library of Congress Control Number: 2022920525

ISBN 978–0–19–761029–9 (pbk.)
ISBN 978–0–19–761028–2 (hbk.)

DOI: 10.1093/oso/9780197610282.001.0001

1 3 5 7 9 8 6 4 2

Paperback printed by Marquis, Canada
Hardback printed by Bridgeport National Bindery, Inc., United States of America

To the memory of Oliver Williamson

Contents

Preface

If you own shares in a limited liability company and vote on the composition of its board of directors at the annual meeting of the shareholders, you are a designer. If you are one of the cofounders of a startup firm contemplating how to split equity among the founding team, you are a member in a group of designers. If you are the founder and the artistic director of a nonprofit theater thinking of how to curate the upcoming season, you are a designer. If you are a civil servant analyzing which parts of prison operations can be contracted out to private firms without jeopardizing the integrity of the prison facility, you are a designer. If you are a student of business administration, sociology, law, psychology, or political science interested in organizations, you may one day be a designer. This is a book written for the designer.

When contemplating design decisions, we invite all designers to embrace the following simple premise: If there are two alternative ways of organizing, choose the option that generates the least amount of waste. The challenge must not be underestimated, because many forms of waste are difficult to uncover. To be sure, the idea of wasting *money* and *time* seems salient. But how about the idea that *attention* and *communication* can be wasted? Or, that sometimes *routines* and *procedures* may develop into forms of "institutionalized waste," that is, waste that has become taken for granted?

Our goal in this book is to enable designers to think of how to identify and minimize all forms of organizational waste to maintain an *efficient organization*. Of all the alternative ways of organizing, the one that produces less waste than the others is, in economic terms, *comparatively efficient*. Importantly, all comparatively efficient alternatives will have flaws, but they are still the ones the designer should choose, at least until a better alternative becomes available.

We distinguish between two kinds of efficiency: myopic and sustainable. The former focuses on short-term gains through some form of exploitation. For example, a powerful buyer improves its cost efficiency by squeezing every penny out of its small suppliers by aggressively renegotiating contracts at contract renewal; an employer demands that employees work overtime without additional pay; those who possess information not available to others use the information asymmetry to their advantage. These are all examples of *myopic efficiency*.

We are not interested in writing about the benefits of opportunistic behavior and short-term gains. On the contrary, our intention is to enable forward-looking designers to organize in ways that promote *sustainable efficiency*: eliminating the excess, not the essential; nurturing cooperation, not jeopardizing it; seeking mutual value creation, not selfish value capture. We still subscribe to self-interest, just not its strong-form manifestations of opportunism and exploitation. We are interested in myopic efficiency only insofar as the honest designer can create governance structures that discourage those inclined to act opportunistically. Nobel Laureate Oliver Williamson, to whom we have dedicated this book, famously counseled that "the world should not be organized to the advantage of the opportunistic against those who are more inclined to keep their promises" (Swedberg 1990, 126). By embracing the objective of sustainable efficiency, our book joins Williamson's cause.

Economist Frank Knight (1941) was the first to describe an economically efficient organization as one that succeeds in eliminating waste. Because we want the word *efficiency* to invoke positive connotations, Knight's description creates the appropriate association.

However, seeking to minimize even the excess may sometimes miss the point of sustainable efficiency. It is well established that designers often consider some forms of excess, or *organizational slack*, desirable even when they seek to be sustainably efficient: (1) industrial firms keep inventories as buffers for demand uncertainty; (2) much like a basketball team wants to have several substitute players available "on the bench," professional service firms maintain a "healthy bench" by assigning no more than, say, 90 percent of their professionals to client projects at any given time; (3) it is well advised not to have organizational members process the maximal amount of information but, rather, "give them some (cognitive) slack;" and so on. Organizations maintain at least some slack for the same reason we all maintain a safe distance to the car in front of us while driving—to buffer against the unexpected.

Organization scholars Richard Cyert and James March ([1963] 1992) noted that non-zero slack makes organizations interesting. We not only concur but also suggest that deciding when and where to introduce slack into an organization and how to govern it belong to the heart of governance and to the designer's agenda.

To be sure, our intention is not to suggest that efficiency should be the designer's only objective. We propose that organizational efficiency can usefully be thought of as analogous to a person's blood pressure. In your annual medical exam, your doctor seeks to obtain an accurate reading of your blood pressure because your blood pressure is relevant, not because it is the most important thing about your health. Then, if your blood pressure is uncomfortably high, the doctor will invite you to a conversation about a possible intervention. At the risk of insulting your intelligence, let us state the obvious: The doctor's prescription does not mean that your life from that moment on should be about how to manage your blood pressure, let alone that the reason for your existence is to maintain a low blood pressure.

Echoing the blood pressure analogy, we do not propose that the purpose of an organization is to be efficient; we merely suggest that efficiency merits attention. With those who embrace the premise that efficiency matters, we engage in a conversation on the ramifications. With those who reject it, we would still try to strike a conversation on the ways in which avoiding waste might be relevant. This, too, is analogous with the doctor-patient relationship. Whether your blood pressure is of interest to you or not, your doctor will try to persuade you to pay attention to it. If you choose to ignore the issue, your doctor immediately withdraws all prescription. At the same time, your decision to ignore your high blood pressure changes neither the doctor's conviction nor the fact that a high blood pressure can be hazardous to your health.

Just as most physicians are convinced blood pressure is relevant to a person's health, we are convinced that sustainable efficiency is relevant to all organizations. We also trust that just like most of us choose to give attention to our blood pressures, most designers are sufficiently motivated to give attention to efficiency. If the organization in question is the designer's own, the motivation arises directly from the fact that the designer is likely the primary bearer of the costs of inefficient organizing. If the designer is in someone else's employ, the chances are there is a contractual or a fiduciary duty to act in the best interest of the organization. Sustainable efficiency can often be argued to be in the best interest of the organization.

To avoid confusion, it is crucial to emphasize from the beginning that an organization need not seek profits for efficiency to become a relevant objective. At its foundation, the pursuit of efficiency is a quest for collaborative value creation. This may involve not only adding economic value measured in dollars, euros, or yen, but also treating patients suffering from depression, teaching children new ways of thinking, or contributing to the rehabilitation of prison inmates. All these may ultimately contribute to the creation of economic value (and possibly profit), but economic value is at best a distant outcome, not the designer's immediate objective.

At the same time, both for-profit and nonprofit organizations often have economic slack in the form of net worth. How net worth is governed must obviously be on the designer's agenda. Therefore, an economic surplus does ultimately become relevant to the designer, just not in the sense of how to *make* it but how to *govern* it.

As a central point of terminology, the word *organization* in this book is not used merely in reference to entities we colloquially think of as organizations. Although organizational entities such as universities, firms, and legislatures are relevant, they do not represent the essence of organization. In this book, the word *organization* has less reference to entities and more to the principles and practices by which those representing these entities organize cooperative relationships with one another. In short, organization *as entity* is relevant but organization *as cooperation* is essential. Accordingly, the efficiency question pertains to efficiency not of entities but of cooperation: Is *this relationship* organized efficiently? This question echoes a well-established position in organization economics that takes the relationship as the unit of analysis.

Since we are both academics trained in business economics, it should not come as a surprise that we invoke economic theories and economic thinking more broadly throughout this book. We have been greatly inspired and influenced by numerous organization economists: Armen Alchian, Kenneth Arrow, Jay Barney, Ronald Coase, John R. Commons, Harold Demsetz, Eugene Fama, Sanford Grossman, Oliver Hart, Friedrich Hayek, Bengt Holmström, Michael Jensen, Gary Libecap, Elinor Ostrom, Edith Penrose, Michael Porter, and Oliver Williamson. Just like we the authors of this book, all these economists have been interested primarily in efficient governance and sustainable value creation through collaboration at various levels of analysis; surprisingly few economists focus on value distribution. Indeed, we suggest that the question of value appropriation—"who gets what?"—requires an extensive analysis of bargaining capabilities, power, influence, and organizational politics. We leave these topics outside the scope of our book.

As interdisciplinary academics interested in practical problems of organization design and governance, we have also been strongly influenced by social scientists more broadly: management and organization scholars, psychologists, sociologists, legal scholars, and political scientists. We have found the works of the following individuals particularly insightful: Chester Barnard, Lucian Bebchuk, Margaret Blair, Alfred Chandler, Robert Clark, Richard Cyert, John DiIulio, Amy Edmondson, Jay Galbraith, Mark Granovetter, Albert Hirschman, Daniel Kahneman, David Larcker, James March, Richard Nelson, Douglass North, Mancur Olson, Philip Selznick, Herbert Simon, Arthur Stinchcombe, Lynn Stout, James Thompson, James Q. Wilson, and Sidney Winter, among scores of others.

As academics, we have both a professional and an ethical obligation to give credit where credit is due. Throughout the chapters of this book, we acknowledge scholarly work by citing the central contributions, as we would in regular academic texts. Therefore, if this book exhibits the characteristics of academic texts, this stems from the central duty of the academic. Do not, however, let these characteristics mislead you to think that this is an academic book written for an academic audience. By citing the relevant research literature, we are merely fulfilling the dual duty of the academic: both conveying the central ideas and identifying their authors.

Citing the research literature ultimately serves the reader as well. We encourage those readers who want to dig deeper into the topics to look at some of the works cited, as they can be sources of further learning and insight. In a book such as ours, we neither want nor can go into deep detail on every topic. All the works cited in this book merit reading as they are highly complementary to our unavoidably limited exposition. We want to emphasize this especially to those readers who are students of organization at universities. The vast majority of the academic articles cited in this book are available in electronic format and can be accessed through publisher's web pages and digital libraries.

The importance of citing the published literature brings us to the motivation for writing this book. With each passing year as educators of management students, executives, entrepreneurs, and organizational leaders, we become increasingly convinced that the numerous foundational messages in the academic literature on organization economics can benefit the designer. The problem is that these messages remain buried in the literature published over the past hundred years in scores of specialized academic texts. Furthermore, the key messages are not found in a particular book or article as much as they are woven into the fabric of broader conversations and debates, each spanning multiple decades and involving dozens of scholars as participants. Understanding any individual message requires an understanding of the broader conversation, not just an individual book or article. If in this book we succeed in translating even a small fraction of these messages into a language that is accessible to the designer, this book will have more than served its purpose.

In Madrid and in Champaign, on June 3rd, 2022
Mikko Ketokivi
Joseph T. Mahoney

Acknowledgments

We dedicate this book to the memory of organization economics giant and Nobel Laureate Oliver Williamson, whose writings have been the single most important influence on the thoughts expressed in this book. This dedication is particularly fitting also because our collaboration as coauthors was sparked by a common interest in Dr. Williamson's theory of transaction costs. That we were introduced to one another by someone neither of us knew well and whom one of us never even met is as mysterious as it is precious.

We are indebted to scores of practitioners whom we have come to know personally and professionally during our careers: in the classroom, in our research projects, through our consulting, or in casual conversations. We thank especially the following executives, managers and organizational leaders, who either generously devoted their time to comment on our chapter drafts, provided illustrative examples, or otherwise engaged us in conversations on the ideas presented in this book: Benjamin Barraza, Deema Bibi, Adrian Blockus, Nigel Brashaw, Salvador Cerón de la Torre, Bastian Gerhard, Brett Hinds, Belinda Holdsworth, Monty Hoxie, Yasalde Jiménez, Sean Joyce, Jussi Kaulio, Ian Kesler, Sheree Kesler, Marja-Liisa Ketola, Patrick Küttner, Sofian Lamali, Markku Lappalainen, Matías Lira, Rauf Mammadov, Shaffi Mather, Carlo Meloni, Jaakko Nevanlinna, Lee Newman, Jeremy Nurse, Alfred Ortiz, Alejandro Pacheco, Suzanne Peters, Salma Qarnain, Efrain Rosemberg, Eila Sailas, Jarmo Salminen, Yasmina Suleyman, Bram van Olffen, Francisco Vazquez, and Joachim von Goetz.

We also thank our colleagues and coauthors in the academic community for providing insightful feedback either on this book or on our work on the economics of organization more generally: Nick Argyres, Janet Bercovitz, Akhil Bhardwaj, Lyda Bigelow, Dan Breznitz, Phil Bromiley, Tyson Browning, Joep Cornelissen, Felipe Csaszar, Suzanne de Treville, Luis Garicano, Ranjay Gulati, Martin Kenney, Peter Klein, Yasemin Kor, Juha-Antti Lamberg, Mike Manning, Saku Mantere, Scott Masten, Kyle Mayer, Jackson Nickerson, Joanne Oxley, Mirva Peltoniemi, Christine Quinn Trank, Petri Rouvinen, Fabrizio Salvador, Roger Schmenner, Brian Silverman, Kalyan Singhal, Deepak Somaya, Andy Van de Ven, Jouni Virtaharju, and Pekka Ylä-Anttila.

We are also grateful to all the anonymous peer reviewers who have given us constructive feedback and invaluable guidance during countless journal review processes. We recognize the double-blind review process as the bedrock institution of the academic community—it is always about the message, not the messenger. As in all our texts, the standard disclaimer applies: All errors, oversights, and omissions remain our responsibility.

Every page of this book echoes the central premise that securing long-term contractual relationships requires a discriminating approach to contracting, conscious foresight, and safeguards to serve as buffers against uncertainty. In precious contrast to the always uncertain and sometimes hazardous world of organizations, the very presence of Eva De Francisco and Jeanne Marie Connell in our lives serves as a constant reminder that in the truly meaningful relationships, this central premise can be tossed to the winds without hesitation.

PART I

FUNDAMENTALS OF EFFICIENT ORGANIZATION

The first part of the book consists of two chapters: chapter 1 ("Introduction") and chapter 2 ("The Efficiency Lens"). The purpose of these two chapters is to lay the conceptual and intellectual foundation for the chapters that follow. Laying the foundation involves an explication of both what this book is and *is not* about. All approaches to the complex topic of organizations—whether economic, sociological, political, or psychological—constitute a way of seeing. Our way of seeing the organization is through the lens of efficiency.

Because the word *efficiency* tends to invoke negative connotations, such as powerful buyers pressuring their smaller suppliers by aggressively renegotiating contracts, employers making employees work more hours without additional pay, and so on, we make the crucial distinction between *myopic efficiency* and *sustainable efficiency*. The objective of the first part of the book is to establish the latter as our primary focus: eliminating the excess, not the essential; nurturing cooperation, not jeopardizing it; and enabling mutual value creation, not unfettered self-interest.

In chapter 1, we clarify our general approach to organization design and governance by explicating five foundational premises, all based on various economic approaches to organization. Most importantly, our focus is on the deliberate and rational choices organization designers should make to ensure sustainable efficiency and value creation. All organizations have a job to do, and the designer's task is to ensure this job is performed in a way that minimizes waste in all its forms. Chapter 1 also serves as a general introduction to the entire book. To this end, an overview of the book's structure and its chapters is provided at the end of chapter 1.

Chapter 2 introduces the Efficiency Lens, an analytical tool that the designer can use to seek efficient organization. The Efficiency Lens consists of three central elements of management, oversight, and risk, their interrelationships, and their dynamics. We apply the Efficiency Lens throughout the chapters of this book.

Finally, to support the first part of the book in particular, there is an extensive Glossary of Terms at the end of the book. In the glossary, we define and describe the central concepts used throughout the book. In order for the book's key messages to become salient to the reader, consistent use of terminology is crucial.

1

Introduction

You stand on the corner of Calle Alberto Aguilera and Calle Acuerdo in Conde Duque, in the heart of Madrid, looking for a taxi to take to a birthday party in La Moraleja, a twenty-minute taxi ride away. As you see a free taxi approaching, you wave your hand to let the driver know that you need transportation. The driver pulls over, you hop in the back seat, and give the driver your destination. The driver nods, turns on the taximeter, and you are on your way. In a world of a billion *transactions*, there is one more.

Even though the chances are you will not spend much time thinking about the specifics of the transaction, let us consider for a moment organization economist Oliver Williamson's (1999, 321) recommendation that "even that which is obvious can sometimes benefit from explication." What exactly happens during the twenty-minute contractual relationship between you and the taxi service provider? What are all the factors that are required to make the transaction work smoothly?

Let us go back to the start of the journey. As you entered the taxi, you made a point of instructing the driver to avoid Paseo de la Castellana, because there is a football game at the Santiago Bernabéu stadium. With eighty thousand football enthusiasts piling up into the stadium, northbound Castellana is going to be in a deadlock. You know the driver is already well aware that there is a game in town (the pre-game broadcast is playing on the radio), but your point was not so much to give the driver instructions as it was to *signal* knowledge; flashing your street smarts at the driver has benefits. The driver, being no stranger to such signaling, realizes your intent but takes no offense; the driver understands that it is reasonable for a customer to worry about being taken, more than just literally, for a ride. Indeed, it has happened to you a few times, and you have picked up a few tricks and have learned to *adapt*.

In addition to learning over time, technology helps. Most of the time, you use the taxi app on your smartphone, which gives you a guaranteed maximum rate if you enter the destination address when you place the order. Moreover, in case the service is not to your expectations, it takes you all of ten seconds to use the app to engage in *ex post monitoring* and submit a

Efficient Organization. Mikko Ketokivi and Joseph T. Mahoney, Oxford University Press. © Oxford University Press 2023. DOI: 10.1093/oso/9780197610282.003.0001

performance evaluation of the driver at the end of the journey. Another pre-caution at your disposal is *ex ante screening*—you may limit the choice of taxis to those with the highest, five-star rating.

On reaching the destination, you pay the driver €20 for the fare, which is smack dab in the middle of the price range the app gave you as you placed the order. You ensure you do not leave anything behind and given your pos-itive experience, reward the driver with a five-star rating on the app. Both transacting parties have received what they expected from the transaction, supply has met demand—*the market clears*—and in a world of a billion transactions, there is one fewer.

From start to finish, there were no resources wasted in the transaction: no surprises, no haggling, and no deception. Furthermore, although both ex-change parties acted out of self-interest (which is what makes the economy run in the first place), neither behaved in a self-serving, opportunistic way. It is not always this smooth, but this is an accurate description of your ex-perience 98 percent of the time. In fact, you do not even remember the last time you had a problem, and the biggest problem you have ever had in the past eight years was once paying roughly €7 more than what you had ex-pected. Nothing to lose your sleep over. You gave the driver a one-star rating, and after blacklisting him, your paths never crossed again. When *specificity* in the transaction is low (when you are not dependent on any specific taxi driver), you can easily and costlessly walk away from an unpleasant en-counter. Therefore, avoiding recurring *transactional hazards* is straightfor-ward. Symmetrically, honest taxi drivers benefit from not having to pick up the same troublemakers time after time. Customers are well aware that taxi drivers rate customers as well, and just as you have access to their ratings, they have access to yours. In this sense, there is no *information asymmetry*.

Let us suggest that the story does not end at getting where you need. We might also wonder whether it would make economic sense for you to own a car. Conducting the *make-or-buy analysis* is not complicated. If you lived in downtown Madrid and owned a car, you would pay at least €250 per month for parking, €80 per month for insurance, and another €120 for gasoline. Finally, as far as the financial investment is concerned, your capital equip-ment would operate at a less-than-10-percent capacity utilization rate (less than two hours a day, on average), spending the vast majority of its time sit-ting idle, depreciating at a rate of €300 per month. It is difficult to think of a more abysmal target for a €30,000 capital investment, particularly since there is an abundant and diverse supply of reliable transportation services in the city. Why *insource* ("make") transportation when you can easily *outsource* ("buy") it?

Having considered the issue in its entirety, spending €500 per month to have a professional drive you around in Madrid sounds less like a luxury and more like economic common sense. This comparatively lower cost is further reduced significantly if you use the subway instead of taking the taxi. The point is that even when a *comparative analysis* involves the most expensive, most convenient, and most flexible transportation outsourcing option, having someone else drive you around is more economical than driving yourself. In addition, when you consider *hybrid governance* options such as a private lease, you find that their total cost is roughly the same as the cost of ownership.

Finally, as you set aside pure self-interest to consider the collective interest and, in particular, the *negative externalities* involved, you cannot avoid the conclusion that while the jam-packed metropolis of over six million people needs many things, yet another private vehicle, to be operated at a very low capacity utilization rate, is perhaps not one of them. You might therefore choose not to contribute to the roughly 10 percent annual growth rate in the number of registered passenger vehicles in Madrid.

For the taxi driver, the world looks very different. Immediately after terminating the transaction with you, the driver is not only free but strongly incentivized to enter into a new transaction with another customer as quickly as possible. The driver wants to make the most out of a capital investment that involves not only the vehicle but also the taxi license, which costs around a €100,000. A casual survey of taxi drivers reveals that an individual driver will work anywhere between eight and fourteen hours each day for five or six days a week.

Given the sizable capital investment, the driver has a *high-powered incentive* to provide a reliable service and to maintain a five-star rating. Another casual survey of taxi drivers reveals that they value and seek to maintain their five-star rating. Furthermore, is it just a coincidence that concurrently with the introduction of the rating system, vehicle cleanliness improved significantly? Or that additional services such as phone chargers, breath mints, and hand sanitizer are now offered to passengers? Might these changes have something to do with the fact that your taxi app lets you provide a star rating not only to the driver but also the vehicle?

In this example of a *mutually credible transaction*, supply met demand, and the contract was completed without unnecessary *ex ante* or *ex post transaction costs.* Both exchange parties not only entered into the transaction voluntarily but were also able to allocate their time and efforts to what they preferred and to what they were skilled at doing. You chose to outsource driving to a professional and spent the twenty-minute ride sending two quick emails and calling the restaurant in La Moraleja to ensure that everything was ready for the birthday celebration.

In sum, the transaction was efficient and mutually beneficial in all relevant respects, even though you probably did not spend a single second thinking about it. This unearths yet another benefit of efficient contracting: It enables efficient allocation of not only our time and money but also our attention. Indeed, sometimes the very act of having to think about something can be a form of waste.

Efficient Organization

The transaction associated with the taxi ride is an example of efficient organization. Efficiency is a relevant concern at all levels of analysis: individuals, organizations, industries, communities, even entire societies. Who would object, at any of these levels, to being efficient?

This book is about efficient organization, where the word *organization* is used in the broadest possible sense. It refers to any form of voluntary cooperation, be it between individuals or broader entities such as firms or other collectives. A massive multinational corporation is an organization, but so is the taxi ride example. The punchline of the taxi ride example was that a comparative economic analysis reveals that it is more efficient for a person residing in downtown Madrid to outsource private transportation to a taxi service than to own a private vehicle.

Because boundary conditions are always essential, let us be explicit about what the efficiency view does *not* cover. In the taxi ride example, we abstracted out questions such as the following: How meaningful is owning, or not owning, a car to you? Do you enjoy, or not enjoy, driving? How skilled a driver are you? How well do you know the city? How highly do you value convenience? Do you have enough money to buy a car? These questions may obviously be of interest to some of us, but because they are not about economic efficiency, they are outside the scope of this book.

The last question in particular merits attention. In the efficiency perspective, and in many economic approaches more generally, various *wealth effects* (Milgrom and Roberts 1992, 35–39) are abstracted out of the analysis. Although this may seem strange at first, a brief reflection should reveal that whether owning a car is economically more efficient than using taxi services does not depend on the wealth of the transacting parties. To be sure, wealthier individuals are both more likely to use taxi services and less likely to be taxi drivers. But we were not interested in the specific individuals involved in the exchange, our aim was to determine which private transportation alternative created less economic waste. Therefore, even though you and the taxi driver were the two protagonists in the example, the story was ultimately not about you or the taxi driver, it was about the comparative long-term cost of alternative forms of transportation. Accordingly, we are not psychologists who "try to get inside the heads" of individual decision makers in an attempt to understand the choices they make.

At the same time, no matter what one's personal preferences are, explicitly analyzing the efficiency implications of one's choices can be useful. That the fixed cost of owning a mid-sized passenger vehicle in downtown Madrid is more than €600 per month came as a surprise to a colleague of ours who owns a private vehicle in Madrid. One reason the total cost may not be salient is because it is scattered over various monthly, semiannual, and annual payments in different cost categories. The total cost becomes salient only if one engages in an explicit calculation. Herein resides a learning opportunity: Becoming better educated about the total cost of car ownership might end up affecting one's personal preferences.

On the Use of Economic Jargon

Philosopher Paul Feyerabend noted in his autobiography (Feyerabend 1995) that philosophers cannot understand one another until they have translated everything into Latin. In light of Feyerabend's remark, what are we to think of the use of terms such as *high-powered incentives, ex ante screening, ex post monitoring, hybrid governance, specificity,* and *negative externalities*? Why speak Latin in a book written primarily for nonacademics?

In the taxi ride example, the terms borrowed from economic theories of organization appeared italicized; there were quite a few of them. The use of unduly sophisticated language is exactly what is wrong with academics, you may think. Were these really essential terms to describe a taxi ride? We suggest that the answer is both *no* and *yes.* The answer is an emphatic *no* in the sense that specialized terminology is not required to *describe* the process of taking a taxi to a birthday party. From the descriptive point of view, speaking Latin is as irritating as it is unnecessary.

But suppose we want to *understand* and *analyze* why a private individual obtaining a personal transportation service from a private entrepreneur was organized the way it was. The particular taxi ride aside, why were there 15,974 taxis in Madrid in 2020? Why is there a market for this type of private transportation? In what sense is it economically rational? Does it help reduce waste? Are there comparatively more efficient alternatives? After our brief economic analysis, we concluded that owning a private vehicle in downtown Madrid surely seems like an economically poor choice. Consequently, we are not surprised at the thousands upon thousands of taxi cabs shuttling the streets of Madrid. The emergence of not only *ride-sharing* but also *car-sharing* arrangements is equally unsurprising. In Madrid, rental cars are currently available at about twenty eurocents per minute by car-sharing services such as ShareNow. These outcomes are predictable consequences of the simple economic reality that owning a private vehicle in downtown Madrid is economically wasteful.

We suggest that when the objective is to analyze and to understand, specialized terminology becomes useful. No matter how strange the terms may at first glance appear, in economic conversations and analyses they have specific meanings and definitions. Economists in particular and academics more generally are skilled at using terms with precision. Indeed, that is how we have been trained, and the reason we "speak Latin" is because we want to ensure the use of terminology is consistent.

If we used colloquial terminology, we would face the problem of different people using the same term in different meanings. Just ask a dozen executives how they define *profit*, and you will get at least a half dozen different answers. Some focus primarily on return on equity, others on return on assets, return on capital employed, or economic value added. We must be careful with the assumption that terminology can be taken as commonly understood. The upside of using specialized terminology is that it gives you, the reader, useful pause and compels you to think about what the concept means and why it is introduced.

Consider the notion that the taxi driver has a *high-powered incentive* to offer taxi services to as many customers as possible during a work shift. As strange as the term may seem at first glance, it succinctly captures an idea that would take considerably longer to describe in colloquial terms. Moreover, suppose we now formally introduce the opposite, *low-powered incentive*. The term is likely immediately understandable to the reader without additional clarification. To make the term and the distinction salient, we might present *hourly wages* as an example of a low-powered incentive; an incentive is low-powered when the payoff does not depend on how the work is performed. *Piece rate* is an example of a comparatively high-powered incentive; under the piece-rate system, the employees' compensation is tied to how they perform the work.

Once we have introduced high- and low-powered incentives (two ends of a continuum), we can now introduce the general term *incentive intensity*. And as we will show in the chapters that follow, incentive intensity is a central design variable.

Let us look at some of the important nuances of incentive intensity that may not be immediately salient. First, in applying a high-powered incentive it is not the *effort* but the *outcome* that is rewarded. Second, incentive intensity is not about whether the absolute levels of compensation are high or not, it only determines how strongly compensation is tied to outcomes. Indeed, the reason taxi drivers in Madrid may work up to fourteen hours a day is because a regular eight-hour shift is woefully inadequate to provide a sufficiently high absolute level of income. In other words, the high-powered incentive motivates drivers to work more, but the fact that absolute levels of pay are low forces them to work *a lot* more. COVID-19 made the situation downright unbearable. One driver told us that in April 2020, he picked up a total of five passengers during a fourteen-hour shift, that is, roughly one customer every three hours. After deducting all fixed and variable expenses, a Madrid taxi driver makes no more than a few euros per trip. Even with a high-powered incentive, the absolute level of compensation may be seriously inadequate.

Once we have understood incentive intensity, we can speak efficiently about incentives without risking confusion. In the case of the taxi driver, the driver is motivated to find as many clients as possible during the work shift. This high motivation is due to a built-in high-powered incentive embedded in the governance structure of taxi services. No extra incentives or motivational pep talk are required, and no additional resources are required to monitor the driver's behavior during the work shift. The effect of a high-powered incentive is relentless self-regulation of the driver's effort, which constitutes a highly efficient mechanism in a decentralized and fragmented organization that consists of over fifteen thousand independent entrepreneurs. In this case, being one's own boss is highly efficient. In some other contexts, it may not be.

Finally, clear definitions and selective use of specialized terminology are also useful whenever it is important to avoid misleading connotations that colloquial terminology sometimes creates. For instance, it is crucial to understand that in this book, *efficiency* pertains to the way in which tasks are organized, and, specifically, whether in performing these tasks, time, resources, or effort is wasted. An efficient organization minimizes waste.

Importantly, minimizing waste is about productivity. Whether being efficient translates into an economic surplus (profit) is an altogether different question, as is the question whether the organization even seeks a profit in the first place. Insofar as efficiency is concerned, profit-seeking is not nearly as relevant as we may think. In fact, a for-profit and a nonprofit organization may often seek efficiency in surprisingly similar ways.

In this book, we use economic terminology, but we do it sparingly, because the aim is not to teach the reader economics, and we do not want to write a book that requires a companion economics dictionary to decipher. We use economic terminology with the primary objective of being able to analyze various decision situations in a rigorous and consistent way. We want to ensure that all economic terms are not only carefully defined but also accessible. To this end, and to make this book self-sufficient in terms of its terminology, we have provided an extensive glossary of key terms at the end of the book.

Five Foundational Premises

The dilemma we face in writing about something as complex as organizations is that all approaches aimed at understanding organization—be they economic, sociological, political, or psychological—offer a limited point of view. Therefore, any individual perspective abstracts out much of what might be relevant for real-life organizations. Indeed, *nothing* is outside the scope of real-life organizations.

Unlike problems that call for solutions, dilemmas call for choices. On the one hand, a holistic approach to organization design sounds appealing, because it would do better justice to the complexity and ambiguity of organizations. At the same time, choosing an eclectic approach runs a risk that is best captured by financial economist Michael Jensen's (2001, 9) critique of the stakeholder literature: "Without the clarity of mission provided by a single-valued objective function, companies embracing stakeholder theory will experience managerial confusion, conflict, inefficiency, and perhaps even competitive failure [. . .] [W]hen there are many masters, all end up being shortchanged."

We agree that without a clear objective, it is difficult to present coherent arguments about organization design and governance. Because we want this book to exhibit a "clarity of mission" (to use Jensen's words), we have chosen not to write an eclectic book that takes different points of view along the way and, predictably enough, arrives at on-the-one-hand/on-the-other-hand-types of conclusions. Although we are in general sympathetic to giving voice to different perspectives on organization design and governance, we focus in this book on economic efficiency.

But what exactly does the focus on efficiency entail? What are the consequences for analysis? Having chosen the focus of efficient organizing and voluntary cooperation, we can delineate five specific premises on which this book rests.

First Premise: Organizations as Deliberately Designed

Even though we find various evolutionary approaches useful and enthusiastically embrace *emergence* as essential to many organizational phenomena, we choose to approach organizations primarily as *deliberately designed* entities. Throughout this book, we use the term *designer* in reference to all those who make deliberate design decisions.

To propose that analyzing organizations as deliberately designed is useful should not be too controversial. For example, in the annual meeting of the shareholders of a limited liability company, we can think of the shareholders as the designers whose task is to make the (incremental) design decision of whether the composition of the board of directors should be changed. In the founding discussions and negotiations of an industrial startup, the prospective founding partners are the designers who make the (foundational) design decision of how many shareholders the firm will have, how equity will be split, and whether both cash and in-kind contributions will be accepted in the purchase of shares.

To clarify, this premise does not suggest that emergent phenomena cannot give rise to design decision situations—they can, and they often do. For example, a buyer-supplier relationship may start as a simple transactional relationship where the buyer chooses one supplier from many alternatives; the identity of the supplier does not matter, in a manner of speaking. However, the relationship may transform over time into one where the specific supplier becomes a preferred supplier; identities start to matter. In the organization economics literature, this process is called the *fundamental transformation* (Williamson 1985, 61). The term is fitting, because there is indeed something fundamental about how the relationship transforms into one where the identity of a particular supplier (or buyer) starts to matter. As a thought exercise, just think how fundamentally the market for taxi services would transform if you as the consumer had to use the same taxicab every time and a given taxi driver could serve only a predetermined set of individual customers.

When we say our focus is on deliberate design, we mean that insofar as the fundamental transformation is concerned, we are not interested in why and how it occurs; the process is likely highly complex and nuanced. We focus on analyzing its governance implications, the kinds of design decision situations it presents, and the kinds of adaptation challenges it creates for the designer. In sum, emergent phenomena may lead to situations where deliberate design decisions are required.

The deliberate design focus, particularly when considered in conjunction with the efficiency premise, also leads us to focus on *remediable problems*. Specifically, when we discuss various organization design decisions, we seek to identify solutions that are not only feasible but have the potential of solving efficiency problems—this is the essence of remediability. This approach is important for at least two reasons. One is that it is sometimes difficult to see how a proposed solution is feasible in the first place. Feasibility might be jeopardized by government regulations, legal requirements, and corporate cultures; sometimes even the organization's information systems (e.g., Goold and Campbell 2002b). The comparatively efficient alternative may not always be feasible from an organizational perspective. For example, it is often not possible for an industrial firm to produce a component in-house ("make"); instead, the firm must purchase it from a supplier ("buy"). A case in point, although national railways such as Indian Railways may own and operate locomotive assembly plants where locomotive assembly and maintenance are performed, it would be simply infeasible for Indian Railways to produce internally many of the components and subsystems required in final assembly (Bhardwaj and Ketokivi 2021).

The other, more subtle reason is that sometimes even feasible solutions ultimately fail to solve problems and improve efficiency. Evidence regarding outsourcing decisions offers a good example. Many companies find, after the fact, that an outsourcing decision turned out to be associated with hidden costs that ultimately made outsourcing less efficient than in-house production. This outcome runs counter to the idea of remediability, which holds that implementing a design decision must result in *net gains*. The intended efficiency gains of a design decision must offset all undesirable (and possibly inadvertent) efficiency losses that the decision might cause in other parts of the organization (Williamson 1975, 79). An industrial firm outsourcing the production of a component to a specialized parts supplier may find that enforcing the buyer-supplier contract on a daily basis has led to additional administrative costs that offset any production productivity benefits.

Focusing on net gains underscores the importance of understanding organization design and governance decisions *in their entirety*—this is one of the central governance principles in the organization economics literature (e.g., Williamson 1996). In chapters 4 and 5, we examine, among other issues, whether the board of directors should be opened to employee participation. In the spirit of investigating net gains, we point out that whereas employee participation on boards may work toward addressing potential problems in the governance of employer-employee relationships, it may create tension and friction elsewhere in the organization.

Second Premise: Start at the *Main Problem*

Should the chief executive officer (CEO) also chair the board of directors? Should a component be outsourced or produced in-house? Should country organizations within a multinational corporation be assigned profit-and-loss (P&L) responsibility? Addressing various organization design and governance questions requires the formulation of a more specific problem that the designer seeks to address. Problems are never a given; instead, an issue becomes a problem only after the decision makers have explicitly agreed on how it should be framed. In this book, we use the term *main problem* in reference to problem framing. Before evaluating potential governance alternatives, the designer must define the main problem.

As an example of formulating the main problem, consider the question whether the CEO should chair the board of directors—this is sometimes dubbed *CEO duality structure* (Rechner and Dalton 1991). In some contexts, CEO duality makes sense, in others the opposite, *CEO independence structure*, is a better option. In the CEO independence structure, the CEO may be a board member but cannot chair the board. But what exactly is the governance problem that the designer seeks to address with CEO duality (or independence)?

Both CEO duality structure and CEO independence structure are organization-specific responses to a specific representation of the main problem. Those advocating the CEO independence structure are more likely to frame the problem as an *agency problem* (Ross 1973; Jensen and Meckling 1976): How does the organization ensure the CEO (the agent) acts in the best interest of the organization (the principal)?

If the main problem is the CEO potentially not acting in the best interest of the organization, the CEO independence structure works toward sufficient separation of powers. The problem of insufficient separation is further exacerbated if the other board members are not independent of the CEO. Even an outside board member may satisfy all the requirements of being formally independent of the firm but simultaneously be in one way or another beholden to the CEO. A recurring concern that several *proxy advisory firms* have expressed regarding Tesla, for instance, is that Tesla's board members have been formally independent of the firm but not truly independent of CEO Elon Musk's influence. Indeed, Tesla's board has faced several lawsuits where shareholders have claimed the board has not acted in the best interest of the company. In 2018, Elon Musk was forced to step down as Tesla's chairperson of the board but remained Tesla's CEO. Clearly, there were concerns that the CEO duality structure was not functioning well.

However, the agency problem is not the only possible problem formulation in the context of board composition. For example, if the organization operates in a highly uncertain and dynamic environment where many important decisions must be made rapidly, unity of command may provide benefits over separation of powers. If all decisions contemplated by top management must be vetted and approved by an independent board of directors chaired by a person whose primary occupation is elsewhere and who spends roughly one day a month attending to director duties, efficient decision-making may be significantly hampered. In such contexts, CEO duality structure may offer the comparatively efficient governance alternative.

Considering the possibility that those adopting CEO duality may be addressing a different main problem than those adopting CEO independence, we do not find it surprising that researchers have found "little or no evidence" (Larcker and Tayan 2015, 134) of the performance impact of CEO duality versus independence. Because CEO duality and CEO independence can both be reasoned decisions given the specifics of the situation, comparing firms with CEO duality to those with CEO independence is ultimately an "apples-to-oranges" comparison. To make the comparison "apples-to-apples," one must analyze a sample of companies that define the main problem in a similar way.[1]

In defining the main problem, it is important to keep in mind that the issue at hand is one of governance, and as such, foundational to the organization. Foundational decisions must be made on foundational grounds. For example, suppose the argument for CEO duality is made on the grounds that because the founding CEO is a skilled individual with unwavering integrity, the concern for an agency problem is minimal. We counsel against such an ad hoc justification. The decision must be made in a forward-looking manner, not merely in light of the organization's current situation. It is myopic to base a governance decision on a transient issue, such as the founding CEO's characteristics and reputation. It is only a matter of time when the founding CEO leaves, and a successor will be appointed. It would be myopic to assume that the successor, or the successor's successor, will present no agency concerns. Governance decisions must be made with conscious foresight to avoid myopia.

Third Premise: Viability Builds on Collaborative Value Creation

The processes by which value is created are distinct from the processes by which it is captured or appropriated. In colloquial terms, the distinction is between "baking the pie" and "dividing the pie." This book is about "baking the pie," that is, ensuring that the organization creates value by securing the cooperation of its most important constituencies. Accordingly, we ask

---

[1] The ubiquitous, vexing dilemma that governance researchers face is that causal effects are notoriously difficult to uncover with empirical analysis. The researcher cannot conduct experiments where governance choices are randomly assigned to organizations in the sample the same way individuals are randomly divided into treatment and control groups in medical experiments. Just how trustworthy would a medical experiment be if individuals could choose whether they receive the treatment or the placebo? In the context of governance, alternative "treatments" are always a matter of choice. But this is not to be viewed as a shortcoming, that they are matters of choice is *the whole point!*

questions such as the following: How do contracting parties enter into relationships? When is the relationship credible in the eyes of the contracting parties? What kinds of safeguards are implemented to avoid contractual hazards? How are conflicts resolved in a way that does not jeopardize the relationship? These questions are aimed at evaluating the extent to which collaborative, value-creating relationships are organized efficiently. When the focus shifts from the entities that organize to the processes of organizing, the *relationship* becomes the central unit of analysis.[2]

In some contexts, the transacting parties seek profits; in others they do not. We propose that insofar as efficient organization of relationships is concerned, profit-seeking is an ancillary concern. Whether avoiding waste is desirable or not should not depend on whether any of the transacting parties are interested in producing a surplus. To be sure, the desire to organize efficiently may be driven by the profit motive, but because value capture is about how much value a specific party is able to appropriate, it misguidedly shifts attention from the relationship and cooperation to the outcomes for *just one* of the participants to the exchange.

As much as possible, we want to keep the focus on securing and maintaining exchange relationships, because it paves the way toward understanding the *viability* of organizations. This objective is consistent with many economic theories of organization that emphasize survival, not profitability. A case in point, two central architects of agency theory, Eugene Fama and Michael Jensen (1983a, 301 [emphasis added]) noted that their central concern was "with the *survival of organizations* in which important decision agents do not bear a substantial share of the wealth effects of their decisions." This quote is instructive not only because it establishes survival as the central concern but also because it points to the separation of decision-making and risk-bearing as the central governance challenge. Whether the organization, or those involved in it, seeks profits or other types of private benefits is a secondary concern.

Some organizational forms are more viable than others. Consider as an example a limited liability company where the same individuals populate

---

[2] Organization economists often take the *transaction* as the unit of analysis (Williamson 1985). In our view, this is the economist's way of expressing that the focus is on relationships; the links of a dyad, not its nodes. Commons (1934, 4) described the objective succinctly: "[E]conomic organization [. . .] has the purpose of harmonizing relations between parties who are otherwise in actual or potential conflict." Along the same lines, Williamson (1996, 365) noted that "the main purpose (which is not to say the only purpose) of economic organization is to infuse integrity into contractual relations."

both the top management team and the board of directors but at the same time, own a very small percentage of shares. In other words, the individuals who make the most important decisions also exercise oversight over their own decisions, without bearing significant risk. Who is going to invest in such a company? To the extent the firm is dependent on raising equity to finance its operations and investments, separating risk-bearing from decision-making without simultaneously separating decision-making from oversight jeopardizes viability. To make the organization viable, one must either populate the board primarily with independent board members or require those populating both the top management team and the board of directors to invest significantly in equity. The appointment of independent board members is standard practice in all publicly traded corporations. Top management and the board investing in equity can, in turn, be found in most small startups where the same individuals run the business, exercise oversight, and bear investment risk.

In economic terminology, this book and its key messages reside on the value creation or *preappropriation* side. Profit is a *postappropriation* measure of performance, because it is what is left over after all contractual obligations have been met and the associated revenue appropriated. It would be awkward to think of organization design and governance in such "leftover terms." Instead, we suggest that the attention be directed, first and foremost, to how organizations create value. Avoiding waste is readily consistent with this objective.[3]

Fourth Premise: Stakeholdership as Reciprocity and Risk

It is common to think of shareholders as the *owners* of the firm. Similarly, shareholders are often considered the only relevant principal and the organization's sole stakeholder because they are the only constituency with rights to the organization's residual.

We find thinking of shareholders as the only constituency with a residual interest both unnecessary and misleading. It is unnecessary because although shareholders may be the most salient constituency with a residual

---

[3] Think of all the economic value that is appropriated from revenue before it is turned into profit: employee salaries, pension payments, suppliers' invoices, insurance, depreciation, and taxes. After all these contractually and legally binding appropriations have been made, the economic surplus emerges as a postappropriation measure of performance.

interest, there may be others. It is further misleading to assume that the agency problem is limited to organizations that have shareholders. In order for an agency problem to occur, all that is required is a principal-agent relationship of some kind. In this vein, Fama and Jensen (1983a, 314) noted that the misapplication of CEO duality structure has consequences that reach well beyond shareholders; it threatens the very survival of the organization.

Definitions of *stakeholder* are as numerous as they are diverse. In this book, we start at the *Cambridge Dictionary* definition, which covers all the aspects relevant to the efficiency argument. Specifically, a stakeholder is "a person such as an employee, customer, or citizen who (1) is involved with the organization, (2) has responsibilities towards it, and (3) [has] an interest in its success."[4] This definition effectively distinguishes stakeholders from other constituencies.

To make the distinction between constituency and stakeholder clear, consider the following relationships:

1. A is B's supplier;
2. A is unilaterally dependent on B;
3. A has the ability to influence B's actions;
4. A is able to extract value from B;
5. A is B's beneficiary; and
6. A creates value for B.

In all these six cases, the three conditions of the definition of a stakeholder relationship may or may not be satisfied. For example, buyers may develop stakeholder relationships with some of their suppliers over time, but merely having a buyer-supplier relationship is not sufficient to transform a constituency into a stakeholder. Similarly, a constituency that creates value for the organization may have a simple transactional relationship with no discernible stakeholder characteristics that warrant the designer's attention. Finally, even though a beneficiary may seem like an obvious stakeholder, beneficiaries tend not to have significant responsibilities toward the organization whose benefits they enjoy, or at least, these responsibilities pale in comparison with the benefits. Children being the beneficiaries of trusts set up by their parents is a good example.

---

[4] www.dictionary.cambridge.org/dictionary/english/stakeholder.

The *Cambridge* definition offers a useful starting point. However, we propose the definition should incorporate reciprocity. Specifically, we should not ask whether A is B's stakeholder but, rather, whether A and B are one another's stakeholders. Furthermore, because stakeholder relationships can involve both individuals and organizations, the definition should incorporate a more general term, such as *party*. Finally, since parties who have responsibilities toward one another are by definition involved with one another, the notion of being involved with one another can be eliminated.

In summary, we modify the *Cambridge* definition as follows: Two parties are one another's stakeholders if they have responsibilities toward one another and are interested in one another's success. We submit that this definition avoids the problem of overpermissiveness that often leads to the conclusion that every constituency is a stakeholder and that everyone is equally important. But if everyone is important, then no one is, and as far as stakeholder issues are concerned, all our work would still be ahead of us.

Prioritization of stakeholders is challenging but essential. We discuss this topic further in detail in chapter 4 where we examine how communities organized the delivery of COVID-19 vaccinations. It would have been ethically untenable to base vaccine delivery on the principle that everyone had an equal right to receive the vaccine. Instead, those with more at stake would have to be prioritized.

We propose that the inability to prioritize stakeholders would have similar consequences as the inability to prioritize recipients of COVID-19 vaccine would have. Specifically, a designer's failure to incorporate the irrefutable fact that some constituencies have more at stake than others will jeopardize the organization's credibility in the eyes of those who have comparatively more at stake. If those with more at stake are critical in value creation (which often is the case), the inability or unwillingness to prioritize stakeholders imminently threatens organizational viability.

Fifth Premise: Focus on Private Ordering

We distinguish between two kinds of context. One refers to the legal and institutional context in which the organization operates. Consider two organizations: DuPont de Nemours, Inc., a US-based publicly traded limited liability company, incorporated in the state of Delaware, and traded on the New York Stock Exchange (NYSE), and the Mondragón Corporación Cooperativa, a massive cooperative organization based in the Basque region of Spain. The two organizations face drastically different legal and institutional environments, and consequently, their designers must respond to the demands of their respective environments. In short, the *institutional context* matters.

Focusing on the institutional context directs the designer's attention to the "rules of the game." For example, the three central sets of rules DuPont must incorporate into its governance decisions are the applicable US federal laws, the applicable laws of the state of Delaware, and the NYSE Corporate Governance Guide. The institutional context is something to which the organization must adapt as a matter of compliance.

Similarly, all companies incorporated in Spain are subject to the same legal requirements. Perhaps largely for this reason, the legal requirements are often general, leaving much to the designer's discretion. For example, Title IV, chapter I, article 210 of the Spanish Corporate Enterprises Act stipulates that "company administration may be entrusted to a sole director, several directors acting jointly or severally, or a board of directors." Furthermore, title IV, chapter VI, article 242 requires that if company administration is entrusted to a board of directors, "the board shall have no [fewer] than three members."

As the Spanish Corporate Enterprises Act effectively illustrates, the institutional context is a source of very general guidelines. For example, consider the question whether to delegate administration to a board of directors and the subsequent decision of how many board members to have. Both are essentially matters of discretion and private choice, or as the economist would put it, matters of *private ordering* (Williamson 1996). This book is about private ordering and, accordingly, the ways in which the *organizational context* matters.

At the founding of the organization, the relevant private-ordering choices are commonly embedded in the organization's founding documents: articles of incorporation, corporate bylaws, and shareholders' agreements. These documents are best thought of as contracts in which the designer seeks to address relevant local and idiosyncratic design questions. Indeed, courts often treat these documents as binding contracts: "[T]he governing documents of the corporation—the charter and bylaws—operate and bind both managers and shareholders as if they had negotiated their terms and signed them, like a common law contract" (Fisch 2018, 377).

It is useful to make the distinction between the institutional and the contractual pillars of efficient organizing. Efficient organization arises from compliance with the institutional rules on the one hand and local contractual adaptation on the other. Although both pillars are relevant and require the designer's attention, we focus in this book primarily on the contractual pillar, that is, the choices that designers make within the boundary conditions set by the institutional pillar. Insofar as the institutional pillar is concerned, the only prescription we give to the designer in this book is the following: Ensure compliance with the requirements and the boundary conditions set by the institutional environment. Accordingly, questions such as whether a US-based corporation should incorporate in the state of Delaware or another state (see Bebchuk and Cohen 2003) are beyond the scope of this book.

The premise in this book, and in many organization design and governance conversations more generally, is that governance challenges must be addressed by individual organizations in their own, idiosyncratic contexts. Focus on private ordering suggests that governance is not so much a legislative and policy issue as it is a private, organization-specific matter. This framing implies that the central focus should be on how the organization seeks to address the local governance problems by making informed choices, which appropriately shifts attention to and emphasizes the responsibilities of the designer.

To further justify why private ordering merits attention, let us examine conflict resolution in interorganizational exchange. Why not just rely on the institutional pillar and resolve conflicts in the court of law? Although the answer may be obvious, there are some nuances that merit attention.

The courts have an indispensable role in supporting conflict resolution in interorganizational exchange. However, relying on them has three general disadvantages: Litigation is time-consuming, expensive, and has potentially a nonexpert presiding over the dispute. The first two should be self-evident. As to nonexperts presiding, the assumption that in the case of, say, a buyer-supplier conflict, the court system will efficiently appoint a judge with the requisite substantive expertise in interfirm business relationships and supply chain structures is wishful thinking. Unless the contracting parties get lucky, they may find themselves in the courtroom with a judge who is not an expert on the substance of the dispute, only the laws that apply to the dispute. Indeed, both legal and economic scholars have suggested that courts sometimes rely on "oversimplified economics" and "unfounded or disproven assumptions" (Leslie 2014, 939), even to the point of suggesting that legal experts at the highest levels of the judiciary may at times be "deeply confused" (Williamson 2002a, 9) about the economics of organization. This critique is not to blame judges but simply to acknowledge that they are experts on law, not economics or business practice.

Instead of referring to the courts (the institutional pillar) for dispute resolution, relying on private ordering (the contractual pillar) may offer the comparatively efficient option. For instance, the contracting parties could stipulate in the contract the following dispute resolution mechanism: If a conflict escalates to a point where negotiation attempts fail and a third party is required, the contracting parties commit to mediation or arbitration instead of litigation. In economic terms, instead of assuming that the institutional environment will provide comparatively efficient conflict resolution, the designer chooses to build in various internal *quasijudicial functions* (Williamson 1975, 30) by which conflicts can be addressed more efficiently: faster, cheaper, and with substantive experts presiding over the dispute.

The designer must also understand that in some cases invoking the institutional pillar will be not only comparatively inefficient but also infeasible. For example, if one division of an industrial firm buys components from another division that belongs to the same parent corporation, the two cannot settle their disputes in court—the corporation would effectively be suing itself.

The private-ordering approach places not the law or the institutional environment but various contracts at center stage. Here, the word *contract* should be understood as a broad term that encompasses all aspects of private ordering—both implicit and explicit—by which two or more parties agree on duties and responsibilities. Indeed, for the purposes of our argument, we find resonance in the sentiment that "the notion of contract is so broad as to include virtually all voluntary social arrangements" (Blair and Stout 1999, 254). This broad definition also underscores the idea that lawyers may not always be the preferred experts to address contractual issues. In this vein, organization scholars Nicholas Argyres and Kyle Mayer (2007) suggested that whereas lawyers may possess superior capabilities to address matters of oversight and control, managers may be better equipped to handle issues such as resource allocation and contingency planning.

Overview of the Chapters

This book comprises eight interrelated chapters organized into three parts. Part I, "Fundamentals of Efficient Organization," consists of the

"Introduction" (chapter 1) and "The Efficiency Lens" (chapter 2). In these two chapters, we introduce the key terminology and the analytical framework, the Efficiency Lens, applied throughout the book. The extensive "Glossary of Terms" at the end of the book serves as a companion to Part I. The main purpose of Part I is to establish the relevance of efficient organization.

Part II, "Governance within and across Organizations," contains three substantive chapters: "Contracting within and across Organizations" (chapter 3), "Stakeholder Analysis" (chapter 4), and "Nonprofit and Public Organizations" (chapter 5). In these chapters, we discuss some of the central themes associated with a governance-based approach to organization. Because contracts, and contracting more generally, are central to governance, the focus is specifically on contractual relationships.

In Part III, "Governance and the Organizational Life Cycle," we examine the governance challenges that organizations face at different stages of their lifecycles: "The Startup Organization" (chapter 6), "The Expanding Organization" (chapter 7), and "The Institutionalized Organization" (chapter 8).

Chapters 3 through 8 form a "matrix" in that the topics discussed in chapters 6 through 8 cut across chapters 3 through 5 (see fig. 1.1). For example, stakeholder issues are relevant in all organizations, no matter at what stage in their lifecycle they may be. At the same time, the stakeholder issues that a small industrial startup faces are different from those faced by large, publicly-traded corporations. In the following, we briefly introduce the content of chapters 2 through 8.

Chapter 2: The Efficiency Lens

In chapter 2, we introduce a general framework and analytical tool we apply throughout the book. The Efficiency Lens consists of three elements—management, oversight, and risk—and their interrelationships and dynamics. We find the word *lens* descriptively accurate, because adopting the efficiency view indeed constitutes a way of *looking at* the organization. The main purpose of the Efficiency Lens is to bring various sources of organizational waste into focus by analyzing how the work gets organized, who exercises oversight, and who bears risk. The overarching objective is to ensure that the organization establishes and maintains credibility in the eyes of those who create value for the organization. Not being able to establish

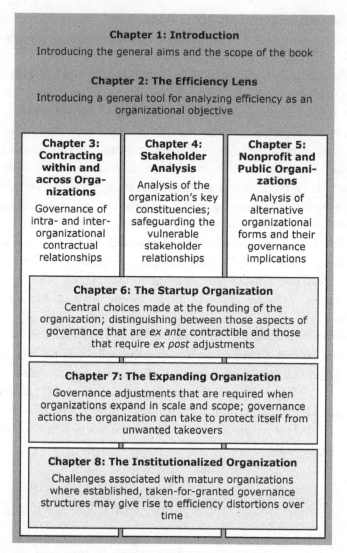

Chapter 1: Introduction

Introducing the general aims and the scope of the book

Chapter 2: The Efficiency Lens

Introducing a general tool for analyzing efficiency as an organizational objective

Chapter 3: Contracting within and across Organizations

Governance of intra- and inter-organizational contractual relationships

Chapter 4: Stakeholder Analysis

Analysis of the organization's key constituencies; safeguarding the vulnerable stakeholder relationships

Chapter 5: Nonprofit and Public Organizations

Analysis of alternative organizational forms and their governance implications

Chapter 6: The Startup Organization

Central choices made at the founding of the organization; distinguishing between those aspects of governance that are *ex ante* contractible and those that require *ex post* adjustments

Chapter 7: The Expanding Organization

Governance adjustments that are required when organizations expand in scale and scope; governance actions the organization can take to protect itself from unwanted takeovers

Chapter 8: The Institutionalized Organization

Challenges associated with mature organizations where established, taken-for-granted governance structures may give rise to efficiency distortions over time

Figure 1.1 The structure of the book

credibility has numerous inefficiency consequences, such as excessive employee turnover, higher cost of capital, underinvestment in R&D, and various contractual disputes, to name just a few common examples.

The Efficiency Lens also helps us give useful definitions and ways of describing both the content and the dynamics of various organizational forms. For example, we can use the Efficiency Lens to define a nonprofit organization as the organizational form with no residual claimant, and to describe the modern corporation as an organization where management, oversight, and risk are materially separated from one another. We can also use the Efficiency Lens to describe governance changes that take place in a startup firm as it grows and heads toward an initial public offering. The Efficiency Lens constitutes the primary interpretative tool throughout all the chapters.

Chapter 3: Contracting within and across Organizations

Contracts and contracting are at the heart of private ordering. In chapter 3, we turn our attention to contracting and the associated costs of transacting. Instead of treating intra- and interorganizational transacting separately, we combine both into one chapter; the designer's choice is often to organize an exchange relationship either within the organization or across organizations. For example, in deciding how to safeguard intellectual property, a high-technology firm may consider either contracting with an external law firm or hiring an in-house counsel. It is useful to contrast the alternatives to determine which is more efficient. In chapter 3, the objective of efficient organizing becomes particularly salient: Alternative forms of contracting can often be explicitly compared in terms of their total cost.

Jointly discussing contracting within and across organizations makes sense also because many intraorganizational contracts have characteristics similar to interorganizational contracts. In their insightful examination of internal transactions, management scholar Robert Eccles and sociologist Harrison White (1988) noted that markets often exhibit authority properties found within firms and that multidivisional firms may contain pricing mechanisms found in markets.

Chapter 4: Stakeholder Analysis

We have found many stakeholder conversations to lack analytical rigor. Consequently, in our exposition of stakeholder issues in chapter 4, we focus specifically on stakeholder *analysis*: What are the criteria by which a constituency becomes considered a stakeholder? How should stakeholders be prioritized? How should the fact that a constituency is considered a stakeholder be incorporated into governance decisions?

Our approach to stakeholder analysis is based on risk in general and *residual risk* in particular. Accordingly, we define as stakeholders those constituencies who, by virtue of becoming involved with the organization, have voluntarily put something at stake. The shareholder of the limited liability company is the obvious stakeholder, but it is often an oversimplification to consider the shareholder the only stakeholder. For example, many contemporary employment relationships allocate more risk to employees, offer lower job security, and incorporate variable compensation as a significant determinant of wages (e.g., Rousseau and Shperling 2003, 2004). Consequently, at least some employees, or employee groups, may have a legitimate residual interest in the organization, just like shareholders. Organizations may also develop stakeholder relationships with suppliers and customers that make relation-specific investments.

In chapter 4, we propose that a systematic stakeholder analysis be conducted to rigorously examine all the relationships the organization has with its constituencies. Further, promoting a constituency to stakeholder status must have implications for how the relationship is governed, lest stakeholder management regress to mere rhetoric. Managing stakeholder relationships calls for the implementation of safeguards that would be redundant (and wasteful) in transactional, arm's-length relationships.

Chapter 5: Nonprofit and Public Organizations

Even though all chapters in this book apply both to for-profit and nonprofit contexts, we dedicate one entire chapter to governance issues outside the conventional corporate context. In chapter 5, we examine the implications of an organization not having a residual claimant who expects a return on investment. Or perhaps more accurately, what are the implications of not having any other residual claimants than the organization itself?

Note that the distinction between for-profits and nonprofits is not about whether the organization creates an economic surplus. In reality, both for-profits and nonprofits make a surplus and have net worth. A central governance question in nonprofits is how a potential surplus is governed in the absence of a residual claimant. Ultimately, managing the surplus is just as relevant to nonprofits as it is to for-profits.

In chapter 5, we also examine the public/private distinction. What does it mean for an organization to be public, and what are the governance implications? Because most public organizations are more accurately described as public-private partnerships, the question is less about what distinguishes a public organization from a private one and more on what kinds of roles public and private actors can assume in these partnerships.

Chapter 5 also offers an important challenge to the analysis of net gains and efficient contracting. This analysis becomes salient as we examine contexts in which the relationships between the organization and its constituencies are not essentially contractual, and where participation in the organization is not necessarily voluntary. In contexts such as psychiatric care, primary education, and incarceration, the designer's primary attention must be to ensure organizational integrity, making efficiency, at best, a secondary concern. The discussions and the examples in chapter 5 provide an important boundary condition for both efficiency thinking and the contractual approach to organizations.

Chapter 6: The Startup Organization

Sociologist Arthur Stinchcombe (1965) famously argued that organizations "are frozen at birth" in the sense that initial conditions have long-lasting consequences. In chapter 6, we examine the design choices made at the founding of the organization: What are the central founding decisions that establish the initial organization design and governance conditions? In this chapter, the importance of understanding private ordering becomes pronounced. The assumption that laws, regulations, and other institutions offer adequate guidance and protection for the designer of a startup is misguided. In chapter 6, we discuss, among other topics, the function of the shareholders' agreement in startup companies.

The general message in chapter 6 evolves around the importance of considering organization design and governance as *ex ante* problems: How does the designer make decisions regarding organization design and governance in a forward-looking manner? Which potential future problems can be folded, either wholly or partially, into an *ex ante* contract? Which problems, in turn, are not *ex ante* contractible, and how should the designer think of them at the moment of the organization's founding? What kinds of safeguards can be implemented in the case of noncontractible issues?

Chapter 7: The Expanding Organization

As the organization grows, the scale and the scope of its activities expand, the need for oversight becomes more elaborate, and many constituencies develop stakeholder relationships with the organization, effectively becoming risk-bearers. In this chapter, we propose that the governance challenges expanding organizations face are ultimately caused not by the expansion itself but the fact that management, oversight, and risk—the three elements of the Efficiency Lens (chapter 2)—gradually separate from one another. For example, although those who make the most important decisions tend also to populate the board of directors in a startup organization, an expanding firm must start appointing independent members to its board of directors, effectively separating management from oversight. Similarly, as the organization expands, not everyone who bears risk can be afforded an oversight role, effectively separating oversight from risk. Not only the expansion of management, oversight, and risk but also their separation requires the designer's attention.

As management, oversight, and risk become separated, the expanding organization may also become vulnerable to takeovers. In chapter 7, we examine the ways in which expanding organizations can seek protection against unwanted takeovers. We also investigate the conditions under which various antitakeover provisions are recommended and whom they ultimately protect. Importantly, whether a takeover is wanted or unwanted is not straightforward; it may be welcomed by some constituencies but strongly resisted by others.

Chapter 8: The Institutionalized Organization

Sociologist and legal scholar Philip Selznick (1957, 16–17) noted that the institutionalization of an activity, structure, or routine involves "infusion of value beyond the technical requirements of the task at hand." Such "infusion of value" may have both desirable and undesirable consequences. In this chapter, we examine the undesirable consequences of institutionalization. To the extent that organization design and governance choices become institutionalized and are no longer being relentlessly questioned, analyzed, and modified, institutionalization may lead to various *efficiency distortions*.

In chapter 8, we examine the reasons why governance choices tend to become taken for granted or otherwise persist over time without being questioned or challenged. We focus in particular on the persistence of the internal organization, that is, the principles and practices that become institutionalized *within* organizations. In our discussion of institutionalization, we further focus primarily on the *inadvertent* sources of persistence. For example, once implemented, the division of tasks by function—*functional structure*—tends to persist over time. One reason for persistence is that functional managers start to protect the interests of their own functions and actively resist change. Although we acknowledge the role of active resistance, we direct the designer's attention to the more elusive source of persistence: the inability to identify comparatively efficient alternatives because the current structure has become taken for granted and "infused with value" beyond the purpose it was intended to serve.

Epilogue

We end the book by a brief reprise of the book's central messages, along with an important reminder of the central boundary conditions in the applicability of comparative efficiency analysis to governance decisions. Even though we promote efficiency thinking throughout the chapters, we find it important to remind all designers of the boundaries of its applicability.

2

The Efficiency Lens

In thinking of how to approach the subject matter of organization design and governance, we are faced with a fundamental challenge: How do we do justice to the vast heterogeneity of organizations? How can we write about organizations and analyze them without arriving at the predictable conclusion that every organization is unique and that there simply is no one right way to organize? All one has to do to conclude that every organization is unique is to glance at a chart that depicts the organization's structure.

At the same time, there are a number of general characteristics featured in all organizations. Insofar as governance is concerned, we suggest that there are three: *management, oversight,* and *risk* (see fig. 2.1). The framework introduced in this chapter—the Efficiency Lens—combines these three, their dynamics, and their interrelationships. The Efficiency Lens is based on roughly one hundred years of organizational research and at least as many years of practical experience and recorded company history. The Efficiency Lens is not based on any specific theory of management or of economics but, instead, incorporates ideas from several theories and ways of approaching organizations from an efficiency perspective.

The main premise in the Efficiency Lens is that in seeking efficient organizing, the designer should adopt three objectives: (1) organizing and coordinating individual activities in the organization efficiently, (2) ensuring that individual activities align with the interests of the entire organization, and (3) safeguarding the interests of those who have something at stake in the organization.

Let us briefly explore the metaphor of a lens by pointing to three distinct events that occur when we observe an object through a lens. All three reveal something essential about the utility of the Efficiency Lens.

The first is that a lens can bring something into focus so that it can be seen more clearly. As the name suggests, the Efficiency Lens brings economic efficiency into focus. In this sense, we can think of the Efficiency Lens as if it were a set of eyeglasses.

Efficient Organization. Mikko Ketokivi and Joseph T. Mahoney, Oxford University Press. © Oxford University Press 2023.
DOI: 10.1093/oso/9780197610282.003.0002

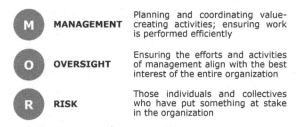

M	**MANAGEMENT**	Planning and coordinating value-creating activities; ensuring work is performed efficiently
O	**OVERSIGHT**	Ensuring the efforts and activities of management align with the best interest of the entire organization
R	**RISK**	Those individuals and collectives who have put something at stake in the organization

Figure 2.1 The three elements of the Efficiency Lens

The second is that a lens can magnify, thus exposing the detailed characteristics of the object of interest. Magnifying is useful as you read the fine print of an insurance policy, for example. In contrast with eyeglasses, when a lens magnifies, it does not bring something into focus as much as it emphasizes something with the purpose of enabling a careful examination of its detail. In this sense, we can think of the Efficiency Lens as if it were a magnifying glass.

Finally, a lens is a useful metaphor because it emphasizes the active role and expertise of the observer. Both a microbiologist and a layperson can view the structure of a coronavirus through the set of lenses of a microscope. To the layperson, the image may appear novel and fascinating, but aside from perhaps learning to appreciate why the word *corona* (crown) was used to name the virus, there is not much more that can be learned. In stark contrast, a microbiologist or a virologist will find the image informative and useful. Therefore, the utility of a lens is fundamentally dependent on user expertise; it is useless to apply a lens without some understanding of what one is looking at. In this sense, we can think of the Efficiency Lens as if it were a microscope.

Building the Efficiency Lens

In constructing the Efficiency Lens, we face a dilemma. On the one hand, we want to use the established terms *management*, *oversight*, and *risk*; inventing new concepts would lead to confusion. On the other hand, because our aim is to provide a general lens applicable to all organizations, we use these terms in meanings that are both broader and more malleable than they are in many conventional treatments on organization design and governance. Consequently, we invite all readers "to reboot their conceptual hard drives."

Rebooting the Conceptual Hard Drive

Let us reexamine some of the taken-for-granted meanings of organizational terminology. This reexamination is particularly important in the context of organization design and governance, where the terminology has a feature that is as frustrating as it is fascinating: Over time, the original neutral meanings of many concepts have acquired conspicuously negative connotations.

What is the first thought that comes to mind as you read the words *centralization, control, hierarchy, authority,* and *bureaucracy*? All five were originally introduced as neutral, descriptive terms, but for some reason, all have been permeated with negative associations. These negative associations have become so widespread that they have made their way into dictionaries. A quick glance at a few online dictionaries reveals that although some of the definitions of *bureaucracy* are neutral (as in "following predetermined rules"), others are evaluative (as in "complicated rules"), even pejorative (as in "excessive red tape"). We counsel the reader to heed the intended neutral definitions.

Why this infusion with negative connotations occurs is a mystery to us. Perhaps its origins are in a recurring, enduring problem we encounter in the popular press on organizations—an obsession with novelty. The rhetoric is familiar enough: Established ways of organizing are outdated as they no longer meet the requirements of contemporary organizations and business environments. Centralization, hierarchy, and bureaucracy belong to the dustbin of history; today's organizations are all about replacing hierarchies with flexible lateral structures, self-management, and informal networks. Alas, a rigorous, dispassionate analysis of organizations reveals that both hierarchies (e.g., Leavitt 2005) and bureaucracy (e.g., Adler and Borys 1996) are essential to all organizations, and that there is a time and a place for centralization (e.g., Alonso, Dessein, and Matouschek 2008). The question is, "When, where, and how?"

As an example, consider centralization and, specifically, the geographic centralization of activities. Some technology firms have concluded that centralizing research and development (R&D) into one large, centralized R&D center is preferred; others decentralize their R&D activities to smaller, specialized, and geographically dispersed R&D units. There is no general prescription or best practice, instead, the degree of centralization constitutes a design decision that, just like all design decisions, must be linked to the main problem the designer seeks to address. In their empirical examination of organizing R&D, organization scholars Nicholas Argyres and Brian Silverman (2004, 929, 930) found that centralized R&D tends to "generate innovations that have larger and broader impact on subsequent technological evolution," whereas decentralized R&D "encourages more proximate ('capabilities-deepening') research." Therefore, there is nothing inherently superior about decentralization (or centralization), everything depends on what the designer is trying to achieve. The same logic applies to all other concepts.

As another example, let us revisit *management*, one of the three central concepts of the Efficiency Lens. Here, we find the writings of Chester Barnard particularly insightful. Barnard was not an academic but an executive who authored a number of prescient and influential works in the early twentieth century, most notably his 1938 book *The Functions of the Executive* (Barnard 1938). We invoke Barnard's work here not only because of his unique and highly influential impact on both the practice of management and research on organizations but also because his approach helps us convey the broader meaning of management.

Above all else, Barnard emphasized that the main function of the organization's top leadership—"the executive"—was to secure the continuing, voluntary cooperation of all those who create value in the organization. With this objective in mind, Barnard's approach to management authority was based not on top-down command but rather on bottom-up consent: "Management's authority, Barnard realized, rested on its ability to persuade, rather than to command" (Mahoney 2002, 164). Moreover, Barnard explicitly warned about the dangers of thinking of organizational authority in terms of directing the work of others: "You put a [person] in charge of an organization and your worst difficulty is that [he or she] thinks [he or she] has to tell everybody what to do; and that's almost fatal if it's carried far enough" (Wolf 1973, 30).

To be clear, the purpose of invoking Barnard's ideas is not to promote persuasion over command and control; this would amount to uncritically replacing one orthodoxy with another. We refer to Barnard's work because he offers a valuable contrast by presenting the broadest possible approach to what management can be. Specifically, coordination of work and exercise of authority can be based on command and control, but they can also be based on persuasion.

Which should it be, then, persuasion or command? Just as in the case of centralization, how to organize management is a design choice. Persuasion may sound intuitively and emotionally more appealing than command, but organization design is not about what sounds good or seems fashionable; it is about what a rigorous analysis of alternatives reveals to be comparatively efficient. Returning to the taxi ride example in chapter 1, owning (or not owning) a car because it feels intuitively or emotionally appealing misses the point of efficient organizing entirely.

The purpose of "rebooting our conceptual hard drives" is to purge our minds of misleading and negative connotations that are unfortunately common in our thinking about organizations. To the end of avoiding negative associations, we invite the reader not only to think of all the concepts that follow in neutral terms but also all contrasts in terms of potentially viable alternatives. Just as there are no "positive" and "negative" concepts in this book, we do not compare "good" and "bad" governance options to one another. The point of a comparative efficiency analysis is to compare feasible alternatives to one another.

Negative connotations are dangerous precisely because they may lead the designer to dismiss an option that may in fact offer the comparatively efficient governance alternative. Students in our business school seminars are caught by surprise when they find out in the classroom discussion on the technology giant Cisco Systems that at the foundation of its organization resides a decidedly old-fashioned, functional structure (Gulati 2010). At the same time, a rigorous analysis reveals that as old-fashioned as it may sound, the functional organization makes perfect sense not only for Cisco but also to many others.

Management

The job of automobile assembly plants is to perform the final assembly of automobiles; the job of a law firm specializing in intellectual property is to enable its clients to manage, protect, and trade and license their patents; the job of a cardiovascular care unit of a hospital is to perform heart surgeries. All organizations have a primary job that needs to get done, and how this work is organized and coordinated is an essential part of governance. The management aspect of governance directs attention to how value-creating activities are divided and coordinated within and across organizations. Furthermore, the Efficiency Lens directs attention specifically to ways in which management should be organized to avoid waste: by avoiding excessive layers, redundancies, excessively complex cross-unit linkages, poorly defined accountability, and so on (e.g., Goold and Campbell 2002b).

In the Efficiency Lens, management does not refer to any specific individual, or individuals, and is not to be interpreted as synonymous with manager or managers. Instead, management refers more generally to *managerial work* that is relevant in all organizations: planning and scheduling, task and resource allocation, coordination, and the like. Whether this work is performed by individuals whose role in the formal structure is that of a manager is an altogether different issue, and a matter of choice. Some organizations choose to employ managers to perform managerial work; others choose not to assign managerial work to a separate class of employees called managers. In addition, in many organizations routinized managerial work such as planning and scheduling may also be automated to a significant degree, that is, embedded in various enterprise resource planning (ERP) systems.

If the idea of organizing without managers sounds utopian, we might note that professional managers have not existed all that long in the history of organizations. Indeed, the formal position of a manager in organizations did not emerge until the 1800s in the context of the industrial revolution. At the same time, management historians Wolfgang Pindur, Sandra Rogers, and Pan Suk Kim (1995, 59) noted that the use of various management techniques, such as systematic written records of business transactions, can be traced back to as early as 3000 BCE.

The Efficiency Lens does not take the formal position of manager as a given; instead, it is presented as one alternative of organizing management. Given the increasing recent interest in *self-managing organizations*, the idea of not having formal managerial positions in the organization should not seem too strange (Lee and Edmondson 2017). Simply put, yes, managers do perform managerial work, but managerial work need not be performed by a person whose business card has the word *manager* on it.[1]

---

[1] Lee and Edmondson (2017, 46) make the point succinctly in their discussion of self-managing organizations (SMOs): "Eliminating 'managers' as a formal role does not mean self-managing organizations are devoid of managerial work. The work of monitoring progress towards organizational goals, allocating resources or projects, designing tasks and organizational structures, and providing feedback to individuals remain vital to effectiveness in SMOs. However, in SMOs, these authorities are formally distributed to individuals in a way that is not permanent, unbounded, or vested in hierarchical rank." Hamel (2011) made similar arguments in his *Harvard Business Review* article provocatively entitled "First, Let's Fire All the Managers." There is nothing utopian about the idea of an organization where employees are in charge of managing their own work. However, we recommend that the designers remain relentlessly comparative: The question, "Does this organization need to hire managers, and if yes, for what purpose?" requires an explicit comparative evaluation of the alternatives.

Of course, many contemporary organizations choose to structure themselves in a way that makes managers central to management. Insofar as individual organizational members are concerned, we include in management not only executives and top management but more broadly everyone involved in the planning and coordination of value-adding activities. In a manufacturing firm, this includes everyone from C-suite executives and middle managers to production supervisors and team leaders. In a hospital, managerial positions are held by hospital administrators and administrative staff as well as those directly providing care to patients (i.e., doctors, nurses, and other clinical staff). To make matters simple, let us suggest that organizational members are a part of management when (1) they have an employment relationship with the organization, and (2) their job description includes at least some planning and coordination responsibilities.

The notion of management is neither limited to top management nor about a person at one level of the organization directing the activities of those at lower organizational levels in a top-down manner. At the same time, the definition does not exclude a top-down approach either. Sometimes planning and coordination are most efficiently performed in a centralized manner by the organization's top managers. A hierarchical top-down organization may constitute the comparatively efficient organizing alternative in stable organizational environments where the organization's task is well defined and unchanging, and where innovation is not a central concern (Burns and Stalker 1961).

Are there still stable environments in today's dynamic world? Of course there are. For example, the demand for public transportation in a given city on a given day is reasonably predictable, and this predictability provides the most important input to those who plan the daily routes and schedules of buses, trams, and trains. We might also point out that the talk about increasing uncertainty, hypercompetition, and other destabilizing factors tends not to survive critical empirical scrutiny. We propose that thinking that we live in special times is a variation on the obsession-with-novelty theme. We invite those who think the world is more dynamic and unpredictable today than it was in the past to look at the evidence.[2]

---

[2] McNamara, Vaaler, and Devers (2003) conducted an empirical analysis using the Compustat Industry Segment Database from 1978 to 1997. Their conclusion was that "managers today face markets no more dynamic and opportunities to gain and sustain competitive advantage no more challenging than in the past." McNamara et al. (2003, 261).

The Role of Technology in Management

Humans are not the only ones to perform work and to add value. Consequently, management is not limited to human beings. Using welding robots in car assembly and artificial intelligence to automate formalized tasks in a law firm are salient examples of technology creating value. Furthermore, just as in the case of employees, we suggest that thinking of technological assets as entities that have a contractual relationship with the organization is useful. Specifically, some productive assets are the property of the organization and appear on its balance sheet. Some of these assets are further employed both in direct and indirect productive uses. For example, just like consumers may choose to borrow against the equity of the house in which they live, an industrial firm may use general-purpose production equipment as collateral in debt financing.

It should be equally clear that an organization can make productive use of assets it does not carry on its balance sheet. For example, it may not make economic sense for a global car rental company to own the entire fleet of hundreds of thousands of vehicles it rents out to customers. Instead, various leasing arrangements likely provide economically more efficient contracting alternatives. Indeed, one foundational question of governance is choosing which assets to own and which to borrow: Which components should a manufacturer produce in-house, and which should it outsource? Does it make sense for a hotel chain to own the buildings that host its activities? How about the land on which these buildings are located? Does it make sense for a business school to rely on visiting faculty to teach its classes? Should oil companies carry a fleet of oil tankers on their balance sheet? These are examples of *make-or-buy decisions*, which constitute an essential part of management.

Fully realizing that using the word *asset* to refer not only to firms and technologies but also to humans may sound awkward; nonetheless, we will do so, because in an economic analysis of organizations, it is useful to think of assets as all the entities, human or otherwise, involved in value creation. This said, nothing in our use of the word *asset* in reference to humans suggests that they should be treated the same way as technology; we merely want to point to the advantages of seeing and analyzing the organization as an entity that has contractual relationships with other firms, value-creating technologies, and human beings.

Oversight

How should a multinational manufacturing firm conduct analyses regarding production location decisions? How is the decision to go public by an initial public offering (IPO) made in a high-technology startup? How should the police department structure the compensation of its police officers? What is the process by which a theater company or a symphony orchestra chooses its program for the upcoming season?

Some questions that organizations face are more foundational than planning and coordinating specific activities (i.e., management) in that they pertain to the general rules, principles, and structures that guide decision making in specific decision situations. It is useful to treat these more general questions separately from questions of management. In the Efficiency Lens, these general questions belong to the domain of *oversight*.

In many conversations, what we call here oversight is equated with governance. However, we consider such a definition of governance unnecessarily narrow. We propose that although oversight is essential *to* governance, it is not the essence *of* governance. We think of governance more broadly in terms of the entire Efficiency Lens: as a triple that encompasses management, oversight, and risk, and how the three relate to one another over time. We hope that the following chapters will show the utility of this broader conceptualization. Most importantly, we cannot write about efficient organization without considering all three factors.

To arrive at a sufficiently broad understanding of oversight, we link its task to three governance issues: (1) the best interest of the organization, (2) residual income, and (3) residual rights of control.

The Best Interest of the Organization

In 2016, Tesla paid $2.6 billion to acquire SolarCity, a company that sells solar energy generation systems. The acquisition created controversy among a number of union pension funds and asset managers whose organizations held stock in Tesla. In 2017, a number of dissatisfied shareholders filed a lawsuit against Tesla's board of directors, alleging that the SolarCity acquisition amounted to a bailout, and that it was Tesla's CEO Elon Musk, his friends, and his family who had benefited from the acquisition. At the time of the acquisition, Mr. Musk chaired SolarCity's board of directors and was its largest shareholder. Further, SolarCity's founders Peter and Lyndon Rive are Mr. Musk's first cousins. Tesla's entire board of directors was named in the lawsuit, but by the time the trial started in 2021, everyone but Mr. Musk had settled the lawsuit out of court.

We do not know whether the lawsuit has merit and take no sides on the substance of the dispute. The trial is ongoing, and it is now the task of the trial judge to decide whether the acquisition was fair to Tesla's shareholders or not. Our point is that the controversy surrounding Tesla effectively raises a foundational governance question: How can the designer ensure that when the organization delegates decisions to its members, the decisions that are made serve not the local interests of those who are trusted to make the decision but, more broadly, the best interest of the entire organization? This is one of the questions that belongs to the domain of oversight. Shareholders filing a lawsuit against the entire board of directors suggests that at least some stakeholders think that there is something seriously wrong with oversight.

There are many reasons why local decisions and broader organizational interests do not align. One possibility is that the decision is made with the explicit intent of serving interests other than those of the organization; the decision maker willfully and deliberately ignores or violates broader organizational interests. Such self-serving behavior lies at the heart of the *agency problem* (see chapter 1).[3]

Although misalignment of the principal's and the agent's priorities may be the direct result of opportunistic behavior by the agent, self-serving behaviors have in our view received disproportionate amounts of attention. There are other, comparatively benign possibilities that merit the designer's attention. Specifically, misalignment of local decisions and broader interests can also stem from the agent being more risk averse than the principal. Consequently, the agent's decision may be more conservative than what the principal would prefer. But reluctance to take risks is not necessarily a manifestation of self-serving behavior or opportunism; the agent may simply be more preoccupied with the survival of the organization than the principal. Particularly in situations where the principal is equated with shareholders who are free to sell their shares in the open market, we might go so far as to suggest that the

[3] In the context of the limited liability company, we commonly think of the shareholders as the principal and managers as the agents. Consequently, the best interest of the organization translates to shareholder wealth. However, this is only one possible formulation of the agency problem.

fact that the agent's preferences and the principal's preferences regarding the organization's survival do not coincide "is not a bug but a feature."

Other, even less deliberate sources of misalignment link to decision makers' limited cognitions. All of us tend to approach decision situations by incorporating primarily the local context in which we operate and the unavoidably limited and specialized expertise and experience we have. We do the best we can, but the limits to cognition, experience, and information—in short, *bounded rationality*—get the best of us. Bounded rationality can lead to misalignment, conflict, and disagreements of an altogether benign variety.

One often hears bounded rationality used as a catch-all phrase to describe all the possible limitations of human decision makers. However, understanding the nuances of bounded rationality has profound implications for governance. Specifically, many conflicts to which opportunism is ascribed may be merely honest disagreements due to different individuals having access to different kinds of information and different bases of expertise. To be sure, not only opportunistic behavior but also honest disagreements can be sources of inefficiency in organizations. Organization economists Armen Alchian and Susan Woodward (1988, 66) elaborate: "Even when both parties recognize the genuine goodwill of the other, different but honest perceptions can lead to disputes that are costly to resolve." They also counsel against immediately interpreting the use of various safeguards such as monitoring as attempts to preempt opportunism: "[M]any business arrangements interpreted as responses to potential 'dishonest' opportunism are equally appropriate for avoiding costly disputes between honest, ethical people who disagree about what event transpired and what adjustment would have been agreed to initially had the event been anticipated" (Alchian and Woodward, 1988, 66).

The problem with failing to understand how bounded rationality operates in decision making is that it may lead to excessively negative readings of a conflict situation and, consequently, an unnecessarily adversarial approach to its resolution. The purpose of checks and balances in organizations or formal contracts between buyers and suppliers is not merely, or even primarily, to curb opportunistic behaviors; they are also a manifestation of the fact that organizations are populated by human beings with severely limited cognitions.

The more benign distortions may occur even in situations where we are explicitly encouraged and genuinely motivated to approach decisions from an organization-wide perspective. It should not come as a surprise that a sales manager "sees" a given organizational problem differently than a production manager, even when the two are explicitly instructed to ignore their specific positions and adopt an organization-wide perspective.[4] As psychologists such as Nobel Laureate Daniel Kahneman (e.g., Kahneman 2011; Kahneman, Slovic, and Tversky 1982) and scores of others have shown, cognitive biases are endemic not just to organizations but to humans more generally. As hard as we try to make rational decisions, our rationality is bounded, and our access to information limited. Insofar as designing organizations is concerned, it is wishful thinking to assume that functional managers can simply shed their functional backgrounds and expertise and approach an issue from an organization-wide perspective. The resultant, unavoidable *position bias* can lead to locally efficient but globally (organizationally) inefficient decisions and solutions (Ketokivi and Castañer 2004).

Keeping the problems stemming from limited cognitions separate from those driven by deliberate opportunistic behaviors is crucial because the two have different antecedents and remedies. In the case of opportunism, the problem is intentional and motivational, and in the case of limitations, inadvertent and cognitive. Governance actions required to curb opportunistic behavior differ from the actions required to address problems arising from cognitive biases. Whereas boards can incentivize top managers to make risky decisions (this is what stock options are designed to do), incentives are generally inefficient when it comes to problems arising from cognitive limitations. However, every designer must take measures to counter various sources of misalignment between individual decisions and the organization's best interest. Ensuring alignment is one of the main tasks of oversight.

Just like management, oversight involves individuals. The most salient part of the organization charged with oversight is a board of some kind. Boards come in different forms and with different names, depending on the context. For-profit limited liability companies have *boards of directors*, universities have *boards of regents*, the Spanish Railway Foundation and the

---

[4] In a classic study of managerial perceptions, organization scholars DeWitt Dearborn and Herbert Simon (1958) had a group of executives from different functional departments of the same manufacturing company read the Castengo Steel Company case used in instruction in business schools in the 1950s. Before discussing the case, the executives were asked to write a brief statement of the problem they thought Castengo faced. The executives were further explicitly instructed to approach the Castengo case from the point of view of the company instead of their own department or function. Yet, most sales executives saw sales as the main problem, production executives saw the problem as one of internal organization, and so forth.

Rockefeller Foundation have *boards of trustees*, the Federal Reserve System has a *board of governors*, and so on. All these boards have a job to do, but this job must be distinguished from the job of management. Board members typically do not have employment contracts with the organization but, instead, fixed-term appointments with little job security. In many limited liability companies, board members may be dismissed without cause at every annual shareholders' meeting. It is often useful to think of those serving on the board not as members but as *stewards* of the organization; we also find the word *trustee* descriptively accurate. The task of a steward or a trustee is to ensure that the members of the organization act in the best interest of the entire organization and all its stakeholders, whoever they happen to be in the specific situation. In short, board membership is a position of trust, not advocacy. We return to the fiduciary (as opposed to contractual) role of boards in chapters 4 and 5.

Just like management consists of both human and nonhuman assets, oversight involves both individuals and groups making decisions (at board, committee, and shareholders' meetings), as well as various rules, guidelines, and procedures. Some of these rules and procedures are provided by the institutional environment, most notably, the relevant laws. However, others are provided by the organization itself as matters of private ordering: articles of association, bylaws, and scores of both formal and informal contracts. Consistent with the Fifth Premise in chapter 1 ("Focus on Private Ordering"), we focus on the organization-specific instruments available to designers to use at their discretion. Thus, in examining the governance of startup firms (chapter 6), for example, we focus less on what the law stipulates and more on what the founders can and should do to ensure efficient governance.

Alignment of local actions within the organization with broader organizational interests is important but not the only function of oversight. We propose that decisions regarding oversight must also address how a potential organizational residual (e.g., an economic surplus) is governed. To this end, the designer must understand the role of residual claims and residual rights of control in oversight.

Residual Claims

In their groundbreaking book *The Behavioral Theory of the Firm*, organization scholars Richard Cyert and James March ([1963] 1992, 42) suggested that organizations become particularly interesting when they exhibit at least some *slack*. In this context, slack refers to some form of excess that is not immediately required to keep the organization functioning.

Imagine an organization that always consumes all the resources available to it just to be able to function. Such an organization would be in many ways simpler than one with slack. What an organization should do with the resources it does not need for immediate use is indeed a central question for oversight—in short, slack must be governed. An organization with zero slack is simpler because governing slack is unnecessary.

Consider the most salient form of organizational slack: An organization creates revenue, and after all contractual and legal obligations have been met, there is something left over. In the corporate context, this leftover is called *profit*, but since our focus here is more broadly on organizations, we use the more general term *surplus*. Nonprofit organizations such as universities often produce an economic surplus, and since it would be confusing to speak of "a nonprofit making a profit," we suggest surplus is a better term.

What kinds of rules guide the decisions regarding the governance of the surplus? In some organizations, someone can make an explicit claim for the residual; these are called *residual claimants*. Residual claims and claimants are most commonly discussed in the context of for-profit organizations incorporated as limited liability companies where shareholders are residual claimants.

Some organizations have residual claimants, others do not, or, more accurately, in other organizations the only residual claimant is the organization itself. In such organizations, a potential economic surplus will be used solely for the benefit of the organization. Fama and Jensen (1983a, 318) proposed this as a straightforward definition of a nonprofit organization, which we adopt in this book as well. Specifically, a nonprofit organization is one that has no residual claimants other than the organization itself. Therefore, the criterion of a nonprofit is not whether or not the organization produces an economic surplus but whether someone is entitled to appropriate it in the form of private benefits. As a general rule, nonprofit organizations—particularly those that receive a favorable tax treatment—are not allowed to grant private benefits. We return to nonprofit organizations, with examples, in chapter 5.

Organization economists Armen Alchian and Harold Demsetz (1972, 789) insightfully asked: "[W]hy should stockholders be regarded as 'owners' in any sense distinct from other financial investors?" To justify their position, Alchian and Demsetz maintained that the primary difference between shareholders and bondholders, as investors, was that the former were more optimistic about the future of the firm. We partly agree with Alchian and Demsetz's position but suggest that shareholders are indeed owners of the corporation in an important sense: They have property rights over residual income. At the heart of ownership is residual income and residual control (Milgrom and Roberts 1990), which introduces the third aspect of oversight: residual rights of control.

Residual Rights of Control

The most elusive aspect of oversight relates to residual rights of control. Whereas residual income and residual claims refer to the economic surplus that is left over after all contractual obligations have been met, the notion of residual rights of control refers to all the considerations that remain unspecified in contracts. This shifts attention from deciding how to govern residual income to decisions about how the organization uses its assets; its materials, its technologies, its employees' time, and so on. Many aspects of how assets are to be used can be written into formal contracts, but long-term contracts in particular are often materially incomplete; they cannot possibly cover every detail, scenario, and contingency. The premise that contracts are often materially incomplete stands at the foundation of many economic approaches to governance.

Consider the scenario where a technology firm retains the services of a law firm in an intellectual property dispute with a competitor. The technology firm and the law firm enter into a materially incomplete, open-ended contract where the law firm agrees to represent the client. The contract is incomplete because many fundamental aspects of the contract, such as contract duration and total price remain unknown and unspecified. Who retains the decision rights over issues not covered in the contract? Here, the attention turns to the discretion and ownership aspects of oversight.

There is a long and rich tradition in the economics literature on what it means to own something. The main point in this literature is that the essence of ownership lies not so much in the legal conception of having title to an asset as it does in the organizational and practical implications of ownership.

This view takes us to the notion of control rights, residual rights of control in particular. In the following sections, we discuss two examples.

Residual Rights of Control in Specialized Industrial Production

Consider a production line that can produce in a single eight-hour shift a total of 150 ice hockey sticks made of carbon fiber and epoxy resin. Suppose further that the production line is highly specialized in that its production technology can be used only to produce said hockey sticks, nothing else. Then consider the design decision of whether the firm that sells the sticks should invest in the production technology and make the sticks in-house or outsource production to a technology supplier. In this example, what are the residual rights of control, and how are they relevant to the designer?

Suppose the hockey stick firm decides to focus on marketing and brand management and outsources stick production to an external supplier. In the buyer-supplier contract, the contracting parties specify contract duration, volumes, prices, delivery schedules, warranties, termination clauses, and other pertinent, contractible issues. At the same time, a lot will remain unspecified, making the contract materially incomplete. For example, it is highly unlikely that the contract will stipulate the geographic location where production takes place, when the sticks will be produced, who supplies the raw materials, how production equipment maintenance is to be arranged, and what kinds of employment contracts the factory employees will have. These unspecified issues can usefully be considered a residual, which we submit the designer should consider analogously with economic surplus when thinking of oversight. However, this residual does not take the form of an economic surplus but, rather, the rights to make decisions. The contractual party that gets to make the decisions regarding the issues not specified in the contract has the residual rights of control. From an organization design and governance point of view, this is the primary implication of ownership: The owner retains the residual rights of control.

Why not focus on ownership in intuitive and conventional terms? "I paid for it, I have title to it, I do as I please with it." Such thinking can be misdirected. The reasoning is as follows.

The expensive and highly specialized production line is designed to produce composite ice hockey sticks, nothing else. Thus, even though the owner of the production line can do with the production equipment "as it pleases," it really has no other option but "to please itself" with the production of ice hockey sticks made of carbon fiber and epoxy resin.[5] But this is exactly the same as what the buyer would have "to please itself with" if it decided to purchase the production technology and produce the sticks in-house. Therefore, no matter who holds title to the specialized technology, it will be used to produce ice hockey sticks.

Particularly in contexts where assets are highly specialized, the notion of "doing as one pleases" loses much of its relevance. We suggest that the relevant difference between in-house production and outsourcing has to do with residual rights of control. Again, both the buyer and the seller would use the specialized production equipment for the purposes of producing ice hockey sticks; there is no material difference here. In contrast, whether the residual rights of control remain with the buyer or the supplier has important implications.

Perhaps the most consequential question with regard to residual rights of control concerns production capacity: How many production lines will the factory host and in what geographic location, or locations? This question looks very different to the supplier and the buyer, and in the case of ice hockey stick production, likely leads to the conclusion that outsourcing will be comparatively efficient. Why?

In the ice hockey equipment business, those selling the equipment to consumers—Bauer, CCM, Warrior, True Hockey—are marketing and brand management firms with little in-house production. Both production and product design are outsourced to large, specialized technology firms in Southeast Asia. Furthermore, these technology firms seek to take advantage of both economies of scale and scope, and in their contracts with particular buyers, they reserve the right to use their technology to supply other buyers as well. Within their residual rights of control are also factory location decisions, supplier selection, workers' employment contracts, planning and scheduling of production, and R&D investments.

The buyers, in turn, understand that economies of scale and scope on the supplier side work to the buyers' advantage as well, even if it means that the same manufacturers also supply the competitors. Outsourcing production to

---

[5] There is also another, albeit less crucial, point about the firm "doing as it pleases" with the assets it owns. If an asset has been offered as collateral for a loan, the firm generally cannot sell the asset without the creditor's blessing. This, too, can be understood in terms of residual rights of control: The creditor maintains significant residual rights of control in decisions pertaining to the sale of the asset.

specialized technology firms that consolidate the production needs of multiple customers into one manufacturing firm is comparatively efficient, because economies of scale in production are such that an individual brand owner producing only to one's own needs would be inefficient. Large scale has the further advantage of making investments in specialized assets and automation attractive. If the small size of the production unit preempts such investments, inefficiency results from underinvestment in technology.

We can also think of residual rights of control from the point of view of factory management incentives. Suppose the buyer contemplates the option of in-house production by vertical integration whereby it would purchase a formerly separate and independent production plant, including all its employment contracts. Vertical integration may create a disincentive, perhaps even an explicit constraint, for plant management to seek clients other than the firm that owns the internal production unit. Perhaps the internal production unit would serve only an internal sales unit to which the sticks would be transferred using an arbitrary transfer price. After vertical integration, the production unit would likely be run as a cost center. Consequently, its profit would become arbitrary because it would depend on an arbitrary transfer price. Making the production plant a cost center instead of a profit center seems like a prudent alternative. But the trade-off is that if instead of assigning the plant profit-and-loss responsibility one only assigns cost responsibility (a budget), the plant management's incentives shift from value creation, innovation, and business expansion to cost control. Such incentive distortions may lead to substantial inefficiency. We return to the more general topic of *efficiency distortions* in chapter 8 where we discuss the governance challenges of established organizations.

Residual Rights of Control in Higher Education

A similar analysis can be applied in the examination of contracting with employees. In fact, the benefits of conceptualizing ownership through residual rights of control become particularly salient when the focus shifts from physical assets to work performed by humans. To be sure, the idea that a consulting firm or a university "owns its employees" is awkward. In contrast, the notion that the organization retains residual rights of control over its employees is salient.

Consider the question of whether a university should use internal faculty (employment contracts) or visiting and adjunct faculty (buyer-supplier contracts) to organize its teaching. Most universities use a combination of both, but there is considerable variability in degrees; some universities rely exclusively on internal faculty, but in others, visiting faculty dominates. There are many factors that account for this heterogeneity, but we suggest that one can gain insight by examining residual rights of control.

The contractual arrangement with visiting faculty is governed as either a one-off or a recurring contractor-contractee relationship. In the formal contract, all activities to be performed by the contractee can flexibly be tailored to fit the specific situation. For example, the contracting parties may agree that the visiting faculty member will teach an elective that consists of fifteen eighty-minute sessions on organization design and governance in the Master of Business Administration Program in the Fall 2022 semester.

The visiting faculty member is contractually bound to perform the specific activities stipulated in the contract but simultaneously retains many residual rights of control, such as what teaching techniques to use, whether to hold a final exam or have the students complete a group project, and how much weight to give to in-class participation in performance evaluation. In higher education, it is generally a good idea to leave residual rights of control regarding activities inside the classroom to the faculty member. Other residual rights of control, such as how many students will be allowed to enroll and where the class will be taught, are left to the employer.

The situation of the internal faculty member is different in a number of relevant ways. One is that whereas internal faculty members enjoy some of the same residual rights of control inside the classroom as the visiting faculty member, internal faculty members may be required to teach some courses using a common syllabus used by other professors as well. For example, a professor of operations management teaching a core MBA seminar on operations management may be required to coordinate syllabus content with other professors teaching the same core seminar, which materially limits the professor's discretion.

Another difference is found in the substance of the formal contract. Internal faculty members' employment contracts are written in comparatively general terms, leaving significantly broader residual rights of control to the employer. For example, the faculty member's employment contract may stipulate a teaching load of one hundred sessions every academic year, without specifying what courses the faculty member is to teach, to whom, and when. Similarly, the contract may require 240 hours of *service* per academic year, leaving the details of what this service entails to the employer's discretion. A professor's service could involve serving on faculty committees or as department chair, advising graduate students, applying for external grants, and the like. Some of the service could also be converted to teaching. Further specification in this case is generally the employer's prerogative; in short, the employer has residual rights of control.

That the university retains the primary residual rights of control does not mean that it should unilaterally dictate how internal faculty members are to allocate their time. If the university is interested in securing the long-term cooperation of particularly those faculty members it does not want to lose, it should be open to *ex post* negotiation and incorporate the faculty members' preferences into all decisions. For example, employment contracts seldom address teaching in the evenings and over the weekends, and it would be ill advised for the university to present unilateral requirements. A better alternative is to provide sufficient financial incentives to secure the cooperation of an adequate number of faculty members willing to devote their evenings or weekends to teaching.

Even though unilaterally dictating what the internal faculty member is to teach and when would likely be myopic, the central governance principle is that the university, not the faculty member, exercises oversight over the allocation of the faculty member's time. Accordingly, in the case of conflicting preferences, the university should be more comfortable challenging the internal faculty member's preferences than vice versa. Faculty members, at least those well versed in the ways of efficient governance, should feel compelled to accept the premise that in their employment relationship, the employer is entitled to exercise residual control, at least as long as it is in the employee's *zone of acceptance*. Hopefully, both contractual parties will be interested in seeking an efficient solution that establishes and maintains mutual credibility.

The upside of using visiting faculty is that no long-term commitments are required. This advantage has allowed universities to adjust to the COVID-19 pandemic. Specifically, whereas the university can selectively renew only those visiting faculty contracts required at any given time, it cannot terminate the contracts of internal faculty without substantive and substantial cause. In fact, in some jurisdictions the bar is set so high that unless the university can establish that the pandemic threatens the very survival of the organization, internal faculty members may contest as illegal any termination or suspension of employment if the main justification is that the employees' contributions are not needed at the particular time. This reasoning applies to private organizations as well: The employer must establish a legal (not merely an economic) basis for termination.

The downside of using visiting faculty is that unlike in the case of internal faculty, visiting faculty cannot flexibly be assigned to different organizational tasks if the situation calls for it. The visiting faculty members make an offer of how their time will be used, and once the university and the visiting faculty member sign the contract, the university has no further discretion. Asking the visiting professor at the last minute to teach another class is both unreasonable and infeasible; canceling the class at the last minute likely constitutes a breach of contract. With internal faculty members, in contrast, the university retains comparatively broader residual decision rights regarding the use of the internal faculty member's time even after the contract has been signed.

Why do we see such diversity in the extent to which universities use internal versus visiting faculty? It is undoubtedly partly a matter of university reputation, as leaning heavily toward using visiting faculty can be viewed as illegitimate. Simply put, a reputable business school has its own faculty, it does not borrow someone else's. However, we suggest that the diversity can also stem in part from different universities thinking differently about the extent to which they seek to maintain residual rights of control. Even though the use of visiting faculty may confer many advantages, a business school that allows itself to become dependent on visiting faculty can lead to highly unstable, fad-of-the-month-type course offerings from one year to the next. A university takes a considerable risk if it lets its curriculum depend on the availability of external contracting parties. Ultimately, this approach might even jeopardize the very survival of the university. In this sense, the reputation and the efficiency perspectives are intertwined.

The General Applicability and Implications of the Residual

The ice hockey production and university teaching examples apply more broadly to decision situations where an organization weighs the options of performing work internally versus contracting it out to external providers. The use of contract workers instead of employees is increasingly common in many organizational settings: The military and the construction industries make extensive use of contract workers; media companies buy content from freelance journalists; real estate and retail companies use independent sales agents instead of internal sales personnel; and so on. In all these contexts, the way in which residual rights of control are distributed among the contracting parties have efficiency implications and, therefore, constitute an important organization design consideration.

Similarly, the advantages and the disadvantages generalize to other settings. If an industrial firm makes a component in-house, it maintains residual rights of control regarding how it manages production. Analogously, if a firm has its own legal department and patent lawyers, it enjoys the benefit of having wide discretion over assigning particular lawyers to particular cases. If an external law firm is used, the client can make proposals for the timeline and request that specific lawyers be assigned to the case; however, the external firm retains residual rights of control on both the assignment of the client team and the timeline. The question of residual control has wide-ranging implications for the governance of contractual relationships.

Focusing on the residual also suggests an intriguing angle to ownership, as it challenges the conventional definition of ownership based on who holds the title to the asset. The conventional definition may be useful in many contexts, but we propose that in the specific context of governance, the residual offers a more useful vantage point to ownership. Specifically, instead of thinking of ownership as having the right to do with the asset as one pleases (as was the case in Roman law), it is more useful to think of ownership in terms of (1) who is entitled to exercise control over the decisions that are not specified in contracts (residual rights of control), and (2) who is entitled to the economic surplus the organization generates (rights to residual claims).

Considering residual rights of control and rights to residual claims separately is important, because as organization economist and Nobel Laureate Oliver Hart (1989, 1766) noted, "these rights will often go together, but they do not have to," which is why the designer must give attention to both. Only an explicit analysis of both residual claims and residual rights of control in the context of the organization will uncover the ramifications in their entirety. Understanding ownership as residual rights of control is particularly relevant in knowledge work contexts, such as professional service organizations. A consulting or a law firm does not own its employees in the conventional sense, but questions of residual rights of control are of foundational importance.

Risk

Numerous individuals and collectives create economic value for an organization and benefit from the organization's existence in one way or another;

we use the term *constituency* to refer to these individuals and collectives. However, the designer must acknowledge that some constituencies have more at stake in the organization than others. Accordingly, we reserve the term *stakeholder* to refer to those individuals and collectives that, by virtue of their participation in the organization, have voluntarily put something at risk, and consequently, have become vulnerable in one way or another. It is imperative that the designer understand the variable degrees of vulnerability among the organization's constituencies.

To us, stakeholder is not a distinct category but, rather, a comparative notion: Some constituencies have *more of* a stakeholder status with the organization than others. Categorizing constituencies into precisely demarcated stakeholders and nonstakeholders is an oversimplification with potentially adverse consequences.

What does it mean to put something at stake in an organization? In what ways do constituencies become vulnerable? We propose a simple thought exercise as a litmus test. Consider all the organization's constituencies, one at a time, and ask the following question: "If the organization unexpectedly ceased to exist, how would the specific constituency be affected?" All constituencies would undoubtedly be affected at least to an extent, but the rigorous designer analyzes degrees (see chapter 4 for details). Consequently, the designer must incorporate the variable degrees of risk into governance decisions. A failure to do so will jeopardize the credibility of the organization in the eyes of those who are asked to put the most at stake.

Note that the issue is not whether a constituency is vulnerable in the general sense but whether the constituency becomes vulnerable *by virtue of joining the organization.* For example, money provides buffers against uncertainty, and those with lower incomes tend to be in the general sense more vulnerable than those with higher incomes. This difference does not, however, mean that those who receive comparatively lower salaries in the organization should be considered vulnerable in the governance sense. The only situation in which low income implies vulnerability in the governance sense is if the employees' low income arises from their membership in the organization. An example is the employee of a startup. Startups are strapped for cash and cannot pay their employees, even CEOs, salaries that are anywhere close to being competitive. The designer must incorporate this discrepancy into governance decisions. In startups, the standard response is to compensate inadequate salaries with an equity stake.

Shareholders as Residual Claimants

The canonical risk taker is the shareholder of the limited liability company. In providing equity financing to the firm, the shareholder is guaranteed nothing, only a claim to the potential residual. Unlike employees and suppliers who are contractually guaranteed to receive *fixed payments* from the firm, the status of a constituency that receives only *residual payments* is comparatively vulnerable. The distinction of fixed versus residual payments is central.

An investor may pay €30 per share for a thousand shares, lose every last penny, and not be entitled to compensation of any kind from anyone; the shareholder is in principle risking everything without a safety net. This risk is partly alleviated in situations in which the shareholder is free to buy and to sell shares in an open market, thus transferring residual claims to another investor. Organization economists speak of "freely alienable" residual claims (e.g., Fama and Jensen 1983a, 312), which individual investors can use to manage risk. If in addition the shares are publicly traded, the price at which shares are bought and sold is unambiguous.

Free alienability enables risk management at the individual investor level. However, this is not what is relevant to the designer who must acknowledge that the organization's residual claimants *as an aggregate* are always vulnerable. Accordingly, the designer's task is not to please any individual investor but, rather, to ensure that the organization maintains its credibility in the eyes of the providers of equity capital in the aggregate. The designer need not worry about losing credibility in the eyes of any individual investor, but a large number of investors losing credibility constitutes an imminent threat to the value of shareholders' equity and, in the long term, the organization's existence.

In startup firms, the stakeholder status of shareholders is even more pronounced for two reasons. One is that there is no market price; all valuations of equity are based on projections of highly uncertain future cash flows. In the absence of unambiguous prices, trading shares becomes subject to difficult negotiations due to asymmetric information. The other reason is that many shareholders' agreements in startup firms place restrictions on the alienability of residual claims. For example, founder-shareholders may be required to offer their shares to other founders before offering them to outsiders. Or, if the company is party to the shareholders' agreement, the company may be entitled to purchase any shares offered for sale at their book value before they can be offered to outsiders. In many startups, the book value of equity is zero, or close to zero. Agreeing to constraints on the alienability of residual claims is an important design decision for a startup firm.

Nuances aside, providers of equity financing certainly have become vulnerable by putting something at stake, which is why they should be considered stakeholders of the limited liability company. At the same time, they are not the only relevant stakeholder, perhaps not even the most important one. Chapter 4 discusses the pertinent governance issues in detail, but we will briefly consider here the idea that an employee can also become vulnerable, and therefore, should sometimes be awarded stakeholder status instead of being considered merely a constituency.

Employees and Risk

Let us apply the stakeholder litmus test to the organization's employees: If the organization ceased to exist, how difficult would it be for an employee, or a specific employee group, to find alternative employment? The answers range from *not difficult at all* to *next to impossible*. Another question is whether the employee, or employee group, would be able to find alternative employment at the same level of income. Again, the answers will vary. The variance in answers to both questions must be analyzed and the implications incorporated into governance decisions.

The two authors of this book are business school professors who teach comparatively general topics of strategy, governance, and operations management to undergraduate, graduate, postgraduate, and executive audiences, using the English language. If for some reason our schools ceased to exist, neither author would have considerable trouble finding new employment in another business school, and neither would have to accept a job that pays less than the current job. Securing new employment might involve inconvenience, such as having to move to another city, but we must not confuse inconvenience with economic risk. It would be hyperbole to propose to the designer of the business school that professors are vulnerable because they would be inconvenienced by the termination of their employment relationships. Professors would be at risk only if their employment relationships *with the specific universities* made them vulnerable. Insofar as this vulnerability is concerned, what is most relevant is that neither author has committed to the kinds of skill sets that would tie us to a specific employer. Just the opposite, our expertise is readily redeployable in many other organizations.

In stark contrast with business schools and their professors, there are numerous contexts in which knowledge and expertise are organization specific, or as is more commonly the case, become organization specific over time. Consider the example of a software development company where engineers are asked to commit to learning and further developing an organization-specific technology, such as a proprietary programming language or unique software products. The engineers know that being skilled in the specific technologies may have considerably less economic value in another organization. Committing to such specificity is a form of employment risk, and something that warrants attention in organization design in general and employment relationships in particular.[6]

In the case of high levels of specificity, it may well be that the employment contract alone will not be sufficient to secure the commitment of some of the key employees. Or, the employment contract will be inefficient in the sense that the salaries must be raised to unfeasibly high levels to offset the perceived employment risk that arises from specificity. In such situations, the organization is well advised to think of its members more broadly than merely in terms of employment contracts where the employees exchange their time and effort for a salary. Unlike investment portfolios, employment portfolios are much more difficult for individuals to diversify, which means employment risk is more difficult to manage. This is why employment risk warrants the designer's attention, particularly in the case of employees the organization would have trouble replacing. In some contexts, employment risk may be more central to the organization's survival than investment risk. This may occur in organizations that do not need to raise equity to finance their operations—professional service firms such as law firms and accounting firms are good examples.

---

[6] This is an authentic example that is based on a conversation one of the authors had with the chief technology officer (CTO) of a software company. The CTO candidly disclosed that the firm faced considerable difficulties attracting talented programmers to the firm due to the specificity involved. Prospective employees understandably viewed the commitment to specificity as risk, for which they demanded a significant price (i.e., salary) premium. Considering specificity is central in the *ex ante* stage when the organization seeks to strike a deal with an important constituency. In the case of the software company, a failure to secure the cooperation of a sufficient number of skilled programmers leads to underinvestment in a strategic technological skill. The author's recommendation to the CTO was to think of the relationship between the firm and the programmers in broader stakeholder terms, not merely as an employment relationship.

Specificity applies to nonhuman assets as well. An example is the use of special-purpose production equipment in a manufacturing firm. Often, investment in special-purpose equipment is justified because it generates more value than general-purpose equipment. The downside is that its economic value in the second-best use may be considerably lower, even nonexistent. An organization that requires firm-specific assets to operate must often rely on equity financing, because lenders will not accept firm-specific technology as collateral.

We conduct a more detailed analysis of risk in its various forms in chapter 4 where we present a proposal for stakeholder analysis. In this analysis, specificity takes center stage.

Negative Externalities and Involuntary Risk

In this book, we focus primarily on risk in contexts where the contracting parties enter into the relationship voluntarily. However, there is an important aspect of involuntary risk, found in situations where risk is imposed without consent. In some contexts, the problem is further exacerbated by the fact that no consent is possible in the first place because the entity on which risk is imposed does not have agency; the environment is the most salient example.

Imposition of risk links to *negative externalities*, or within an organization, to *negative spillover effects*. In a negative externality, something that an organization does has unintended and undesirable effects on entities that do not have a contractual relationship with the organization. A case in point, the Great Pacific Garbage Patch consists of 1.6 million square kilometers— about the size of Mexico—of plastic waste, such as bottles, bags, and the like. This obviously constitutes a risk to the environment, to wildlife, and to the residents of the Pacific islands. Furthermore, it is a risk that has been imposed without consent.

How should the designer approach the situation in which the organization's actions impose a risk on the environment? Should the environment be considered a stakeholder? If the designer answers in the affirmative, how should the designer incorporate the interests of a stakeholder that is not a contracting party in the conventional sense? The question whether noncontracting entities having neither discernible identity nor representation should be considered stakeholders is complex, and we have no definitive answers. But we can propose a number of questions and issues to address.

On the one hand, the natural environment is an important part of every organization's environment, and taking responsibility for protecting those unable to protect themselves seems like a prudent general principle. At the same time, it is difficult to think of this responsibility in stakeholder terms. If the environment is a stakeholder, what are the organization's responsibilities toward the environment, and the environment's responsibilities toward the organization? Trying to formulate the question in contracting terms runs into considerable difficulties.

It seems that if the environment is to be considered in stakeholder terms, a different approach is required. The general question of negative externalities boils down to the question whether externalities should be viewed through the lens of contracting (private ordering), legislation and policy (public ordering), or moral obligation. The answer is that it is likely a combination of all three, and all three have implications for governance. However, the nonobvious question we present to the designer is, "In what ways should negative externalities be incorporated into governance as matters of private ordering?"

There is no consensus on the issue. Those who suggest private ordering is less relevant tend to point to the centrality of public ordering: "The existence of organizations that advocate for the environment, such as the Environmental Protection Agency and the Department of the Interior as well as the Sierra Club and the National Resources Defense Council and others, renders stakeholder status for the natural environment redundant or unnecessary" (Phillips and Reichart 2000, 188–89). Those who take the opposite position tend to suggest that "human proxies for the non-human environment" (Phillips and Reichart 2000, 189) are necessary but not sufficient (see also Starik 1995).

One need not but take a quick look at the pollution indexes across the globe to reach the conclusion that the public measures taken to protect the environment are woefully insufficient. However, we must remain intellectually rigorous and acknowledge that this does not imply that private ordering provides a comparatively efficient alternative. Whether further reinforcing public ordering (through legislation, policy, and polity) is efficient compared to private ordering requires further analysis. Those who think that public institutions are inefficient should also consider the possibility that the same inefficiency applies to private-ordering initiatives. In his scathing *Harvard Business Review* essay,[7] management scholar Kenneth Pucker observed the following:

---

[7] https://hbr.org/2022/01/the-myth-of-sustainable-fashion

Few industries tout their sustainability credentials more forcefully than the fashion industry. But the sad truth is that despite high-profile attempts at innovation, [it has] failed to reduce its planetary impact in the past 25 years. Most items are still produced using non-biodegradable petroleum-based synthetics and end up in a landfill [. . .] [G]overnments need to step in to force companies to pay for their negative impact on the planet. (Pucker 2022, summary paragraph)

The challenge of discussing environmental concerns in terms of private ordering in for-profit corporations is that these concerns ultimately tend to become subservient to shareholder interests. Legal scholars Lucien Bebchuk and Roberto Tallarita (2020, 109) are spot on in observing that in for-profit corporations "consideration of [environmental concerns] is a means to the end of shareholder welfare." Given both top management and director compensation in large corporations is heavily equity based, the dispassionate analyst must consider the possibility that private ordering as a response to negative externalities may amount to an "illusory promise" (Bebchuk and Tallarita 2020, 91).

Finally, even though invoking the moral aspect introduces an entirely new dimension to the conversation, let us suggest that it can usefully be linked to efficiency. A case in point, the taxi ride example in chapter 1 implicitly embraces the general moral responsibility of waste avoidance in individual decisions. In this sense, there is no immediate reason why efficiency cannot be compatible with considerations of what is ethically justified. This topic is discussed in more detail in chapter 5.

How Management, Oversight, and Risk Relate to One Another

Having defined the three key elements, we now turn attention to their interrelationships, which are just as central to governance as are the concepts themselves. Of particular importance is the extent to which management, oversight, and risk are separated from one another. Let us consider two examples.

Consider first the proportion of board members who should be independent outsiders. In Efficiency Lens terms, the question is about the extent to which oversight should be separated from management and risk.

At least some separation seems necessary, because a board member who is also involved in management may run into conflicts of interest in the boardroom. Suppose the board of a manufacturing firm contemplates the decision to close one of its factories. The CEO may have a vested interest in closing the plant, particularly if this strategic move will have a positive effect on financial performance and, consequently, the CEO's non-equity-based bonus compensation.

A board member who also represents risk may similarly be unable to approach the question impartially. For example, union representatives on the board will likely see the plant closure primarily as having negative outcomes to their constituencies. Even though the union representatives' concerns are valid, as board members they do not represent the union but the entire organization. Indeed, under the law, board members have a duty of loyalty and care not to their constituencies but *to the corporation* (Clark 1985; Blair and Stout 1999). Consequently, the very notion of *union representative* is problematic; so are *shareholder representative* and *stakeholder representative*, for that matter. Under the law, every board member is a representative of the organization, not its individual stakeholders.

Consider second the scenario of a risky strategic acquisition decision. To what extent should those making the decision also bear the consequences if the acquisition fails and destroys value instead of creating it? This question is about the degree to which management overlaps with risk. On the one hand, we can see how having no overlap between the two could be viewed as problematic. Specifically, is it fair to have someone who had nothing to do with the decision bear the financial consequences of failure? On the other hand, it is important to see also the problems that overlap creates. If members of the top management team faced significant economic consequences in case the investment failed, the predictable consequence is that they would become highly risk averse in their decisions. Such investment paralysis might eventually jeopardize the survival of the entire organization.

More generally, we propose that not only can we express central governance decisions in terms of how management, oversight, and risk are related, but also the definition of efficient governance boils down to the question, "What constitutes a credible configuration of management, oversight, and risk?" By *configuration*, we refer specifically to how the three elements are interrelated and the extent to which they overlap. Let us examine two illustrative examples: the sole proprietorship and the open corporation.

The Sole Proprietorship

The simplest organization is one where management, oversight, and risk are completely overlapping (fig. 2.2). Those who make the most important decisions bear all the relevant risk and, therefore, are readily incentivized to exercise oversight and control over their own decisions. The closest to this ideal is the one-person organization incorporated as a sole proprietorship. The sole proprietor has all the incentives to get the job done in an efficient way; there are no conflicts of interest, and because there are no agency relationships, there are no potential agency problems either. In a sole proprietorship, management, oversight, and risk are for all practical governance purposes embedded in just one person.

Even in the case of the sole proprietorship, management, oversight, and risk are, strictly speaking, not fully overlapping. Even a one-person organization incorporated as a sole proprietorship must relinquish a number of central oversight functions to other entities, such as accounting firms and tax authorities. It is simply not good governance to let even the smartest and most honest sole proprietor accountants perform financial audits of their own firms. Therefore, management and oversight are always only partially overlapping.

Similarly, due to externalities and spillovers, the sole proprietor is not the only entity exposed to risk. For example, an incompetent or careless sole proprietor accounting consultant can expose clients to unnecessary risks, even litigation. Therefore, management and risk are not completely overlapping either. This potential hazard gives rise to various institutional safeguards. In the field of accountancy, a forward-looking client is well advised to seek the services of certified accountants, even if they are more expensive. Indeed, in some countries only certified persons actively applying their certified skills are allowed to use the label *accountant*, which provides an important safeguard that does not exist in many other settings. We conjecture that one of the reasons the title *consultant* sometimes raises suspicions is because its use

 In the sole proprietorship, one person is not only in charge of management and oversight but is also the primary risk bearer; there is no separation of the three elements of the Efficiency Lens.

Figure 2.2 The configuration of a sole proprietorship viewed through the Efficiency Lens

is not regulated in any way. Tales of shady chartered professional accountants are much less frequent.

The Open Corporation

At the other end of the complexity spectrum is the organization where management, oversight, and risk are separated from one another (fig. 2.3). A large, publicly traded limited liability company is an example. In some conversations, these organizations are dubbed public corporations or public limited companies. We prefer using the word *open* instead of *public*, because from a governance perspective, the fact that the corporation's shares are publicly traded does not make the organization public in the relevant sense. Because most publicly traded corporations are private organizations, we find the term *open corporation* descriptively accurate (Fama and Jensen 1983a, 303).

Due to the fragmented ownership common in most open corporations, management owns a very small fraction of shares; therefore, management is materially separated from risk. As of December 28, 2020, Apple CEO Tim Cook—the person in charge of the most important strategic decisions— owned 837,374 shares of Apple stock, which represented 0.02 percent of all outstanding shares. If Mr. Cook made a bad decision and the value of Apple's equity plummeted, 99.98 percent of the direct financial consequences alone would fall on individuals and groups most of whom had no role in the decision. If we considered other financial consequences, such as Apple employees losing their jobs, Mr. Cook's share of the loss would be even smaller. Separation of management and risk should have profound organization design and governance implications.

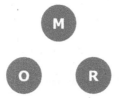

In the open corporation, management, oversight, and risk are materially separated. Separation of management and oversight may be mandated by external institutions.

Figure 2.3 The configuration of an open corporation viewed through the Efficiency Lens

One implication of risk separating from management is the necessity of separating management from oversight as well. The most conspicuous manifestation is the fact that aside from the CEO, it is uncommon for any other member of management to serve on the open corporation's board of directors. Instead, directors are outsiders employed in other corporations.

Focus on Material Separation

Given that management, oversight, and risk are neither completely overlapping nor completely separated, the designer must direct attention to the question whether the observed degree of separation is of material importance. To determine whether separation is material, we offer a simple litmus test: Is the separation sufficient to merit a governance response? If the answer is *yes*, then the separation is material.

The separation of management from risk in the open corporation is material precisely because it necessitates a governance response, specifically, material separation of oversight from management. An organization where management is separated from risk but not from oversight is not credible in the eyes of risk (see fig. 2.4). A look at just about any corporate scandal illustrates the point.

One way to make sense of the events that took place at the Enron Corporation at the turn of the millennium is to think of it as insufficient separation of management and oversight when management and risk were materially separated. A plausible reason for Enron's failure as an organization was the fact that the integrity of the most important individuals in charge of oversight (chairperson of the board Kenneth Lay) and management (CEO Jeffrey Skilling) was fundamentally compromised. The primary consequences of Enron's decline and bankruptcy fell on those bearing risk. The two obvious groups affected were the shareholders, who lost a total of $74 billion, and the

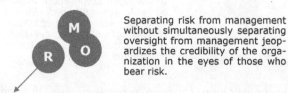

Separating risk from management without simultaneously separating oversight from management jeopardizes the credibility of the organization in the eyes of those who bear risk.

Figure 2.4 A non-viable configuration of management, oversight, and risk

Enron employees, who lost their jobs. Those hit the hardest were employees who were also shareholders; the pension plans of twenty thousand Enron employees who lost their jobs were massively affected, some annihilated.

In summary, in the publicly traded corporation, the separation of management and risk is always of material importance and requires the designer's attention; the obvious response is to separate oversight and management powers from one another. In contrast, in a sole proprietorship, separation of management from risk is not materially important. Although the sole proprietor may not, strictly speaking, be the sole risk bearer, the amount of risk sole proprietors carry tends to be sufficient to incentivize them to deeply care about the fate of the organization. Being the primary risk bearer gives the entrepreneur the requisite high-powered incentive to make business decisions that are in the best interest of the organization, and indirectly, in the best interest of all those who bear risk.

The Dynamic of Management, Oversight, and Risk

The third characteristic of the Efficiency Lens has to do with how management, oversight, and risk, and their interrelationships, evolve over time. A technology startup heading toward an IPO is a good example. On the IPO path, there are three distinct but related dynamics (fig. 2.5):

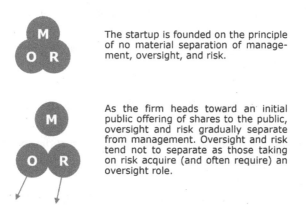

The startup is founded on the principle of no material separation of management, oversight, and risk.

As the firm heads toward an initial public offering of shares to the public, oversight and risk gradually separate from management. Oversight and risk tend not to separate as those taking on risk acquire (and often require) an oversight role.

Figure 2.5 The dynamic of a startup viewed through the Efficiency Lens

1. As a startup organized as a private limited liability company heads to-ward an IPO, it must add nonfounders and noninvestors to its board, which means that management and oversight begin to separate. At the IPO, the requirement for separation is explicit: The governance guidelines of stock exchanges consistently require that at the time of the IPO, the majority of board members be independent.

2. An IPO implies that ownership will become more dispersed as it is opened to outside investors. This increased dispersion of owner-ship means that those who make the key decisions will bear a smaller portion of the overall risk, which reduces the overlap between man-agement and risk. This alone requires that the organization must also reduce the overlap between management and oversight. An organiza-tion where management and oversight are highly overlapping with one another but nonoverlapping with risk is not viable.

3. As risk and oversight separate from management, they tend not to move in opposite directions, because new investors are reluctant to take on risk unless they are awarded an oversight role. Separation of oversight and risk accelerates when the startup nears an IPO, because ultimately the firm must comply with stock exchange governance guidelines that require clear separation of oversight from both management and risk.

Consistent with the First Premise from chapter 1 ("Organizations as Deliberately Designed"), we approach the dynamics of management, over-sight, and risk as a series of deliberate design choices that seek to maintain the credibility of the organization in the eyes of its central stakeholders. As the startup example shows, separation of powers is the outcome of conscious, deliberate decisions that modify the composition of the board of directors.

Summary: Defining Governance

It may seem strange to offer a definition of a key term at the end of a chapter instead of the beginning. But with a concept such as governance, we find it impossible to define the term without first discussing and elaborating the underpinning foundation on which it stands. After having introduced the Efficiency Lens, we are prepared to offer our definition of governance.

Cambridge Dictionary defines governance as "the way that organizations or countries are managed at the highest level, and the systems for doing this."[8] It is hard to find much utility in this definition. Furthermore, the idea of defining governance as the way an organization is managed is unnecessarily narrow and potentially misleading.

The challenge with defining governance stems from the fact that in its abstractness and generality, governance is analogous with concepts such as sport, classical music, or mental health. These terms are not so much concepts to be defined as they are umbrella terms whose domains must be circumscribed. For instance, most discussions of what classical music is and what it is not will likely involve a discussion not of definitions but, instead, of composers and compositions that belong to its domain. This process is not so much about defining what classical music is as it is about circumscribing its domain. Indeed, *Cambridge Dictionary* "defines" classical music not by offering a formal definition but by specifying its general domain as "a form of music developed from a European tradition mainly in the 18th and 19th centuries."[9]

We suggest that a useful way of approaching governance as a concept is not to try to offer a definition but to provide a list of questions that circumscribe its domain. We circumscribe governance with three interrelated questions:

1. Who in the organization is trusted to make the most important decisions about how activities are organized, how resources are allocated, and how performance is evaluated? In Efficiency Lens terms, who is in charge of *management*?
2. What general guidelines and principles govern decision making to ensure that decisions are made in the best interest of the organization? In Efficiency Lens terms, how is *oversight* organized?
3. What safeguards are in place to ensure the cooperation of the organization's most important constituencies, particularly those who have voluntarily put something at stake? In Efficiency Lens terms, how does the organization address stakeholder *risk*?

Note that since these questions circumscribe governance primarily in terms of private ordering, it would be inappropriate to offer this definition as universally applicable. We readily acknowledge that those who view governance from an external point of view will emphasize compliance,

---

[8] https://dictionary.cambridge.org/dictionary/english/governance
[9] https://dictionary.cambridge.org/dictionary/english/classical-music

law, regulation, and policy. A good example of an externally oriented definition can be found in the Organisation for Economic Co-operation and Development's (OECD) principles of corporate governance:

> Effective corporate governance requires a sound legal, regulatory and institutional framework that market participants can rely on when they establish their private contractual relations. This corporate governance framework typically comprises elements of legislation, regulation, self-regulatory arrangements, voluntary commitments and business practices that are the result of a country's specific circumstances, history and tradition. (Organisation for Economic Co-operation and Development 2015, 13)

An externally oriented approach to circumscribing governance is fully understandable given OECD's emphasis on public policy and international standards. OECD's definition differs from ours not because we disagree with one another but because we take an internal and OECD an external perspective. However, we view the two approaches as ultimately complementary. For instance, our private-ordering view elaborates the self-regulatory arrangements, voluntary commitments, and business practices mentioned in the OECD definition. Furthermore, in the discussion of startup governance in chapter 6, we show how important it is for the designer to understand how external rules and regulations impose limits on private ordering. In short, private ordering occurs in a broader institutional context that both enables and constrains private choices.

PART II

GOVERNANCE WITHIN AND ACROSS ORGANIZATIONS

In his groundbreaking 1937 article "The Nature of the Firm," economics Nobel Laureate Ronald Coase made a profound observation regarding the organization of industrial production. When an industrial firm decides to produce a component in-house instead of buying it from an external supplier, it is effectively choosing between transacting internally (within the firm) and transacting in the market (across firms). Indeed, a market transaction and internal production are "alternative methods for co-ordinating production" (Coase 1937, 388).

In many contexts, the designer faces a similar choice of contracting either within the organization or across organizations. The aim of chapter 3 is to show how these contracting decisions and choices can be subjected to a comparative efficiency analysis. To this end, chapter 3 focuses specifically on the costs of contracting.

In chapter 4, we take a contractual approach to stakeholder management. An organization has numerous constituencies, some of which are more critical to the organization's viability than others. This chapter turns attention to those constituencies that put something significant at stake by striking a relationship with the organization. We call those with the most at stake the organization's stakeholders. The purpose of the stakeholder analysis discussed in this chapter is to evaluate which constituencies have most at stake and how their cooperation can be secured by implementing the requisite governance safeguards. Informed prioritization is essential to stakeholder analysis.

In chapter 5, we analyze the for-profit/nonprofit and public/private distinctions from a governance perspective. A nuanced analysis reveals that from the point of view of efficient governance, these distinctions, although important, are not as central as one might think. This is because most nonprofits generate an economic surplus (just like for-profits do) and most public organizations are in fact public-private partnerships. Consequently, in addition to understanding and evaluating the general organizational form, the designer must analyze the organization's governance microstructure. An examination of nonprofits and public organizations also helps explore the central boundary conditions of the efficiency approach.

3

Contracting within and across Organizations

Think of the most substantial purchase you have ever made. For most of us, it may have been the purchase of a house or an apartment. The chances are that both before and after the purchase, you incurred various costs directly related to the transaction. Before the transaction took place, you searched for suitable alternatives and negotiated with prospective sellers. You may also have incurred the cost of implementing various safeguards to avoid exposure to hazards. Symmetrically, the seller incurred various costs, such as searching for a buyer and implementing safeguards on the seller's side. All the costs incurred before the transaction are *ex ante transaction costs*.

After you made the purchase, you may have discovered that the contract with the seller turned out to have a number of gaps and omissions that did not clearly assign responsibilities in the event of unexpected disturbances. Perhaps the house you bought turned out to have hidden flaws that were not known to you at the time of the sale. As you raise the issue with the seller, the seller appeals to *caveat emptor* ("let the buyer beware") and maintains that the flaws could have been discovered by reasonable inspection. All the time and the effort you and the seller spend on settling the dispute after the transaction has occurred results in various *ex post transaction costs*.

This chapter is about the costs of transacting. In the context of governance, attention turns to a comparative analysis of alternative ways of organizing a transaction. Because many transactions can be organized as either intra- or interorganizational, the designer can seek efficiency by comparing the costs of the two alternatives and choosing the comparatively efficient alternative. As table 3.1 illustrates, the designer often faces the situation of having to choose either the intra- or the interorganizational mode of transacting. Both options involve *ex ante* and *ex post* transaction costs that the designer should incorporate into the decision of how to structure the transaction or the relationship.

Efficient Organization. Mikko Ketokivi and Joseph T. Mahoney, Oxford University Press. © Oxford University Press 2023.
DOI: 10.1093/oso/9780197610282.003.0003

Table 3.1. Examples of Intraorganizational and Interorganizational Contracting as Alternatives

Contracting activity	Intraorganizational mode	Interorganizational mode
Organizing business school teaching	Using internal faculty	Contracting with visiting and adjunct faculty
Producing a component needed in automobile final assembly	Using an internal division to produce the component in-house	Using an external vendor to supply the component
Protecting the intellectual property of a high-technology firm	Having an internal legal department with the requisite expertise	Contracting with an external law firm specialized in intellectual property
Long-haul transport of goods on trucks	Using a private fleet of company trucks and company drivers	Contracting with external owner-operators
A real estate company organizing transactions between buyers and sellers	Hiring internal sales representatives as salaried employees	Contracting with independent sales agents who work exclusively on commission

British economist and Nobel Laureate Ronald Coase (1937) was the first to point out that transacting within and across organizations are in many instances alternatives to one another. What may now seem like a trivial point turns out to have profound implications for the governance of contractual relationships.

In Efficiency Lens terms, contracting decisions are usually thought to belong to the domain of management. Specifically, whether to perform an activity in-house or to outsource it to an external organization is a matter of planning and coordinating the value-adding activities. However, we seek to establish in this chapter that oversight and risk are always relevant in these decisions as well. Consequently, the examples depicted in table 3.1 are ultimately not merely management decisions but indeed governance decisions that involve management, oversight, and risk. Furthermore, the Efficiency Lens prescribes the designer to choose the comparatively efficient governance option, which in the case of intra- versus interorganizational contracting becomes particularly salient; the alternative governance modes can be compared directly to one another in terms of their *total costs*.

Whether a contracting activity occurs within or across organizations is based on the legal conception of the organization. If the transacting parties are two separate legal entities (e.g., separate firms), the transaction is interorganizational; otherwise, the transaction is intraorganizational. Adopting the legal conception tends to emphasize some aspects of the contracting situation while abstracting out others. Because it is in our view instructive to understand what is being abstracted out, we begin this chapter by contrasting the efficiency logic with three other dominant logics: power, competence, and identity.

Four Lenses to Organizational Boundaries

In their comprehensive review and analysis of organizational boundaries, organization scholars Filipe Santos and Kathleen Eisenhardt (2005) noted that the legal conception of organizational boundaries readily lends itself to an efficiency analysis. Once the organization is defined in terms of its legal boundaries, we can analyze whether the costs associated with crossing the boundary are so high that they should be incorporated into the decision of whether to organize the exchange as an intra- or an interorganizational transaction.

In addition to the efficiency approach, Santos and Eisenhardt (2005) presented three other ways of conceptualizing organizational boundaries (identity, power, and competence), which could be applied to the contracting situations in table 3.1 to bring something essential about the situation into focus. In fact, an entire book could be written to discuss any of these three perspectives, which prompts us to give them voice here.[1]

To make all four perspectives salient, we apply each in turn to examine the question whether a business school should organize its teaching activities by employing internal faculty or by procuring teaching from the outside by contracting with visiting and adjunct faculty, or by some combination of the two. We start with the identity, power, and competence logics and then contrast them with the efficiency logic.

---

[1] Just like the efficiency view, the three other views are based on and informed by decades of academic research; Santos and Eisenhardt (2005) provide an excellent summary. To those interested in reading more on the three other views, we recommend the following texts as the central intellectual contributions (contributions within each view are listed in a chronological order): (1) Power: Thompson (1967), Pfeffer and Salancik (1978), Pfeffer (1987), Clegg, Courpasson, and Phillips (2006); (2) Competence: Penrose (1959), Chandler (1967, 1972), Porter (1985), Chandler (1990), Barney (1991), Kaplan and Norton (2008), Gamble, Peteraf, and Thompson (2021); (3) Identity: Albert and Whetten (1985), Weick (1995), Hatch and Schultz (2004), Gioia et al. (2013).

Identity Lens: What Is a Business School?

Consider a prospective master's student contemplating the choice of which business school to choose for his or her MBA degree. The decision is consequential, because tuition fees in top MBA programs are easily the same magnitude as the person's annual net salary postgraduation. Imagine then that the student visits a business school's website and, perusing the faculty pages, discovers that the primary affiliation of every faculty member is in another organization; all classes are taught by visiting faculty. Will this inspire confidence or concern? Probably the latter. A legitimate business school has its own faculty.

We submit that both students and faculty subscribe to this view. Those of us teaching in various business school programs prefer not to have colleagues change from one semester to the next. Instead, we like to get to know our colleagues, their fields of expertise, their teaching styles, and so on. We further benefit from cooperation and collaboration when we design our syllabi to ensure that those who teach the same course are sufficiently consistent in their content and approaches. This need for consistency across colleagues is a question of organizational identity, and the associated lens through which boundary decisions are viewed could be labeled the *identity lens*. The identity lens emphasizes both the collective identity of the organizational members as well as the image the organization projects to those outside the organization. The key question is, "Who are we?"

Power Lens: On Whom Is the Business School Dependent and How?

The business school, as an organization, is dependent on skilled teachers to commit their time and efforts to teach classes. To what extent will these individuals have power over the decisions of what to teach, to whom, and when? Will the business school want to depend on the same individuals, or different individuals, over time? Should the business school prefer long-term or short-term contracts? More specifically, does the business school want to depend on individuals whose commitment is secured by way of comparatively longer-term employment contracts, or on individuals with whom the business school enters into comparatively shorter-term buyer-supplier contracts?

The form of the contract has power implications. As we pointed out in chapter 2 in conjunction with the discussion on residual rights of control, even though business schools do not instruct their teachers on the content and the style of their teaching, they can exercise more residual control over internal faculty than over visiting faculty.

When organizational boundaries are approached from a power perspective, the central question concerns the degree to which the organization becomes dependent on others and, consequently, relinquishes some of its autonomy. Consider again a business school that relies heavily on contracting its teaching out to adjuncts and visiting faculty. If the school is dependent on short-term contracts with external professors, how are curriculum decisions made? Will the person who taught the organization design elective last year come back to teach this year as well? In case the professor is not available, are there other external professors who could be contracted to teach the same class? Will they teach using the same syllabus as the professor who taught the class the previous year, or will they want to teach using their own syllabus? If they want to use their own syllabus, does the scope of the elective change?

It is clear that decisions regarding what to do internally and what to outsource link to considerations of autonomy, and losing autonomy is a cause for concern. These decisions are the central issues considered within the *power lens*.

Competence Lens: How Can the Business School Achieve Its Strategic Goals?

Most business school deans would likely agree that the central objective of business school activities is to offer high-quality education. Accordingly, the school should balance between the use of internal and visiting faculty in a way that secures the highest quality of education, as measured by how much students learn and how highly they value their degree in postgraduation surveys. Understanding these outcomes is the focus in the *competence lens*.

There are many ways in which business schools seek to excel in providing their students with a meaningful and useful learning experience. In contemplating the question of how to organize teaching in particular, the competence lens would direct our attention to the quality of the students' classroom experience and, consequently, teacher competence both individually and collectively. Many business schools boast of their faculty, and indeed, faculty scholarship is one of the central metrics used in business school rankings. No matter what business school deans may think of the validity of business school rankings and the metrics employed, everyone acknowledges that they are influential.

Insofar as using internal versus external faculty is concerned, the key question from the competence perspective is, "Which option leads to better student learning outcomes?" As we think back to all our teaching in business schools over the past thirty years, we conclude that students do not base the evaluations of their learning experience so much on the individual classes they took as much as they reflect on their entire learning journey. Therefore, whether students genuinely learn the skills that are taught in the classroom depends on the totality of their classroom experience; the structure and sequencing of the entire degree program matters just as much as, if not more than, the content and the delivery of any individual course they take. Consequently, we suggest that having an all-star roster of individual teachers (whether internal or visiting) is no guarantee of a high-learning outcome. Instead, organization matters as well, which provides a segue to the efficiency lens.

Efficiency Lens: Is the Business School Well Organized in Its Teaching?

Consider the task of organizing the school's teaching for the upcoming academic year. Who is going to teach which courses? How should the syllabus of the mandatory core MBA seminar on strategic management be revised? How much discretion is given to individual teachers to include their preferred topics in the common syllabus? Which electives will the Operations Management department offer? How does the organization ensure that the individual professors' teaching loads meet the minimum required for the academic year? What should the sequencing of classes in the highly technical Business Analytics concentration be?

These are all questions of coordination, which takes time and effort. The efficiency perspective turns attention to how this coordination is organized. To the extent coordination is hampered by delays, confusion, scheduling conflicts, limited availabilities, lack of commitment, teacher turnover, self-serving behaviors, and the like, coordination costs increase and the organization creates waste. The efficiency logic prescribes that coordination costs and avoidance of waste be incorporated into design and governance decisions.

It is straightforward to see how the costs of coordinating teaching can link to the mix of internal and external faculty. Specifically, if the exact same team of internal faculty members teaches the classes from one year to the next, the resultant continuity introduces stability, repeatability, and familiarity that all work to lower coordination costs. The individuals involved know one another and one another's competences, they have experience coordinating (and being coordinated) at the specific school, they have likely had many informal conversations about course syllabi, topics, teaching materials, and so on. Planning is easier when those involved in planning know one another and have participated in the process in the past. Familiarity lowers adjustment costs and breeds efficiency.

At the same time, hiring internal faculty involves long-term contracts, which may be comparatively more costly than short-term contracting with visiting faculty. In the efficiency logic, all relevant costs should be incorporated into the comparative assessment of alternatives.

Efficiency Lens vs. the Other Lenses

We consider the four lenses primarily complementary rather than competing. To be sure, efficient coordination likely ultimately contributes to the business school achieving its objective of providing high-quality education to students. Further, a business school faculty with a strong common organizational identity and ethos may alleviate coordination problems arising from subgoal pursuit and self-serving behaviors. Finally, much like a highly vertically integrated industrial firm that produces internally most of the components required in final assembly, a business school that is not fundamentally dependent on specific individuals external to the organization for their contributions is more likely to be able to coordinate its activities more efficiently.

Compatibilities and complementarities notwithstanding, focusing on efficiency is important, in fact, so important that we thought the topic merits the writing of an entire book. On the question of organizing teaching in business schools, it is our impression and experience as faculty members that business schools sometimes tend to apply the competence logic with zeal by paying disproportionate attention to outcomes that students directly experience and evaluate.

We do not want to downplay the importance of student experience but suggest a slight redirection to organizational outcomes, if only to complement the attention to student outcomes. This redirection invites an analysis of governance decisions and formulation of the main problem as one of efficient organization. This redirection further shifts attention from strategic outcomes to organizational ones. Strategic outcomes (e.g., business school rankings) and organizational outcomes (e.g., coordination efficiency) are related and likely complementary, but they are *not* the same thing. It seems logical to get the organizational outcomes right before turning attention to the strategic outcomes.

The efficiency logic does not suggest that the designer should minimize coordination costs, only that they should be incorporated into the efficiency analysis as part of the total cost of transacting. Coordination costs, and transaction costs more generally, must be considered in conjunction with all other relevant costs. Optimization of individual cost categories leads the designer to the familiar suboptimization trap.

In the case of the internal versus external faculty decision, a central cost category is teacher compensation. For the sake of argument, let us assume that an analysis of compensation costs favors contracting with external faculty. After all, in the case of an employment relationship, the employer incurs many costs that it would forgo if the teacher was hired as an external service provider. In addition, employment relationships tend to involve longer-term commitments. However, the efficiency logic suggests that this potential comparative cost advantage must be considered in conjunction with the potential increase in coordination costs.

To coordinate the teaching activities of external faculty members, the business school would likely have to implement an administrative structure to coordinate and contract with visiting faculty. To this end, some universities have established an entire department assigned to coordinating visiting faculty, led by the associate dean of visiting faculty. Importantly, the salaries of these administrative personnel should not be considered general overhead costs. In the spirit of activity-based management, the costs of administering visiting faculty should be incorporated as a relevant cost category in the decision of whether to use internal or external faculty.

An important revelation that systematic research on the costs of organizing has produced over the past sixty years is that transaction costs may sometimes be so consequential that they tilt the efficiency analysis from favoring one design alternative to another.[2] It should go without saying that the total cost of organizing teaching (not an individual cost category such as teachers' salaries) should drive the decision. However, the challenge is that because the costs of organizing are an elusive cost category (indeed, often assigned to overhead), designers may focus on the more salient direct cost categories, such as teachers' salaries. Focusing on just one relevant cost category leads to suboptimization.

The problem of ignoring total costs is relevant to all organizations. In many industrial supply chains, firms tend to engage in make-or-buy decision analyses regarding components by considering only the comparatively salient component prices and direct production costs, thus ignoring the costs of coordination. A comparative analysis of external-supplier prices and internal-supplier production costs may point toward buying a component from an external supplier instead of producing it internally. At the same time, the cost of managing the buyer-supplier relationship may sometimes offset this comparative advantage.

The Costs of Economic Exchange

Suppose you walk into a grocery store with the intent of engaging in a simple (spot market) contract by which you exchange $3 of your wealth for a carton of milk. You enter the store, get the milk from the refrigerator, pay $3 at the register, and walk out.

The transaction in this example is so simple that we seldom stop to think about it. Simplicity stems from two factors that most of us take for granted. One, prices are salient. We know how much a carton of milk is supposed to be priced at retail, and those who do not can find out at a negligible cost. In economic terms, the *price system* works to the buyer's advantage in the transaction. Two, in most countries we can trust that the quality of dairy products is intact. In the United States, for example, both federal and state

---

[2] Economic research on coordination costs has been conducted mainly under the rubric of *transaction cost economics* (Williamson 1975, 1985, 1996). Some of the central academic publications that have taken stock of the empirical research results include Shelanski and Klein (1995), Rindfleisch and Heide (1997), Silverman (2002), Macher and Richman (2008), and Cuypers et al. (2021).

governments have established and maintain safety regulations for dairy products; violations are heavily sanctioned (e.g., Sumner and Balagtas 2002). The *system of institutions* supports the exchange as well.

Because of the price system and the system of institutions, there is little uncertainty associated with the grocery store transaction. For all practical purposes, the cost of the transaction itself is negligible. Of course, you pay $3 for the product, but that is the cost of the product, not of the transaction. Finally, even if upon arriving at home you realize the milk you purchased is past its expiration date, the transaction is easily reversible and the *ex post* problem of inferior quality readily remediable. There is nothing transactionally complex about buying a carton of milk.

The dairy product transaction looks simple to us because it is supported by an institutional structure. Those who live in the developing countries, or travel in them, know that simplicity is in fact only ostensible. Specifically, absent the proper system of institutions, buying even dairy products may become so complex and risky that many will refrain from purchasing and consuming them. In economic terms, the *market fails*: Even though both supply and demand exist, the transaction will not take place. Market failures are always cause for concern, which is why a general understanding of the price system and the institutional environment warrants the designer's attention.

Consider in contrast a situation where the exchanging parties cannot fully rely on the institutional pillar and must address contracting as a matter of private ordering, thus relying on the contractual pillar instead (see chapter 1). As an illustration, let us briefly put ourselves in the position of a purchasing manager of an automobile manufacturer seeking a supplier for ten thousand automatic transmission assemblies, priced at roughly a thousand dollars per unit. The assemblies are make- and model-specific and must be designed and engineered to model specifications. This means neither their precise quality nor their exact price is necessarily known *ex ante*. Furthermore, the purchasing manager may or may not have prior experience with the pool of candidate suppliers. In this situation, both the buyer and the supplier expose themselves to a potentially significant contracting hazard.

Ex Ante and Ex Post Costs

All contracting costs have a comparatively salient *ex ante* and a comparatively opaque *ex post* side. *Ex ante* costs consist of all the costs the contracting parties incur as they engage in negotiation, drafting, and agreeing upon the contract that will be used to govern the transaction. Transacting parties often incur *ex ante* costs even before they find one another. Indeed, various search costs can be significant, even in seemingly simple situations, such as trying to find a good lawyer, piano instructor, or therapist.

If the two transacting parties are legally separate entities, the relationship will likely be governed by a formal contract, which involves both legal and managerial effort and expertise. All the attention allocated to the transaction upfront counts as an *ex ante* transaction cost. The *ex ante* cost can be thought simply as the cost of "setting things up."

Ex post costs involve all the costs that occur after the inception of the contractual relationship. These costs link to the daily execution of the contract, monitoring, enforcing, renegotiation, and conflict resolution. Conflict resolution may range from the comparatively inexpensive renegotiation and joint problem-solving to the more expensive forms that involve third parties: mediation, arbitration, and litigation. In cases where contractual parties to the dispute act in bad faith, *ex post* transaction costs may skyrocket.

Finally, terminating a contract may also have a cost, particularly if after contract termination, one or both parties need to find a replacement exchange partner. Just think of the hassle associated with replacing your lawyer, piano instructor, or therapist. Potential *switching costs* should be considered *ex post* transaction costs as well.

When both *ex ante* and *ex post* transaction costs are incorporated into a comparative efficiency analysis of alternative governance structures, the designer may well realize that the costs are so significant that they have material implications for the decision. For example, a make-or-buy analysis based solely on the comparison of supplier prices and internal production costs may favor outsourcing a component, but a fuller analysis that incorporates both production and transaction costs may well make insourcing comparatively efficient. Consequently, it is not surprising that organizations find outsourcing decisions not to lead to the kinds of cost savings that were envisioned. Higher transaction costs associated with outsourcing offers a plausible explanation.

Ex Ante and *Ex Post* Costs as Design Choices: The Case of Insurance
We counsel the designer not to take *ex ante* or *ex post* costs as givens but, instead, treat them as matters of choice. As a general rule, it is more efficient to prevent a problem from occurring than having to address it after it has

occurred. Purchasing insurance offers a salient example of *ex ante* and *ex post* problems, and an illustration of how the designer can turn an *ex post* problem into an *ex ante* problem. In the following, we first discuss the general notion of *ex ante* versus *ex post* costs, and subsequently, *ex ante* versus *ex post* aspects of transaction costs in particular.

Obtaining a comprehensive insurance coverage policy for one's automobile ensures that no matter what undesirable event happens, be it collision, theft, or a tree falling on the car, the economic consequences will be manageable. An insurance policy effectively turns the *ex post* cost of a potentially unmanageable economic loss into a more palatable *ex ante* cost of having to pay monthly insurance policy payments. Predictably enough, since most of us are both risk- and loss-averse, our preference is to address significant economic loss as an *ex ante* problem. We may have only a vague idea of the probability of getting into a car accident, but we take out an insurance policy as a safeguard, just in case.

In other insurance situations, we accept the *ex post* problem as manageable and effectively self-insure instead of shifting the risk of total loss to the insurance company. When we purchase a smartphone, how many of us pay the additional $50 for an extended warranty that covers hardware failures and offers an express replacement service after the standard one-year warranty has expired? In this case, many of us find the risk reasonable to bear ourselves. A total loss of a smartphone is something most of us are willing to self-insure, and the manufacturer's standard warranty is sufficient to safeguard the transaction.

The logic of insurance effectively illustrates the *ex ante* and *ex post* aspects of an economic problem, and how an *ex post* problem can, if desirable, be converted into an *ex ante* problem. In addition to effectively establishing *ex ante* and *ex post* costs as partial substitutes, a brief examination of the transaction costs involved in the insurance case is useful.

In the insurance case, the *ex ante* transaction costs would consist of the costs of drafting and approving the insurance policy and ascertaining the value of the insured assets. As anyone who has taken out an insurance policy knows, these costs are, for all practical purposes, negligible. Indeed, it is in the best interest of both the insurer and the insured that the *ex ante* process of insuring property is not overly cumbersome.

In contrast, those who have filed insurance claims for substantial losses know painfully well how significant *ex post* transaction costs may be. For example, consider a car accident that involves personal injuries and where the settlement one person receives is paid through another person's insurance policy. Disagreements and bad faith make the situation even worse and may result in litigation in which massive *ex post* transaction costs are incurred. In fact, not only litigation but also other forms of dispute resolution such as arbitration can be cumbersome, risky, and costly: Legal scholar Thomas Stipanowich (2010) dubbed arbitration "the new litigation" due to the fact that over time, arbitration has lost some of the benefits it had as an *alternative dispute resolution* (ADR) mechanism.

The reason we self-insure smaller losses is twofold. One reason is that the economic consequence is manageable. Why insure something you can, in some sense, afford to lose? But the other is that filing an insurance claim takes time, and the outcome is uncertain. How much are we willing to spend in terms of *ex post* transaction costs, which typically consist of having to spend time filing claims? At any rate, this effort should be considered jointly with the size of the prospective settlement. In some cases, self-insurance may present a more efficient alternative.

When *Ex Post* Costs Skyrocket: The Case of the Faulty Ignition Switch

Ex post transaction costs consist primarily of the effects of unexpected events not foreseen at the inception of the contract. Sometimes these unexpected events are so consequential that the *ex post* transaction costs may not only skyrocket but also seriously strain the contractual relationship. Nowhere is this more evident than in the infamous case of the faulty ignition switches in General Motors (GM) automobiles.

Delphi Automotive, a manufacturer of ignition switches, used to be a part of GM. In 1999, it was spun off in an IPO. As an independent company, Delphi continued its operation as an external supplier to GM. In early 2014, GM had to recall 800,000 of its small cars due to faulty ignition switches. The problem turned out to have catastrophic consequences: The faulty ignition switches were ultimately credibly linked to more than one hundred fatalities and hundreds of injuries. GM ended up paying over $2 billion in fines, penalties, and settlements.[3]

---

[3] https://www.nytimes.com/2017/04/24/business/supreme-court-general-motors-ignition-flaw-suits.html

Fully acknowledging that all economic ramifications pale in comparison with the human tragedy involved, an examination of the economic consequences can be instructive. Whereas poor-quality inputs are always cause for concern due to their direct cost consequences, we want to turn attention here to the complications that arose from the supplier and the buyer of the ignition switches being two separate firms.

Had Delphi still been a part of GM at the time of the recall, the situation would have been comparatively simpler. For one, there would have been no need to litigate whether the final assembler or the part supplier was at fault, because both would have been part of the same legal entity. Even though it would have been of little consolation to the victims and their families, having GM and Delphi be part of the same firm would at the very least have paved the way toward swifter dispute resolution. For example, the victims would not have had to face the choice of whom to litigate, GM or Delphi. Some sued GM, others Delphi, yet others named the two as codefendants.

Furthermore, whatever disputes GM had with Delphi could have more efficiently been addressed within GM as matters of internal management and oversight instead of cross-organizational negotiation or litigation. In this sense, organizations have important *quasijudicial functions* that expedite internal conflict resolution (Williamson 1975, 30). Finally, there would have been just one CEO, GM's Mary Barra, appearing before Congress in 2014 to speak on behalf of both GM and its internal supply division Delphi. In summary, the GM-Delphi example shows that many potentially massive transaction costs are *ex ante* hidden, because they do not manifest until something unexpected happens. Uncertainty has profound implications for the *ex post* costs of transacting.

Why did GM and Delphi not safeguard against uncertainty by vertical integration? Why did GM decide to divest Delphi? The main reason cited for the divestment was that other auto manufacturers refused to contract with Delphi as long as it was part of GM. It might have been transactionally more efficient for GM not to divest Delphi, but this would have had drastic adverse consequences to Delphi's revenue. Governance decisions are never made in isolation.

Did the problem with ignition switches have something to do with the fact that GM and Delphi were separate companies? Evidence suggests that GM as an organization exhibited a history of failing to address quality problems. At the same time, there is no evidence that the problems with the ignition switch were *caused* by the introduction of a legal boundary between GM and

Delphi, and that if Delphi had been an internal GM division instead of an external supplier, the quality problems would have received more attention. In fact, external vendors are often scrutinized *more* rigorously than internal suppliers. It seems implausible that the quality problems were caused by the fact that the transaction was interorganizational; negligence seems like the more plausible explanation.

The Importance of Oversight

A key lesson in the GM-Delphi case pertains to oversight. As we noted earlier, even though make-or-buy decisions are often thought of as matters of management, oversight is relevant as well. The faulty ignition switch case importantly illustrates how questions of oversight may be decisive. Understanding the aftermath of the faulty ignition switch case requires an understanding not only of the management but also the oversight of the GM-Delphi relationship.

In the GM-Delphi case, the central question of interest was ultimately not who designed and manufactured the part (issues of management) but specifically how oversight was exercised. Even though Delphi not only manufactured the switch but also owned the associated intellectual property rights, GM was in charge of design specifications and approved both the final part specifications and its installation into GM automobiles. During a congressional hearing in 2014, Delphi CEO Rodney O'Neal maintained that GM should be held responsible, because it had a central oversight role in approving the design.[4]

As another example where a technical failure can plausibly be linked to oversight, consider the explosion of the Challenger space shuttle in 1986. To attribute the disaster to the failure of the solid rocket booster sealing—this was the immediate cause—overlooks the organizational failures that preceded the technical failure. The Rogers Commission that investigated the disaster described it not as a technical failure but as "an accident rooted in history" (Rogers et al. 1986, 120).

There is indeed a parallel to the ignition switch case in that there were concerns that the infamous "O-rings" used in the rocket booster sealing (supplied to NASA by an external supplier) were not necessarily flawed in

---

[4] Hearing before the Subcommittee on Consumer Protection, Product Safety, and Insurance of the Committee on Commerce, Science, and Transportations, United States Senate Hearing 113-715, July 17, 2014.

their design but unsuitable to be used in the specific operating conditions. Once again, attention turned to oversight: Who approved the design of the O-rings and their installation into the space shuttle? Who approved the launch?

The general governance question in the Challenger case pertains to the rules and procedures that govern the launch decision process at NASA. Another investigation into the Challenger disaster by the U.S. House of Representatives Committee on Science and Technology echoed a more general concern: "There is no clear understanding or agreement among the various levels of NASA management as to what constitutes a launch constraint or the process for imposing and waiving constraints [and that] it is not always clear who has authority or responsibility" (Fuqua 1986, 144). It is also instructive to observe that the report pointed to problems in the incentive structures of buyer-supplier relationships: "The [supplier contract] is a cost-plus, incentive/award fee contract [which] provides far greater incentives to the contractor for minimizing costs and meeting schedules than for features related to safety and performance" (Fuqua 1986, 144). The target in these critiques was not the specific decisions associated with the launching of the Challenger but, rather, the organizational rules and principles that governed decisions and contractual relations at NASA more generally—in short, matters of oversight. Understanding the key distinction between the management and the oversight of a contractual relationship is central.

The Determinants of Transaction Costs

Contracting across an organizational boundary tends to be more costly than contracting inside the boundary. Complications arise from the fact that an organizational boundary tends to be also a legal boundary, which means the contracting parties in an interorganizational transaction represent different legal entities. The representatives of separate legal entities are further contractually obligated to act in the best interest of their respective organizations, which may cause friction in the relationship. This friction is attenuated if the contracting parties are part of the same legal entity, such as the same parent corporation.

The reason transaction costs should be incorporated into the analysis is that the comparative efficiency of intraorganizational contracting may be offset if the external supplier or service provider enjoys a productivity advantage due to economies of specialization and economies of scale. A case in point, Bridgestone and Continental are more efficient in car tire production than any automaker. In 2020, Bridgestone's tire-related revenue was $27 billion, which means it produced several hundred million tires that year. If GM produced a set of tires for each of its seven million cars it sold annually, the total number of tires would be only 28 million, an order of magnitude smaller than Bridgestone's production volume. Due to economies of scale and economies of specialization, interorganizational contracting may be preferred even in cases where transaction costs are higher.

A fundamental question is whether the cost of transacting can be so high that the comparative advantage of intraorganizational contracting exceeds the external supplier's productivity advantage, thus suggesting that internalizing an activity would be more efficient even if productivity was lower. To address the question, the designer must analyze the drivers of transaction costs. The extensive research literature on the governance of transactions has revealed three primary drivers: frequency, uncertainty, and specificity. Note that all three are characteristics of the exchange relationship, not the contracting parties.

Frequency of Transacting

Transaction costs tend to increase as a function of the number of transactions. Importantly, this is not merely a matter of volume but, specifically, of the number of transactions. For example, a supplier delivering a total of one thousand units to the buyer once a month is different than the same supplier delivering 250 units per week. When frequency increases, so does the need for planning and scheduling, as well as the hazard of delays and other disruptions.

Even though frequency is in many ways the most salient of the three drivers, its effect on governance decisions is elusive. Higher frequency means higher cost, but at the same time, it can also justify investment in more complex and specialized governance structures. For example, suppliers often appoint key account managers to handle the most important customer accounts. This is analogous with the idea that large production volumes may justify investments in automation. Williamson (1985, 60) elaborates: "[T]he cost of specialized governance structures will be easier to recover for large transactions of a recurring kind."

The link between transaction frequency and the appropriate governance decision remains tenuous. In their extensive review of the research literature on transaction costs, organization scholar Jeffrey Macher and legal scholar Barak Richman (2008) noted that not only has transaction frequency received less attention than uncertainty and specificity, but also the effects of frequency on the governance mode are contested. These mixed empirical results are plausible because, on the one hand, an increase in the frequency of transactions provides a large "shadow of the future" in which contractual parties have an incentive to meet their contractual obligations so that they do not lose promising future business transactions, which can favor efficient interorganizational contracting. On the other hand, increasing frequency, dedicated investments, and more costly governance can be justified, which can favor intraorganizational governance.

Uncertainty

Increasing uncertainty tends to make intraorganizational contracting more efficient due to comparatively lower *ex post* transaction costs. However, instead of thinking of uncertainty in the general sense, the designer must unpack the concept and look at its diverse sources and manifestations. Here, we highlight uncertainty of three different kinds: technological, behavioral, and demand uncertainty.

Technological uncertainty has to do with changes and developments in technology that are often difficult to anticipate. In the case of two firms engaging in R&D collaboration, for example, technological uncertainty is likely the most significant reason why the collaborating firms must adapt over time. Technological uncertainty is driven by the simple fact that the pace and the direction of innovative activities are unpredictable.

Behavioral uncertainty suggests that it is generally impossible for one exchange party to predict how the other party will behave in an unforeseen circumstance that the contract does not cover. Behavioral uncertainty can occur not only because of self-serving and opportunistic behaviors but also because of honest disagreements as the contractual parties fail to converge in their expectations. Because of behavioral uncertainty, there is a need for contractual safeguards. Safeguarding against the unpredictable directs attention to situations in which the contracting parties find themselves in unforeseen and unprecedented circumstances that are outside the scope of their contract. How does one contracting party know how the other will behave in a situation that has not occurred before? How does the party know how it will *itself* behave in an unprecedented situation? Such unpredictability is the essence of behavioral uncertainty and can lead to significant *ex post* transaction costs.

Finally, buyer-supplier relationships are affected by demand uncertainty. A case in point, demand for automobiles is significantly affected by factors outside the control of the exchange parties; input prices, interest rates, and general consumer confidence are but a few examples. The number of seats that GM will need from its seat supplier Adient in any given month or year is not only variable but also unpredictable. Demand unpredictability leads to various *maladaptation problems* such as order cancellations (Williamson 1983, 526), which requires contractual safeguards.

The research evidence of how uncertainty affects governance modes is mixed as well, which is likely due to the fact that different researchers look at different dimensions of uncertainty. Furthermore, different dimensions associate with the decisions in different, context-dependent ways. For example, some forms of technological uncertainty may point to the intraorganizational mode as comparatively efficient, but other forms, such as the possibility of technological obsolescence, may have just the opposite effect.[5]

The other reason for the mixed evidence is that uncertainty tends not to operate on the governance mode independently of other factors. For instance, uncertainty presents a contractual hazard primarily in contexts where specificity is present as well. We therefore counsel the designer not to draw any conclusions based on uncertainty alone. More generally, any one-factor-at-a-time approach to governance decisions is likely to mislead the designer. Even though the designer can benefit from thought exercises of the consequences of "tweaking one factor at a time," governance decisions call for an examination of the organization *in its entirety*.

Specificity
Whenever contracting parties commit to something that makes them dependent on one another, specificity builds up. For example, an industrial

---

[5] Strategy scholars Srinivasan Balakrishnan and Birger Wernerfelt (1986) suggested that the effects of technological uncertainty must be analyzed by disaggregating technological uncertainty into its constituent subdimensions. They proposed that even though increasing technological uncertainty tends to be associated with a higher likelihood of transacting within the organization (i.e., vertical integration), technological obsolescence has the opposite effect: As the likelihood of technological obsolescence increases, the expected benefits of the investment decrease, as do the benefits of vertical integration. Therefore, when the likelihood of obsolescence increases, interorganizational transacting may become comparatively efficient.

supplier may build its subassembly plant next to the customer's final assembly plant. In making the relation-specific investment, the supplier commits to specificity: The economic value the subassembly plant generates would suffer greatly should the exchange relationship terminate. Specificity is about the difference of the value of an asset, skill, or activity in its best versus second-best use.

Specificity takes many different forms (Williamson 1985). The location-specific investment is an example of *site specificity*. The supplier may also commit to *physical asset specificity* by investing in tools and technologies that can only be used to serve the specific customer. Employees in turn may commit to *human capital specificity* by developing organization-specific skills.

Specificity links directly to the cost of switching from one contracting party to another. Low switching costs alleviate the contractual hazard arising from uncertainty, because undesirable behavior by the other contracting party can be remedied by switching suppliers. In the taxi ride example in chapter 1, the passenger need not worry about the behavioral uncertainty of a specific taxi driver. If the passenger has an unpleasant experience with a particular driver, all one has to do is to use different drivers in the future. The likelihood of the same driver picking up the same customer again is very low anyway. The same applies to drivers having an unpleasant experience with a particular passenger. In sum, competitive markets produce efficiency because with many alternative suppliers and customers, "large numbers" provide a sufficient safeguard and curb opportunistic behaviors.

Of the three drivers of governance decisions, asset specificity is corroborated by strong and unambiguous evidence. In their review of the research literature, Macher and Richman (2008, 42) noted that incorporating asset specificity has significantly improved our understanding of why contracting parties favor intraorganizational contracting to serve the purpose of efficient governance. Here, understanding that contracting parties would be wise to provide mutual commitments to become bilaterally dependent due to relation-specific investments is central for maintaining efficient governance. We therefore counsel the designer to give careful attention to specificity. At the same time, specificity should be considered in conjunction with other relevant factors, most notably uncertainty.

The General Governance Decision

Whether a parts supplier should be an independent company or an internal division of the final assembler is the canonical example of the make-or-buy decision. The efficient governance decision is one that is lower in its total cost, where all *ex ante* and *ex post* costs relevant to the transaction are incorporated.

The make-or-buy decision is but one manifestation of the general question of how to govern a contractual relationship. There are numerous variations on the theme of efficient contracting, and making connections is useful. Williamson (1994, 86 [emphasis added]) elaborates:

> [Seeking efficiency] is mainly responsible for the choice of one form of capitalist organization over another. It thereupon applies this hypothesis to a wide range of phenomena—vertical integration, vertical restrictions, labor organization, corporate governance, finance, regulation (and deregulation), conglomerate organization, technology transfer, and, more generally, to *any issue that can be posed directly or indirectly as a contracting problem*. As it turns out, large numbers of problems that on first examination do not appear to be of a contracting kind turn out to have an underlying contracting structure.

In this section, we explore in detail what this general contracting structure is and how it can be applied.

Table 3.2 gives examples of contracting situations that range from managing buyer-supplier relationships and R&D alliances to the organization of the legislature (Ketokivi and Mahoney 2017). All these examples involve central governance decisions that two (or more) contracting parties must collectively make. We further propose that contracting efficiency is relevant concern in all these decisions, only the manifestations and drivers differ. Table 3.3 summarizes the efficiency criteria and efficiency drivers for each example.

In the following sections, we discuss four of the examples in Table 3.3 in detail: vertical integration, corporate diversification, R&D collaboration, and the legislature. We cover the corporate governance example in detail in chapter 4 in conjunction with the discussion of stakeholder analysis. We invite the reader to engage in a similar reflection and analysis of the remaining two, franchising and corporate finance.[6]

---

[6] Rubin (1978) discussed the franchising example and Williamson (1988) corporate finance.

Table 3.2. A Selection of Governance Contexts with the Corresponding Governance Questions and Contracting Parties[a]

Context	Representative governance question	Contracting parties
Vertical integration	Which components should a manufacturer outsource and which should it make in-house?	Buyer and supplier
Franchising	Should the franchising fee that the franchisee pays to the franchisor be based on franchise revenue or profit?	Franchisor and franchisee
Corporate diversification	Which individual businesses should the corporation own?	Horizontally equivalent firms
Corporate governance	Who should have a seat on the corporation's board of directors?	The firm and its stakeholders
R&D collaboration	When should R&D collaboration between two firms be organized as a joint equity alliance instead of collaborative contracting?	Alliance partners
Corporate finance	Which assets are financed through debt and which through equity?	The firm, lenders, and providers of equity
Legislature	What kinds of cooperation and exchange should occur among members of Congress?	Members of the legislature

[a] Adapted, with some modifications and additions, from Ketokivi and Mahoney (2017). Reprinted with permission from Oxford University Press © 2017.

Vertical Integration

Which components should the final assembler produce in-house, and which should it purchase from external suppliers? Should a firm have its own legal department to handle intellectual property issues, or should it contract with an external law firm? Should a university hire internal faculty or contract with adjunct and visiting faculty? More generally, how should the organization approach the make-or-buy decision?

In contemplating the make-or-buy decision, two cost categories become relevant. One is the cost of performing the activity itself: producing a component, providing legal advice on an intellectual property dispute, teaching a course at the university, and so on. Comparing the production costs of the feasible governance options is a salient part of the analysis.

The more elusive part is the analysis of the cost of contracting. In industrial production, if the parts needed in final assembly are standardized and

Table 3.3. Examples of Governance Decisions, Efficiency Criteria, and Efficiency Drivers

Context	The efficiency criterion	Efficiency drivers
Vertical integration	Is the degree of vertical integration set such that the total cost of governing the buyer-supplier relationship (the sum of production costs and transaction costs) is minimized?	Productivity and coordination
Franchising	Do the franchisor and the franchisee have the proper incentives to create value through the operations each manages and controls? Is free riding discouraged?	Incentive alignment within and across organizations
Corporate diversification	Do the individual business units create collectively more value when they are divisions of the same corporation, as opposed to operating as separate businesses?	Economies of scope within the organization
Corporate governance	Does the composition of the corporation's board of directors secure the long-term cooperation of the corporation's stakeholders?	Cooperation of the organization's stakeholders
R&D collaboration	To manage uncertain interfirm collaboration, is a joint equity alliance a more flexible governance mode than collaborative contracting?	Flexibility to address unanticipated disturbances
Corporate finance	Does the mix of debt and equity financing minimize the cost of capital?	Cost of capital
Legislature	Do members of the legislature, individually and collectively, serve the interests of their constituencies?	Alignment of legislative work with constituency interests

alternate suppliers are available, then purchasing the parts would amount to little more than "ordering them from a catalog." The issue becomes more complicated for customer-specific parts that require customer-specific engineering. Parts are no longer simply picked from a catalog. Instead, they are designed, redesigned, and exchanged in collaborative long-term relationships. Car seats and entire car interiors are good examples in the context of automobile assembly. These relationships include various relation-specific investments, which are usually comparatively easier to manage if the buyer and the supplier are divisions of the same firm. Internal disputes are alleviated by the fact that they are subject to corporate intervention. In contrast, if the transacting parties are separate firms, such managerial intervention is not possible. Furthermore, in the case of internal transactions, there is also a strong incentive to address problems through internal organization because litigation is not an option—courts do not hear or settle internal disputes.

The obvious designer's mistake is to engage in suboptimization by basing the decision exclusively on a comparison of production costs. Analyses that incorporate only the direct costs of production tend to point to outsourcing as the more efficient option, because specialized suppliers often enjoy economies of scale and scope not available to the buyer. But because transaction costs in interorganizational transacting are often higher than in intraorganizational transacting, failing to incorporate the costs of contracting may mislead the designer to consider outsourcing preferable even when it is less efficient in terms of total cost. Indeed, many outsourcing decisions have not led to the kinds of cost savings first envisioned. It is possible that the differences in contracting costs are significant enough to offset any productivity advantages.[7]

Finally, we should note that the comparative analysis does not require *make* and *buy* to be the only options; an efficiency analysis can incorporate hybrid governance forms, such as leasing. In their study of shoemaking machinery, organization economists Scott Masten and Edward Snyder (1993) concluded that the manufacturer of shoemaking machines should structure its contracts with those who use the machines (the shoemakers) as long-term leases. The reasoning was that a lease would help avoid possibly costly haggling over prices and free-riding concerns on both the buyer and the seller side. Leasing the machines instead of buying them would be more lucrative to the shoemaker, because "[r]eceiving payment up-front, a manufacturer has no interest, beyond its reputation, in the ultimate performance of its product" (Masten and Snyder 1993, 42). But if the equipment were leased and maintenance performed by the party that designed and built the equipment, these performance concerns would be alleviated.

Making the lease long term would be beneficial to the equipment manufacturer who has invested significant resources in the design and further development of the machines. Masten and Snyder (1993, 38) noted that at the time, United Shoe was one of the five largest patent holders in the United

---

[7] The comparison should also incorporate potential differences in the quality of internally produced and externally procured parts. But since we are operating under the assumption that *make* and *buy* are feasible alternatives, the premise is that in both cases, quality is adequate. If this is not the case, then the obvious choice is the option where quality is adequate.

States. A long-term lease would serve as a safeguard to the manufacturer because having to commit to a long-term lease would incentivize the shoemaker to ensure the machines would also be used.

In summary, a long-term lease would strike a balance between the interests of the two contracting parties: "[L]easing makes the incentives to develop and support quality machinery largely self-enforcing and thus avoids the practical limitations of contractual guarantees" (Masten and Snyder 1993, 42). The long-term lease would thus offer a similar built-in high-powered incentive on the seller side we observed in the taxi ride example in chapter 1.

Corporate Diversification

Volkswagen Group consists of the Automotive Division and the Financial Services Division. The Automotive Division is further divided into the Passenger Cars Business Area, the Commercial Vehicles Business Area, and the Power Engineering Business Area. Finally, the Passenger Cars Business Area consists of the individual brands such as Volkswagen, Audi, Škoda, Seat, Bentley, and Porsche (Volkswagen Group 2020).

Why does it make sense for Volkswagen Group to house all these different car brands—*horizontally equivalent activities* in economic terminology— under the same corporate umbrella? In 2020, Volkswagen Group sold a total of one million Audis for a total of €50 billion of revenue. What, if anything, would be different if Audi operated as an independent automaker?

It should not come as a surprise that individual car brands are not managed independently of one another within Volkswagen Group. Because passenger car brands have similar technological needs such as fuel efficiency, significant amounts of R&D effort can be shared and leveraged across individual brands that "not only work *with* each other, but also *for* each other on key technologies, forming cross-brand networks of expertise to address topics of importance for the future" (Volkswagen Group 2020, 145 [emphasis added]).

Obviously, nothing would stop Audi and Volkswagen from collaborating even if they did not belong to the same corporation. Therefore, the central governance question is not whether the brands should collaborate but, rather, whether the collaboration should be organized within the same firm or across independent firms. The efficiency view suggests that due to the highly intensive and idiosyncratic needs for collaboration that likely involves frequent joint problem-solving, sharing of classified information, and proprietary intellectual property, bringing both brands under the same corporate umbrella is comparatively efficient. To be sure, having a legal boundary in between two car brands would not prevent collaboration, but it might cause significant inefficiencies due to the contracting hazards it would present. Williamson (1979, 250) elaborates the efficiency logic: "The nonstandardized nature of these transactions makes primary reliance on [interorganizational] governance hazardous, while their recurrent nature permits the cost of the specialized [internal] governance structure to be recovered." Interpreted in the context of Volkswagen Group, the complex corporate governance structure is justified because the advantages it bestows more than offsets the costs, resulting in net gains.

Note also that the question here is not whether the individual car brands enjoy a competitive advantage in the marketplace or whether Volkswagen Group's individual business units and car brands are profitable. The question is squarely on the efficiency of coordination: Are horizontally equivalent activities more efficiently structured as intra- or interorganizational relationships? Whether the efficiency Volkswagen Group gains from internalizing horizontally equivalent activities has competitive implications would require an analysis that is outside the scope of this book. Also, combining horizontally equivalent activities is not always beneficial. In the auto industry, Volvo Cars seems to be doing much better as an autonomous car brand than it did when it was a division of Ford Motor Company.

R&D Collaboration

Consider a scenario where two technology companies with partially overlapping interests seek the best way to structure joint R&D. Two alternatives are collaborative contracting and a joint equity alliance. In the former, the relationship would be governed through a series of contracts that specify each party's rights and responsibilities. In the latter governance alternative, a separate legal entity—a joint limited liability company—would be established. Both companies would make contributions to its equity and appoint members to its board of directors. Which alternative is comparatively efficient?

Let us start at the main problem the designers of the collaboration are trying to solve. In the case of risky R&D collaboration, a common way of framing the governance problem is in terms of how the contracting parties will address issues that may arise unexpectedly during the collaboration. If the relationship is governed by collaborative contracts, addressing issues that the contracts do not cover presents a recurring contractual challenge. If these emergent issues are frequent, the contracting parties may find themselves committing lots of resources and attention to negotiations and exception management.

Under conditions of high uncertainty, the joint equity alliance has several benefits. For example, the contracting parties need not write complex contracts, because they can assign problem-solving responsibility to the alliance's board of directors which is entrusted to address problems whenever they arise. Furthermore, because board members have a fiduciary duty of loyalty and care to the alliance, the contracting parties can expect fewer agency problems. Finally, contributions to joint equity can be thought of as safeguards by which the contracting parties signal their strong commitment to the collaboration (Gulati and Singh 1998).

In summary, whereas governance efficiency in the vertical integration centered on production and coordination costs, in the case of R&D collaboration efficiency pertains to the ability to address unanticipated developments in interfirm collaboration. A joint equity alliance is the comparatively efficient response under conditions of high uncertainty. If uncertainty is lower, as may be the case in short-term collaborations, collaborative contracting may be preferred.

Organizing the Legislature

In their insightful economic analysis of the legislature, political scientist Barry Weingast and management scholar William Marshall (1988) concluded that exchange in the United States Congress was organized in a seemingly efficient way. But what does it mean for a legislature to be efficient?

It is useful to start at the fact that lawmakers have considerable incentives to exchange support with one another. Indeed, legislators often actively seek "trading partners" to further the interests of their own constituencies. The question is not whether the legislature makes smart decisions and passes high-quality laws but, rather, whether legislators, individually and collectively, are able to introduce legislation that serves the interests of their respective constituencies. The question is not one of *quality* of the decisions but, rather, the *alignment* of legislative work with the interests of the electorate.

The exchange of votes runs into severe problems in daily legislative practice. The issues of interest of two "trading partners" do not come up for a vote simultaneously, which makes packaging bills into a single "market exchange" infeasible. When trading is nonsimultaneous, how can the legislator whose turn is to deliver first trust that the other will deliver later? Opportunism aside, what if an unforeseen circumstance, such as the failure to get re-elected, led to a situation where the other party was simply unable to fulfill its side of the bargain? Enforceability of bargains becomes problematic, and the simple market form of exchange becomes inefficient.

The ubiquitous *committee system* found in legislatures around the world provides a comparatively efficient alternative, because it provides protection against uncertainties associated with market exchange. In many ways, the legislature functions more like a firm than a market. Just like the R&D department of an industrial firm focuses on product and service development tasks and the sales and marketing departments on revenue creation, the United States House Committee on Energy & Commerce controls the agendas within its jurisdiction by deciding which bills to bring to the House floor for a vote.

An important function of the committee system is to introduce stability that enables comparatively more efficient legislative bargaining. Although it is by no means perfect (no governance alternative is), it can be argued to be more efficient than simple market exchange, because it addresses the nonsimultaneity problem. If all trades had to occur simultaneously in the very same bill, the ability of legislators to serve their constituents would be significantly hampered. The stability that the committee system provides contributes to efficient organization.

Conclusion: Toward Understanding the Entire Organization

Suppose we analyze all the organization's contractual relationships and examine whether they are structured as intra- or interorganizational. In figure 3.1, there are a total of 16 tasks, seven of which are conducted within the organization and nine by external actors. For the sake of argument, let us assume T1–T7 represent seven different R&D teams of a research lab that collaborate both with one another as well as with nine other research teams (T8–T16) belonging to external organizations.

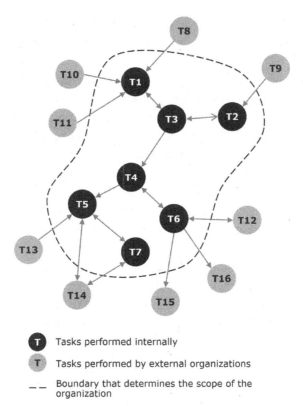

T Tasks performed internally

T Tasks performed by external organizations

_ _ Boundary that determines the scope of the organization

Figure 3.1 Organizational boundary and the scope of the organization

Some of the relationships are more intensive than others in terms of the collaboration requirements. Perhaps the relationship T4↔T6 requires intense daily communication, joint problem-solving, and sharing of facilities for the collaboration to be successful; the double-headed arrow indicates *reciprocal interdependence*. In contrast, the relationship T3→T4→T5 may represent a series of supplier relationships where T4 requires inputs from T3 in order to supply T5; the single-headed arrows indicate *sequential interdependence*. Finally, T1 may be responsible for simply pooling the contributions from three external suppliers T8, T10, and T11; the set of single-headed arrows leading to T1 (T8→T1, T10→T1, and T11→T1) indicate *pooled interdependence*. The three types of interdependence were first introduced to the analysis of organizational relationships by sociologist James Thompson (1967).

The efficiency logic predicts that one is likely to find the most intensive interdependencies in intraorganizational relationships. Importantly, intensity is not merely a function of interdependencies stemming from the *workflow* (the conventional view) but also by interdependencies that have their roots in the *organization* (our view), that is, transaction frequency, uncertainty, and relation-specific investments. Indeed, not only reciprocal but also pooled and sequential interdependencies in the workflow can be associated with strong reciprocal organizational interdependencies. For instance, the relationship T3→T4→T5 may be comparatively simple in terms of its sequential workflow interdependency, but there may be organizational factors that necessitate the internalization of all three activities. All three activities might involve proprietary knowledge possessed only by the organization's best internal experts.

At the same time, some contractual relationships may be characterized by strong interdependencies and still remain interorganizational. Task T14, for example, may be a task that is infeasible for the organization to internalize, because it relies on a technological competence the organization could not internalize even if it were desirable. These relationships may give rise to contracting hazards, and therefore, require special attention from the designer.

The implications of figure 3.1 are profound. Having mapped all the relevant tasks, their interdependencies, and their contracting modes, what emerges is an understanding of the *entire organization*. Specifically, having conducted an efficiency analysis of all the relevant contractual relationships, we will have made sense of not only individual contractual relationships but also the scope of the entire organization. Some organizations have broader scopes because many transactions are so complex that they are prohibitively expensive to manage through interorganizational contracting. Others have narrow scopes due to the relative ease at which contractual relationships across organizational boundaries can be governed. To understand contracting is to understand the organization in its entirety.[8]

---

[8] The organization economist would say that we have arrived at a *theory of the firm*. The purpose of a theory of the firm is to explain why organizations exist in the first place and what determines their scope (Holmström and Tirole 1989).

4

Stakeholder Analysis

One of the authors of this book chaired the board of an industrial startup. In his discussions with factory workers, it dawned on him that employees had no idea how equity operated in a limited liability company. The workers had never owned shares, and understandably, the notions of residual claimancy and residual risk as well as the distinction between fixed and residual payments were alien to the young engineers and technicians. The workers did not know how fundamentally vulnerable shareholders were due to being entitled only to residual payments. The employees had understandably analyzed their own employment risk, but acquiring an understanding of shareholder risk led to productive conversations regarding the broader notion of stakeholder risk and, in particular, how important it was for the startup to maintain a buffer of positive shareholders' equity; not to be distributed to the shareholders but to ensure the small, risky organization's survival.

The conversations were not only about informing employees on the economic realities of a high-risk startup. One of the prospective employees taught the board an important lesson about how becoming an employee would effectively commit him to site specificity (see chapter 3). The man, in his early thirties, had two children ages four and six. Becoming an employee at the plant would require that he either commute a total of sixty miles every day from his hometown to the plant or relocate his family to the small town where the plant was located. The former would effectively have added an hour and a half to his workday. However, the latter would have meant that his family would commit to their six-year-old child starting school in a new town. It is reasonable to view this decision as the employee committing to specificity, even though it was only indirectly related to the man's potential employment contract. The man took the job, commuted for a few months, and then resigned. It was fully understandable that he was reluctant not only to accept employment at a high-risk startup but also to commit to site specificity.

Unfortunately, many stakeholder conversations are about constituencies engaging in advocacy to protect their interests. In an attempt to counter

Efficient Organization. Mikko Ketokivi and Joseph T. Mahoney, Oxford University Press. © Oxford University Press 2023. DOI: 10.1093/oso/9780197610282.003.0004

purely self-interested behavior on all sides, we present in this chapter a framework aimed at helping the designer conduct an explicit stakeholder analysis by a comparative assessment of the vulnerabilities of the organization's constituencies. A central objective of a dispassionate analysis is that the organization's stakeholders become aware not only of their own risk but also the risk that other stakeholders bear.

It is perhaps realistic to assume that self-interest will likely continue to dominate stakeholder conversations. However, our objective is to transform hardball advocacy into informed, reasoned advocacy. To this end, we emphasize throughout this chapter both the importance of analysis and what legal scholars Margaret Blair and Lynn Stout (2001, 404) labeled *other-regarding behaviors*, not only by the designer but by all constituencies and stakeholders. The problem with the purely self-interested approach to stakeholder management is that a self-interested constituency will always find a way to argue for a stakeholder status. Other-regarding constituencies, in contrast, will evaluate their own position by an explicit comparison to other constituencies. This comparative analysis goes to the very essence of value-creating cooperation.

In addition to downplaying advocacy, another objective is to overcome the unfortunately common problem in stakeholder conversations: the adoption of excessively expansive approaches that tend to be "so broad as to be meaningless and so complex as to be useless" (Orts and Strudler 2002, 218). In many conversations, the word *stakeholder* is simply used as rhetorical shorthand to convey that someone, or something, is important. To counter this lack of nuance, in addition to analyzing the stakeholder status of the organization's constituencies, we also examine specific governance responses available to the designer in safeguarding the most important stakeholder relationships. Awarding stakeholder status to a constituency is meaningless unless it is associated with a governance response of some kind.

Most fundamentally, a nuanced analysis is needed for stakeholder governance to become practically relevant for the designer. To this end, we start this chapter by making the distinction between an organization's stakeholders and its constituencies more generally. We evaluate the potential stakeholder status of a constituency by asking whether a constituency has voluntarily put something at stake by joining the organization. Legal scholars and business ethicists Eric Orts and Alan Strudler (2002, 217–18) crystallized what it means to be a stakeholder of an organization: A stakeholder "holds a bet or a wager on the outcome of an enterprise." Our version of stakeholder analysis adopts a similar approach.

To be sure, some constituencies of the organization can make the claim of having voluntarily put something more at stake than others. Stakeholder analysis is therefore ultimately a matter of analyzing degrees, not categories: Some constituencies have *more of a stakeholder status* than others. This comparative approach paves the way toward informed prioritization of stakeholders, which is essential to governance decisions.

Designers face numerous dilemmas in prioritizing constituencies, and a dispassionate look at stakeholder interests reveals fundamental incompatibilities; a benefit to one stakeholder may come at the expense of another. In fact, if stakeholder interests were compatible, there would be no need for stakeholder analysis, or stakeholder governance for that matter. Instead, the designer would simply select the governance alternative that benefits all stakeholders. Such idealized thinking amounts to "a mischaracterization of reality" (Bebchuk and Tallarita 2020, 129).

Only partially overlapping and at times conflicting interests constitute a *stakeholder dilemma*, which presents the designer with governance alternatives each of which has at least one undesirable consequence. The designer must resist attempts to escape difficult choices and trade-offs by appealing to the idea of balancing stakeholder interests. Jensen (2002, 251) bluntly described *balancing* as a "hurrah word" that "cannot ever substitute for having to deal with the difficult issues associated with specifying the trade-offs among multiple goods and bads."

This chapter echoes Jensen's call and counsels the designer to approach stakeholder issues analytically. The greatest threat in failing to prioritize is that the organization risks its credibility in the eyes of those who have the most at stake. In many organizations, those who have put the most at stake tend to be both critical to the viability of the organization and particularly difficult to replace. A stakeholder approach that either deliberately or inadvertently ends up trying to pacify those with less at stake poses an immediate threat to viability.

Stakeholders vs. Other Constituencies

We consider any individual or collective that has a contractual relationship with the organization a *constituency*. Constituencies have duties toward the organization, and for the organization to be credible in the eyes of the constituency, the organization must offer something in return. Barnard (1938) wrote about the importance of organizations offering all its constituencies the proper *inducements* in exchange for the *contributions* the organization asks in return. Barnard (1938, 93) further linked inducements and contributions directly to organizational efficiency and viability: "[E]fficiency of an organization is its capacity to offer effective inducements in sufficient quantity to maintain the equilibrium of the system. It is efficiency in this sense and not the efficiency of material productiveness which maintains the vitality of organizations." Barnard's position is fully consistent with the aims of this book.

In the case of most constituencies, inducements and contributions can be adequately addressed and secured in formal contracts: employment contracts, buyer-supplier contracts, licensing agreements, leases, and the like. The need for a more nuanced analysis arises when constituency relationships involve nontrivial degrees of risk, which gives rise to the need to implement additional safeguards to secure the cooperation of the risk-bearing constituency. Some of these safeguards can be enfolded into the formal contract. For example, employee job security may be introduced by the employer committing to a long-term employment contract.

However, sometimes all formal contractual arrangements fall short of providing the requisite inducements. Some relationships involve so much risk that adequately safeguarding them must extend beyond formal contracts and become embedded in the very design of the organization. The relationship between the limited liability company and its shareholders offers the canonical example.

The Shareholder as a Stakeholder of the Limited Liability Company

Inducements in the case of employees take the form of fixed salary payments once or twice a month. If the employer defaults on these payments, employees have multiple alternatives for recourse. If negotiations fail and the employer still refuses to pay, the employees can take the employer to court. If litigation is ineffective, they can take the corporation to bankruptcy; upon liquidation of the corporation's assets, employees would be among the first to be compensated. In bankruptcy proceedings, not only the firm but also its top executives and board members could be held liable.

Bankruptcy would, of course, ultimately have adverse consequences for the employees as well, but the central governance point is that due to strong institutional forces bolstering employment contracts, the employer is *ex ante* strongly incentivized to maintain the contractually guaranteed inducements to its employees. In the case of organizational demise, everybody loses, including those making decisions on behalf of the organization in its management and oversight functions. This should properly incentivize management to ensure that the organization makes all its contractually required fixed payments.

Consider in contrast the shareholders. What contractual safeguards do they have? More fundamentally, what kind of a contract do they have with the firm in the first place? The firm is asking for financial contributions in the form of equity financing, but what inducements does it offer in return? If these inducements are not maintained, what recourse do shareholders have?

Whereas employees are contractually guaranteed to receive fixed payments from the top line of the income statement, shareholders receive only residual payments from the bottom line in case there is something left over. It is illegal to pay dividends unless all other contractual obligations are met; if there is no residual, there can be no dividend. Organizations cannot give any guarantees to shareholders that they will receive residual payments. This risk makes shareholders a contractually disadvantaged and a highly vulnerable constituency—shareholders have essentially no protection.

In the absence of a formal contract, the organization must embed in its governance structures the requisite inducements to shareholders to secure their contributions. One common safeguard is to make the board of directors a governance instrument of the shareholders. Specifically, the organization signals credibility toward shareholders by appointing a board of directors whose primary task is to secure the rights of the residual claimants. Therefore, although the corporation can make no promises of residual payments, it can assign its board the role of ensuring that residual interests are incorporated into governance. The vulnerability of the shareholder has prompted a governance response, and therefore, the shareholder has been converted into a stakeholder possessing a safeguard.

Buying shares in a limited liability company is an obvious bet or wager on the outcome of the organization, but there may be others. What are they? What bets and wagers have others made on organizational outcomes? Do employees make a bet when they sign the employment contract and exchange their time and effort for fixed salary payments? Do suppliers make a wager as they agree to supply products and services to the buyer? The aim of a stakeholder analysis is to analyze all bets and wagers and work out the governance ramifications.

Consistent with Orts and Strudler's (2002) idea that the bets and wagers are made specifically on organizational outcomes, we offer residual risk as the starting point of a stakeholder analysis. Just like the assessment of risk in general, the analysis must incorporate the magnitude of residual risk each stakeholder bears; the associated comparative analysis provides the foundation for stakeholder prioritization. If designers start at the premise that a constituency either is or is not a stakeholder, then the predictable outcome is that every constituency is classified as a stakeholder, and all the designers' work is still ahead of them; if everyone is important, then no one is important. Prioritization of COVID-19 vaccine delivery provides a useful illustration.

COVID-19 Vaccine Delivery: Efficient and Transparent Prioritization

It is difficult to disagree with the general principle that the COVID-19 vaccine should be offered free of charge to everyone who wants it. However, this principle is analogous to the idea that everyone is a stakeholder, and as such, is useless to the designer of the COVID-19 vaccine delivery organization. If everyone is entitled to the vaccine, who should get it first? Should vaccinations be given on a first-come, first-served basis? This approach would be not only unethical but also potentially dangerous.[1] Not surprisingly, we are not aware of a single country, state, municipality, or other jurisdiction where a detailed, reasoned, and transparent prioritization was not implemented and clearly communicated to the public.

It seems prudent to prioritize healthcare professionals, essential workers, senior citizens, and individuals with compromised immune systems, over others. To this end, the COVID-19 Vaccination Plan issued by Illinois Department of Public Health (2021, 13) stipulated the following: "Local public health jurisdictions should plan to collaborate with their regional healthcare coalition, hospitals, long-term care and/or assisted living facilities, and other potential vaccine providers that serve frontline essential workers

---

[1] To those who believe that the first-come, first-served principle is efficient in situations where a lot is at stake, we recommend entering "Black Friday crowd rushing into the mall" into a search engine and watching a few videos of how people behave when the primary thing at stake is a discount on a smartphone. What would happen if the first-come, first-served principle was applied in a matter involving personal health?

in their jurisdiction to ensure full coverage of vaccine first to the designated priority groups and then to the general public."

In the state of Illinois, which was in our view sufficiently representative of most jurisdictions, the first priority group consisted of healthcare workers and long-term care facility residents and staff; the second consisted of persons over sixty-five years old, front-line essential workers, persons between the ages of sixteen and sixty-four with high-risk medical conditions; and so on. In all these groups, the key terms were specified in great detail to make prioritization exceedingly transparent. For example, *healthcare worker* was defined using the Centers for Disease Control and Prevention (CDC) definition as "paid and unpaid workers in healthcare settings who have the potential for direct or indirect exposure to patients or infectious materials." Note that this definition did not require that the person necessarily work with patients.

Similarly, high-risk medical conditions were listed in detail: diabetes, pulmonary disease, cancer, and heart condition, among others. Smoking was also included as a high-risk medical condition, which was a source of some controversy. We propose that the prioritization of smokers offers an excellent opportunity to exercise other-regarding stakeholder thinking.

It may be appealing for a nonsmoker to criticize the prioritization of smokers. Why should people receive preferential treatment simply because of a personal health choice they had made? The designers of the vaccine prioritization principles were well aware that prioritization of smokers would stir controversy and, consequently, fully understood the importance of communicating an explicit justification to the public. The justification for prioritizing smokers was based on two related issues. One was the scientific finding that cumulative smoking exposure (measured by pack-years) had an empirically corroborated adverse association with COVID-19 outcomes (e.g., Lowe et al. 2021). The other was that vaccine delivery would be prioritized such that the comparatively more vulnerable receive protection first regardless of the origin of their vulnerability.

For the sake of argument, suppose that the designer had begun to classify dozens, if not hundreds, of preexisting conditions based on whether they had plausibly resulted from a personal choice. Is obesity a personal choice? How about diabetes, the origins of which can in part be traced to personal choices? High cholesterol? How much more challenging would the (already highly complex and contested) prioritization protocol become? The guiding principle in vaccine delivery was that designers considered only the hazard the preexisting condition presented, regardless of its source. In other words, vaccine delivery would be addressed exclusively as a matter of public health, not a judgment of personal choices. Incorporating personal choices would not only have been ethically questionable, but it would also have led to prohibitively complex governance structures.

Having followed the discussions on vaccine prioritization closely, we observed that as a general rule, other-regarding behaviors were more the rule than the exception. The twenty-one-year-old college athlete with no respiratory issues readily understood and accepted that a sixty-five-year-old with asthma had more at stake. Both should have the right to receive the vaccine, but it was clear that the designer would incorporate into governance decisions the fact that the sixty-five-year-old asthmatic must be prioritized over the twenty-one-year-old college athlete.

We submit COVID-19 vaccine prioritization as an instructive example of why both explicit stakeholder prioritization and other-regarding behaviors are essential to governance decisions. Everyone can argue to be ultimately at risk, but some are more at risk than others. We further propose that the question "Who needs the organization the most?" is sufficiently analogous with the question "Who needs the vaccine the most?" Accordingly, in evaluating the potential stakeholder status of an employee, an investor, a supplier, or a customer, we ask, "How would the person or entity in question be affected if the organization ceased to exist?" Employees would lose their jobs, investors would lose their wealth, suppliers would lose customers, customers would lose suppliers, and communities (municipalities, states, nations) would lose tax revenue. That some would lose more than others should be clear. For example, some employees would be able to find alternative employment very quickly, with little or no reduction in pay. But others might have considerable problems finding new employment, particularly if their skills are highly organization specific. To arrive at an informed understanding of stakeholders, the analysis must involve a detailed examination of the implications of organizational failure. This is why the focus turns specifically to organizational *outcomes*.

Defining Stakeholder

Management scholar Bidhan Parmar and colleagues (2010, 412) insightfully noted that "[r]ather than seeing the definitional problem [of stakeholder] as a singular and fixed, admitting of only one answer, we instead can see different definitions serving different purposes." This is exactly why trying to formulate a generally applicable definition is not useful. For the purposes of our exposition, we formulate a definition that helps the designer think of ways by which the organization can ensure that the requisite bets and wagers the organization needs from its constituencies are in fact made. For the industrial startup whose survival hinges on successfully raising equity to finance highly specific technological assets, the most important bets and wagers likely involve investments in equity; for organizations that rely on organization-specific innovation and R&D, bets and wagers may involve not only equity financing but also employees committing to organization-specific skills. The failure to attract the requisite bets and wagers means the organization underinvests in some of its central activities, which jeopardizes viability.

Once all constituencies have made all the bets and the wagers that link to organizational outcomes, they will also have developed a residual interest and therefore become, by definition, interested in the organization's success. Similarly, especially in cases where constituencies commit to specificity and become difficult to replace, the organization symmetrically develops an interest in their success. As a result, the conditions of a stakeholder relationship (see chapter 1) are fulfilled: By virtue of having responsibilities toward one another and being interested in one another's success, the contracting parties have become one another's stakeholders. The magnitude or the intensity of the stakeholder relationship can be established by examining the size of the bets and the wagers made.

We maintain that our approach to stakeholder analysis avoids the problem of both being too narrow and being overpermissive. To illustrate the approach, we use in the following publicly available information to conduct a stakeholder analysis of HP Inc., a global provider of personal computing devices and accessories in both business-to-business and business-to-consumer markets.

A Stakeholder Analysis of HP, Inc.

In its 2020 annual report, HP (2020, 4) described its business as follows:

> We are a leading global provider of personal computing and other access devices, imaging and printing products, and related technologies, solutions and services. We sell to individual consumers, small- and medium-sized

businesses ("SMBs") and large enterprises, including customers in the government, health, and education sectors.

Based on this description alone, it is straightforward to see how HP is involved in a large number of diverse long-term contracts and relationships with employees, suppliers, customers (consumers, businesses, and other institutions), communities, governments, investors, banks, and the like. Indeed, HP's 131-page Sustainable Impact Report (HP 2019) discussed the diversity of HP's stakeholders in great detail. The complexity and the vast heterogeneity of stakeholders provides us with a great opportunity for conducting a stakeholder analysis. We first briefly discuss HP's own approach and then extend it by our own efficiency-based analysis.

HP's Perspective in Brief

In its Sustainability Impact Report, HP (2019, 5) listed the following entities as stakeholders: HP employees, suppliers and supply chain workers, local and global communities, customers, channel and retail partners, recycling vendors, and regulators. Interestingly, the 131-page report mentions shareholders only once and does *not* list shareholders as stakeholders. However, we think it is not only reasonable to count shareholders as stakeholders—their wagers are unambiguous—but also ultimately misleading to make a distinction between the two. Our position is that the stakeholder status of all constituencies, shareholders included, has a common origin in residual risk.

The Sustainability Impact Report also reveals that HP engages in explicit analysis of stakeholder issues: "We identify appropriate stakeholders based on factors such as expertise, willingness to collaborate, reputation, location, and sphere of influence" (HP 2019, 14). Moreover, the focus is on engagement: "We gain valuable insight through our regular engagement with a range of stakeholders—including employees, investors, suppliers, customers, peer companies, public policymakers, industry bodies, nongovernmental organizations (NGOs), sector experts, and others" (HP 2019, 14). This approach squares perfectly with our idea of focusing on mutual value creation and collaboration. We want to add to this idea the importance of assessing residual risk.

At HP, stakeholder issues are elevated to the top management and board levels. Most notably:

> HP's Board of Directors' Nominating, Governance and Social Responsibility (NGSR) Committee oversees the company's policies and programs relating to global citizenship and the impact of HP's operations; provides guidance and recommendations to the Board on legal, regulatory, and compliance matters relating to political, environmental, global citizenship, and public policy trends; and reviews the annual Sustainable Impact Report. (HP 2019, 15)

Publicly available documents do not describe in detail how HP prioritizes its stakeholders. In the following section, we use publicly available information in conjunction with the Efficiency Lens to make inferences about which particular relationships might be more likely to exhibit stakeholder characteristics.

A Stakeholder Analysis of HP's Constituencies

Prioritization of constituencies should be performed not only across but also within constituency groups. In fact, we propose that prioritization within categories is both more meaningful and has better tractability than prioritization across categories. The question, "Which specific employees, or employee groups, should be considered stakeholders?," is more tractable than the question, "Are shareholders more important stakeholders than employees?" We consider the latter question ambiguous not because it is difficult to compare an employee to a shareholder but because to compare the two is to compare two heterogeneous groups to one another. Put differently, fine-grained within-group analyses must precede any between-group comparisons.

Suppliers
We estimate the total number of HP's suppliers to be around a thousand, at least in terms of the order of magnitude. It is further immediately clear from basic accounting data that suppliers in the aggregate are crucial to HP's business. We estimate HP's total annual spending in its supply chain—purchase of components, products, and services—to be at the very least 40 percent

of HP's annual revenue.[2] Not surprisingly, HP openly acknowledges that it not only depends on third-party suppliers, but also that its financial results would suffer if it failed to manage its suppliers effectively, and that the "business could be negatively impacted if key suppliers [were] forced to cease or limit their operations" (HP 2020, 16).

The magnitude of HP's purchasing costs clearly establishes that HP is fundamentally dependent on its supply chain; if purchasing costs were 4 instead of 40 percent of revenue, we would be less concerned. However, it does not immediately follow that suppliers, as constituents, are also stakeholders. The idea that HP would have a thousand external organizations as its stakeholders would lead to prohibitively complex governance structures. Consequently, significant prioritization must take place.

What would happen if HP lost Company X as its supplier? What would happen if Company X lost its HP account to another vendor? It is always important to analyze stakeholder relationships through the lens of bilateral dependency because relationships characterized by strongly unilateral dependence do not qualify as stakeholder relationships. Specifically, it makes little sense to label HP's relationship with Company X a stakeholder relationship if Company X is a supplier of standard parts that HP can purchase from a dozen other vendors. To be sure, Company X might like to claim a stakeholder relationship with HP, but since the arm's-length relationship with Company X constitutes no risk to HP, awarding stakeholder status would direct unwarranted attention to a simple transactional relationship, and possibly away from the genuinely complex relationships that merit the designer's attention.

What kind of a cost would HP incur if it had to replace Company X with a new supplier? Supplier switching cost offers a salient metric for evaluating the potential stakeholder characteristics of a buyer-supplier relationship. Furthermore, bilateral dependency would prompt us to ask the symmetrical question, "What kind of a cost would Company X incur if it had to find a new buyer to replace HP?" In some buyer-supplier relationships, switching costs are negligible; in others, they are astronomical.

HP's annual reports provide insight into the prioritization of suppliers and the identification of those suppliers that are likely considered stakeholders.

---

[2] In 2020, HP's revenue was $56 billion and cost of revenue $46 billion (82 percent of sales). Cost of revenue consists primarily of purchases and wages of those employees working directly on the generation of sales. We hypothesize purchases to be the single most important source of costs, which is why we estimate it to be at least 40 percent of revenue. Obviously, this is merely our own estimate.

A good litmus test for whether a supplier is a stakeholder is whether its name appears on the 10-K form.[3] If a supplier is mentioned by name, its identity matters, and a stakeholder status is more likely.

Suppliers whose names appear repeatedly on HP's 10-K form are AMD (a supplier of x86 processors; mentioned four times in the 2020 10-K form), Canon (a supplier of laser print engines and laser printer cartridges, mentioned eleven times), Microsoft (a supplier of software products; mentioned five times), and Intel (a supplier of x86 processors; mentioned four times). Not surprisingly, HP (2020, 6) openly admits to being "dependent upon" these suppliers. In the case of AMD, Canon, Microsoft, and Intel, switching costs are so high that losing these suppliers would likely threaten HP's survival.[4]

AMD's, Canon's, Intel's, and Microsoft's annual reports reveal a symmetric dependence on HP. For example, HP is Intel's third-largest customer, accounting for 10 percent of Intel's $78 billion revenue in 2020. HP cannot afford to lose Intel as a supplier, but we are almost certain that the feeling is mutual.

At the other end of the supplier spectrum are scores of vendors that HP (2020, 5) described as follows: "For most of [the products and components we purchase], we have existing alternate sources of supply or alternate sources of supply are readily available." The switching costs with regard to these suppliers are intentionally kept low by managing them as market transactions instead of long-term contracts. In general, switching costs offer a straightforward tool for analyzing the stakeholder status of suppliers.

---

[3] Form 10-K is an elaborate document each publicly listed company must file with the Securities and Exchange Commission every year. The 10-K form is a source of useful information on the company's business environment, strategy, management, and financial data. It is also useful in conducting a rudimentary stakeholder analysis.

[4] In the early 2000s, one of the authors worked with a manufacturer that performed the final assembly of tractors. The manufacturer bought most of the components and subsystems from external suppliers. One of these suppliers designed and manufactured tractor cabins, one of the most expensive subsystems in the final assembly. Furthermore, there was only one supplier of cabins, which made the final assembler highly dependent on the specific supplier. Given that each cabin was customized, cabins had to be delivered on a just-in-time basis from the supplier's factory to final assembly. By the early 2000s, the buyer-supplier relationship had been ongoing for fifty years, and predictably enough, developed all kinds of relation-specific features. When the general manager of the final assembly operation was asked how long it would take for his factory to replace the cabin supplier, the manager replied, without missing a beat: five years. He then added: "We had no option but to put all our eggs in one basket, so my task is to watch that basket!" To be sure, five years would be sufficient to take the company to bankruptcy many times over.

Customers

An identical switching-cost analysis can be applied to customers. The stakeholder status of customers becomes salient in the HP case when we consider the large institutional and corporate clients. For example, CDW Corporation is a multibrand provider of information technology solutions to various institutional customers (e.g., government, healthcare, and education). A Fortune 500 company with annual sales of $20 billion in 2020, CDW is also one of HP's large corporate clients, and we suspect the relationship exhibits many characteristics of a stakeholder relationship. But since HP is CDW's supplier, we have essentially covered this issue in the previous discussion on suppliers. HP is mentioned several times—and referred to as CDW's *partner*—in CDW's 10-K form.[5]

Considering customers as stakeholders does raise an interesting additional question not covered in the previous section on suppliers: When should the specific customer category of consumers be considered stakeholders? The intuitive answer may be *always*, but we propose the answer is actually *rarely*.

Suppose you purchase an HP laptop computer. Does this make you a member of the HP organization? No. What obligations do you have toward HP? None. What obligations does HP have toward you? Aside from having to ensure that the laptop works the way it is expected until the warranty period ends, not much else. It is hyperbole to describe a relationship with no discernible reciprocal characteristics or bilateral dependency as a stakeholder relationship. Of course, we are fully aware that corporations often consider not only customers in general but consumers in particular their stakeholders. We dare suggest this is simply to convey the sentiment that consumers are an important constituency because without consumers there will be no viable business. To those who disagree with our position that consumers are rarely stakeholders, we present the following challenge: Show us how consumer interests are incorporated into governance structures, and where the important safeguards that secure the rights of consumers are implemented.

---

[5] On its 10-K form for the 2019 fiscal year, CDW stated the following: "[S]ales of products manufactured by Apple, Cisco, Dell EMC, HP Inc., Lenovo and Microsoft, whether purchased directly from these vendor partners or from a wholesale distributor, represented approximately 60% of our 2019 consolidated Net sales [. . .] The loss of, or change in business relationship with, any of these or any other key vendor partners, or the diminished availability of their products, including due to backlogs for their products, could reduce the supply and increase the cost of products we sell and negatively impact our competitive position" (CDW Corporation 2019, 11). We have no doubt that it is in the best interest of both CDW and HP to safeguard the critical buyer-supplier relationship through bilateral credible commitments.

To be sure, HP must take care of its consumer customers; after all, consumers are a significant source of revenue. In the 2020 fiscal year, HP's revenues from consumer hardware were $2.5 billion. But just as in the case of suppliers, high volume must not be confounded with stakeholder status. We see no discernible governance implications in the HP-consumer relationship. HP's relationships with large institutional clients are obviously an entirely different matter, because business-to-business relationships often involve significant bets and wagers on both sides. In business-to-consumer relationships, it is difficult to see bets and wagers that would require the designer's attention.

We suggest that as a general rule, consumers are unlikely to be stakeholders of the companies whose products and services they use. The simple reason is that switching costs tend to be negligible both to the consumer and the organization. We might in fact go even so far as to suggest that not being a stakeholder is what consumers *should* prefer. Imagine the scenario of not only being dependent on the use of a personal computer (as many of us are) but also being dependent specifically on one provided by HP. Why would you choose to commit to such specificity? What are the benefits of such "lock-in" to you? Will they offset the increased switching cost such that net gains are obtained? With most consumer products, voluntarily putting something at stake with a particular brand seems like an unnecessary wager.

HP laptops are not cheap, but it is an overstatement to suggest that by buying one you have put so much at stake that you should be able to claim stakeholder status. If HP ceased to exist, you would have no trouble finding another brand of computers. Besides, HP ceasing to exist would not mean that your HP laptop would be immediately useless. IBM laptops certainly did not stop functioning on May 1, 2005, when IBM sold its PC hardware business to Lenovo.

Symmetrically, it cannot possibly be surprising to learn that the owners and executives at HP would lose no sleep over losing you as a customer. Even though HP is dependent on both businesses and consumers buying its products, it depends on the consumer market only in the aggregate; the cost of switching from one particular consumer to another is negligible. Only a mass exodus of consumers would be a cause for concern. To be sure, this sometimes happens, but we propose that the failure to incorporate consumers as stakeholders is not the reason.

We do not know whether HP's leadership considers consumers stakeholders in our meaning of the term. However, insofar as efficient organization is concerned, we do not see how it would be justified for HP to elevate consumers to a stakeholder status. Symmetrically, no economic-efficiency rationale suggests that consumers should seek to put anything at stake at HP. One does not need to become HP's stakeholder to use HP's products, and HP does not have to consider the consumer a stakeholder to sell its products and to take care of all its customers' needs. The relationship between the two is purely transactional.

The fundamental problem in thinking of the relationship between corporations and consumers in stakeholder terms is that the relationship is typically asymmetric. When the consumer becomes "locked in" to the specific supplier of products or services, the supplier becomes in no appreciable way dependent on the individual consumer. This is hazardous to the consumer, because the supplier can effectively hold the consumer hostage:

> [O]nce the relationship has begun, the supplier will be isolated to some degree from competition and will be in a position to "hold up" the consumer. . . . Generally, after the consumer has entered into the relationship with the producer, [he or she] will find [himself or herself] vulnerable to price increases or the threat of termination; the producer will be in a position to price discriminate in an attempt to capture [more value]. (Goldberg 1976, 439)

Employees

For the purposes of an efficiency analysis, it is instructive to consider employees and suppliers as analogous: Employees can usefully be regarded as "supplying" their time and efforts in return for compensation. Accordingly, an employment contract is, in some sense, a special case of the more general buyer-supplier contract. Furthermore, just like in the case of analyzing suppliers and customers as stakeholders, the focus should be on switching costs on both sides.

Who are the employees HP cannot afford to lose because they would be difficult to replace? These are the employees whose relationship with the organization should be considered in stakeholder terms instead of being viewed merely through the lens of an employment contract.

Are those who create greater value to HP more likely to be stakeholders than those who create less value? This is not necessarily the case. The question of stakeholder status is not about how much value an employee creates but whether the employee possesses skills that are organization specific. It is not value but specificity that makes the employee more difficult to replace.

In discussing employee skills, it is crucial to distinguish between *specificity* and *specialization*. As an example, consider the orthopedic surgeon working at the Johns Hopkins University in Baltimore. The surgeon is both highly specialized and highly valuable to the hospital. At the same time, the surgeon's technical skills are not organization specific.[6] The surgeon can easily seek employment at other hospitals, and symmetrically, the hospital may look to hire a replacement surgeon from another hospital. Committing to specialization makes individuals *profession specific*, committing to specificity makes them *organization specific*. Because the profession (orthopedic surgery) is a broader entity than the organization (Johns Hopkins University), those who commit to organizational specificity tend to be more difficult to replace, because the pool of replacement candidates is smaller.

Individuals who have committed to specialization are found throughout the HP organization; it is probably reasonable to suggest that all HP employees are specialized in one way or another. But where might we find individuals who have committed to specificity? In an attempt to pinpoint the parts of HP's organization where specificity might be found, it is useful to start with the question of what is distinctive about the organization.

Strategy scholars C. K. Prahalad and Gary Hamel (1990) suggested that an organization distinguishes itself from the rest through its *core competences*. For example, Prahalad and Hamel (1990, 83) described Honda's and Canon's core competences as follows: "It is Honda's core competence in engines and power trains that gives it a distinctive advantage in car, motorcycle, lawn mower, and generator businesses. Canon's core [competences] in optics, imaging, and microprocessor controls have enabled it to enter, even dominate, markets as seemingly diverse as copiers, laser printers, cameras, and image scanners." In Prahalad and Hamel's logic, core competences become embedded in core products, which are then leveraged to create revenue in the corporation's business units.

But if the organization's core competences make the organization unique, then it is only logical to look for commitments to organizational specificity within these competences. Commitments to specificity may be technological

---

[6] Surgeons work as members in surgical teams. Over time, a fundamental transformation may occur as team members learn to work together. As a result, some specificity may develop, and moving to another organization would involve having to learn to work with a new surgical team. However, the surgeon's general technical skills, while highly specialized, are not team or organization specific.

(physical asset specificity), but to the extent they involve employees developing and nurturing organization-specific skills (human capital specificity), these employees should be considered not merely constituencies but indeed stakeholders. The organization cannot expect employees to commit to specificity without the requisite safeguards.

By applying Prahalad and Hamel's logic, we find it plausible that in the case of HP, human capital specificity is found in HP's Printing Segment, and in particular, within the units that develop graphical solutions to deliver "large-format, commercial and industrial solutions, and supplies to print service providers and packaging converters through a wide portfolio of printers and presses (HP DesignJet, HP Latex, HP Indigo and HP PageWide Web Presses)" (HP 2020, 70). It is likely that at least some of HP's technical experts who work on commercial and industrial printing solutions possess skills that are in varying degrees HP specific, because printing and imaging have always been at the core of HP's strategy. Not surprisingly, this segment is also where many of HP's central patents are found. Those employees whose work is related to HP's intellectual property are also likely to exhibit human capital specificity. When employees commit to the development of organization-specific technologies, they make an unambiguous wager on organizational outcomes.

Financiers

Which providers of capital have a stakeholder relationship with HP, and why? Here, it is instructive to examine the kinds of contracts financiers have with the firm. The obvious distinction is between the providers of debt and equity capital. Even though the debt-equity categorization is a simplification and there are many hybrid forms of financing that exhibit features of both (e.g., Pratt 2000), the distinction is still analytically useful. Specifically, whether the financing instrument is "pure" debt or "pure" equity or some combination of the two, understanding the essence of the contractual relationship with the financier is central. Insofar as governance is concerned, understanding the difference between fixed payments and residual payments becomes central. The starting point for a stakeholder analysis is provided by "pure" debt representing the "unqualified obligation to pay" and "pure" equity the "unlimited claim to the residual benefits of ownership" (Pratt 2000, 1067).

With providers of debt capital, HP enters into a formal contract that stipulates the material conditions of the debt: amount, interest, payback schedule, collateral, and the like. Lenders will seek contractual safeguards, collateral being the obvious example. Furthermore, there is also a well-developed aftermarket for debt instruments, which means that the lender can transfer its contract with HP to another lender. Consequently, because the relationship with lenders can be safeguarded through a formal contract, it is difficult to see why lenders should be considered stakeholders in any but the most extreme of circumstances. Lenders should be considered stakeholders only if they genuinely make bets and wagers on organizational outcomes—this is seldom the case.

Just like in the case of suppliers, customers, and employees, we can analyze this further by asking the question, "How would the lender be affected if HP ceased to exist?" Here, it is relevant to note that lenders receive preferential treatment over shareholders in bankruptcy proceedings. Specifically, if HP were to declare bankruptcy, its debt obligations would not disappear, they would only be transferred to the bankruptcy estate. Bankruptcy, therefore, does not mean that the lender faces an immediate loss. There are well-developed safeguards in place.[7]

Stakeholder analysis of financiers leads to a very different result when providers of equity capital are considered. In short, shareholders are promised nothing and can, at least in principle, lose everything. If HP were to declare bankruptcy, HP's shares would in all likelihood be worth nothing, which means no obligations to shareholders would be transferred to the bankruptcy estate. Even in the case something was transferred, shareholders would remain residual claimants, the last in line to receive benefits from the estate. Bankruptcy proceedings seldom result in there being a residual because corporations tend not to declare bankruptcy when their net worth is significantly positive.

The wagers that shareholders make on organizational outcomes are so salient that it is straightforward to see why shareholders should, as a general rule, be considered stakeholders. Furthermore, in comparison with suppliers, customers, employees, and lenders, shareholders are the comparatively disadvantaged contracting party in that they are recipients of only

---

[7] One of the authors of this book was an investor in a consumer-products firm that declared bankruptcy. In the bankruptcy, shareholders lost everything when the shares lost all their value; suppliers lost as some of their invoices were left unpaid; employees lost as they did not receive all their paychecks and the firm failed to make even the mandatory pension payments on the employer side; customers lost as they did not receive products for which they had already paid. In stark contrast, not a single bank incurred an economic loss. With the requisite safeguards in place, banks had fully avoided exposure to residual risk. Of course, we do not wish to suggest banks never lose money in bankruptcies; the point is that they not only have access to safeguards others do not (e.g., collateral), but they are also more informed and skilled in implementing these safeguards.

residual payments. At the same time, the problem resides in the failure to see the other, less conspicuous wagers that other constituencies make. Designers should be compelled to examine stakeholder issues in their entirety, which means analyzing all wagers made, not just the immediately observable and salient ones. Once all wagers have been identified, the designer should think of how to safeguard them through the appropriate governance responses.

Governance Responses to Stakeholder Interests

Identifying the organization's stakeholders is merely the first step. The second, more challenging step, is to work out the governance implications: How should stakeholder interests and stakeholder prioritization be incorporated into governance? What kinds of safeguards are needed to secure the most critical relationships that exhibit residual risk?

The enduring problem with stakeholder conversations is that they tend not to have actionable implications for governance decisions. For example, suppose the designer concludes that a group of employees should be considered stakeholders. What are the governance implications? Should these employees be awarded a formal role in oversight, such as representation on the board of directors? Furthermore, does broader board participation offer a remediable solution to an efficiency problem, that is, will net gains be realized for the organization? The designer must understand that governance is not a system that can be "tweaked" one factor at a time; instead, individual decisions tend to have various indirect, systemic effects.

In this section, we discuss the governance implications of stakeholder analysis. In the discussion, we focus on the third question that circumscribes the essence of governance (see chapter 2): What are the reciprocal credible commitments that secure the continuing cooperation of the organization's constituencies in general and its stakeholders in particular?

The premise in structuring exchange relationships is that the contracting parties seek a solution that *aligns* with the central characteristics of the specific relationship. In seeking alignment, the designer must be able to *discriminate*, that is, to understand the efficiency implications of the feasible alternatives in the given context. In economic terms, the designer must seek *discriminating alignment* in governance decisions (Williamson 1991, 277).

We propose incorporating commitments to specificity and vulnerability as the central characteristics of the organization's relationship with a given constituency. Those who have by virtue of joining the organization become vulnerable have made a credible commitment toward the organization; the organization must reciprocate by properly safeguarding the relationship. The resultant mutual credible commitments secure the cooperation of the constituency.

For contracting to be efficient, the relationship must have the requisite safeguards to secure the cooperation of the contracting parties. In the following, we discuss the different ways of safeguarding employment relationships, buyer-supplier relationships, and relationships with financiers.

Safeguarding Employment Relationships

Because employment relationships are heterogeneous, they also vary greatly in the degree of safeguarding required. This variation can be linked directly to levels of specificity and contract duration.

Think of your first summer job, whether it was mowing lawns, selling ice cream, or delivering newspapers. The essence of your employment relationship was little more than you offering your free time in exchange for monetary compensation in an intentionally transient relationship. Such a simple contracting setup allows the contracting parties to draft an essentially complete employment contract; it is hard to see justification for burdening the relationship with additional safeguards. The only relevant governance choice is whether a low- or a high-powered incentive is preferred. If you mowed lawns, the chances are the employer (or your customers) paid you based on the number of lawns you mowed (a high-powered incentive). In ice cream sales, an hourly rate (a low-powered incentive) is probably more appropriate. If compensation was based on the number of customers served, the worker might mysteriously call in sick on cold and rainy days, only to miraculously recover when the weather got warm and sunny again. Linking employee compensation to arbitrary factors such as the weather tends to be inefficient.

At the other end of the spectrum are employment relationships where employees commit to specificity by developing and nurturing skills that create strong bilateral dependency between the employee and the organization. Organization-specific skills have low redeployability, and therefore, committing to them must be considered a form of risk—they are bets on organizational outcomes. One way for the designer to think about discriminating alignment is to acknowledge that employees committing to human capital specificity have a legitimate residual interest. Accordingly, one option is to award employees a formal residual claimant status.

In limited liability companies, employee stock ownership plans are one alternative of awarding employees a residual-claimant status; opening the board of directors to the group of employees who represent organization-specific skills is another. The latter would effectively make some employees not merely residual claimants but also trustees of the organization. Employees would participate in the ratification of management decisions and would exercise oversight over their implementation. In the governance literature, employee participation in oversight is sometimes discussed under the rubric of *codetermination*. Countries such as Germany have mandated codetermination for companies that have more than five hundred employees. The most salient manifestation of codetermination is employee participation on the board of directors.

Codetermination in Germany (and a number of other countries) is legally mandated, but there is no reason why the designer could not incorporate codetermination as a private-ordering response as well if it offered an efficient governance alternative. Williamson (1985, 303) pointed to the informational advantages of employee representation on boards: "[Employee] membership on boards of directors can be especially important during periods of actual or alleged adversity, especially when firms are asking workers for give-backs. Labor's board membership might mitigate worker's skepticism by promoting the exchange of credible information." In this sense, employee participation can function as an instrument for securing the credibility of management decisions in the eyes of employees. This credibility is essential in situations where employees commit to specificity.

Opening up the board of directors for broader participation is a "heavy-duty" measure that will likely have undesirable systemic effects. However, there are also targeted options available to the designer. These more targeted measures can be implemented at the level of both the individual employment contract and a collection of similar contracts. In some European countries, for example, contracting with employees is subject to externally mandated industry-wide standards embedded in various collective-action agreements. The private-ordering counterpart to externally mandated obligations is *multiunit bargaining* where a representative of employees (typically a union) negotiates with a specific employer on behalf of an entire group of employees whose contractual relationships with the organization are appreciably similar.

For example, the general agreement between the United Automobile, Aerospace and Agricultural Implement Workers (UAW) and General Motors (GM) is a seven hundred-page document that contains scores of rules and principles that protect unionized GM employees. The agreement stipulates, among other things, that the employer is not allowed to locate outside suppliers at a plant if it "conflicts with UAW assigned operations that could cause a loss of jobs" (UAW-GM 2015, 655). Similarly, the employer's discretion regarding sale of assets belonging to the bargaining units (e.g., a specific plant) is severely restricted.[8]

Negotiations between employers and employees frequently involve deep-seated and adversarial power dynamics. However, in our attempt at understanding efficient organization, we direct the designer's attention here squarely to the cooperative aspects of employer-union relationships and private-ordering approaches to codetermination. We choose to view these relationships less as hardball advocacy and more as genuine attempts at safeguarding contractual relationships under conditions of bilateral dependency. We are not surprised that the need for multiunit bargaining arises in oligopolistic industries in particular (Davidson 1988): When an industry is dominated by a small number of employers, the chances are their key activities involve various kinds of specificity, including human capital specificity. The automobile industry and commercial airlines are representative examples.

Safeguarding Buyer-Supplier Relationships

A similar specificity examination can be applied to relationships with suppliers and customers. Even though the nature of specificity in buyer-supplier relationships is more likely to involve physical asset specificity and dedicated assets instead of human capital specificity, the designer's task remains essentially unchanged: Contractual relationships that involve specificity merit the designer's attention because they may require additional safeguarding.

---

[8] "[T]he Company will not close, idle, nor partially or wholly sell, spin-off, split-off, consolidate or otherwise dispose of in any form, any plant, asset, or business unit of any type, beyond those which have already been identified, constituting a bargaining unit under the Agreement" (UAW-GM 2015, 356).

Arm's-length buyer-supplier relationships that involve neither specificity nor residual risk require no additional safeguards; when switching costs are low, the availability of alternative sources of supply provides the requisite protection. Symmetrically, suppliers having alternate sources of demand for their products and services safeguards the supplier side. All additional safeguards would be redundant and, therefore, a form of waste. For this reason, neither the taxi driver nor the passenger needs to safeguard the contractual relationship; there is little at stake and a negative experience can be addressed by blacklisting the specific exchange partner.

Specificity changes everything. The case of shoemaking (see chapter 3) provides an excellent example of contracting parties seeking discriminating alignment under conditions of specificity (Masten and Snyder 1993). The long-term lease arrangement between the shoemaker and the equipment manufacturer safeguarded the high levels of physical asset specificity. Specifically, the shoemaker agreeing to a long-term lease and committing to using the shoemaking machines ensured that the equipment manufacturer's massive investments in R&D would not be wasted. The shoemaker would in turn benefit from the equipment manufacturer's continuing commitment to further developing the machinery. Another benefit was that the equipment manufacturer would be incentivized to perform adequate maintenance on the equipment, because the manufacturer only leased the equipment to the shoemaker. If the shoemaker had bought the machines, the equipment manufacturer might still have performed maintenance but would have lower incentive intensity since it would have given up title to the machines.

Some relationships are so hazardous that the exchange is most efficiently organized as an intraorganizational relationship. As an example, consider the oil refining value chain (Klein, Crawford, and Alchian 1978). Suppose an oil company owns and operates the oil fields and the refineries, both of which are subject to considerable site specificity and physical asset specificity. Suppose further that an oil pipeline is the only way of transporting the oil from the fields to the refineries. The oil company operating the oil fields and the refineries might be well advised to integrate vertically into pipelines as well; contracting with an external firm for pipeline service would expose the oil company's highly specific assets to an economic "holdup problem" (Goldberg 1976) by the pipeline service company. Owning and operating not only the oil fields and the refineries but also the pipelines would effectively eliminate the holdup problem. Vertical integration is the ultimate "heavy-duty" governance mechanism for safeguarding complex transactions that involve high degrees of specificity.

Unlike in the case of securing the cooperation of employees who exhibit high human capital specificity, board membership is seldom considered in the case of buyer-supplier relationships. As the United Shoe example shows, even significant commitments to specificity can be addressed through carefully tailored and specialized buyer-supplier contracts. It is hard to think of a situation in which a buyer-supplier relationship should be safeguarded by awarding the buyer an oversight role in the seller's organization, or vice versa. Williamson (1985, 308) elaborates: "Considering the variety of widely applicable governance devices to which firms and their suppliers have access, there is no general basis to accord suppliers additional protection through membership on the board of directors [. . .] [T]he governance structure that firm and supplier devise at the time of contract [. . .] will afford adequate protection." Williamson's point applies equally if we replace the word *supplier* with the word *customer*.

Safeguarding Relationships with Financiers

In contrast with contractual relationships with employees, buyers, and suppliers, it is awkward to think of contractual relationships with financiers in terms of specificity. Neither lenders nor providers of equity commit to specificity when they finance an organization. However, they do expose themselves to varying degrees of financial risk. Therefore, instead of analyzing the contractual relationships with financiers through the lens of specificity, let us turn to the general notion of vulnerability and look at whether the financier receives fixed or residual payments. Those who receive fixed payments require fewer safeguards than those entitled only to residual payments; in fact, the contractual guarantee of a fixed payment *is* a safeguard in and of itself.

The organization's lenders have a comparatively complete contract with the organization. The loan agreement guarantees the creditors fixed payments of interest and capital. The lender may also require the borrower to offer collateral, such as general-purpose equipment or the organization members' personal property, to guarantee the loan. In case the organization defaults on the fixed payments, lenders have powerful tools at their disposal to recover their investments: They can take the borrower to court, make claims for the collateral, or, if everything else fails, take the borrower to bankruptcy. Even in the event of a bankruptcy, the organization's debt obligations will not disappear, they will instead be transferred to the bankruptcy estate. In summary, debt financing can usually be sufficiently safeguarded through a formal contract that guarantees fixed payments.

Providers of equity face a completely different set of circumstances. Unlike lenders, shareholders receive only residual payments from the organization. Because the existence of a residual is a performance outcome subject to uncertainty, it is essentially noncontractible: The organization simply cannot contractually commit to a certain return on investment to the shareholders. Furthermore, if the organization is taken to bankruptcy, only residual claimancy (no contractual obligations) will be transferred to the bankruptcy estate.

The relationship between the organization and providers of equity must be safeguarded. Absent sufficient safeguards, who would ever contribute to the equity of the organization? A common way of safeguarding the rights of the residual claimant is through participation on the board of directors. In contrast, there are no compelling reasons why providers of debt financing should be awarded board seats.

The Paradox of Stakeholder Participation

Both the specific topic of shareholder participation and the more general notion of stakeholder participation on the board of directors have received considerable attention in governance practice and research. Some scholars and practitioners maintain that the board should be an instrument of the shareholders, whereas others suggest it should be opened for broader stakeholder participation.

In a stark departure from both views, we propose that it is fundamentally misguided to think of board membership in terms of participation. In fact, we submit that the very notion of participation on boards is paradoxical. Unpacking the paradox requires that we make the distinction between stakeholder interests and stakeholder representation.

What does the suggestion that the organization's most important stakeholders should be *represented* on its board of directors ultimately mean? Does it mean that the largest shareholder gets to appoint their agent to the board of directors to secure the specific shareholder's interests? Similarly, should companies whose employees commit to high levels of human capital specificity let the employees appoint their agent to the board to ensure employee interests are incorporated to board-level decisions?

We are constantly amazed at how casually those engaging in stakeholder conversations and debates gloss over the fact that the only constituency the board member represents is the organization. This is not only a governance principle but it is also *the law*: The only beneficiary of the board member's fiduciary duty of loyalty and care is the organization, not the constituency that appointed the member.

It is hazardous to confound stakeholder interests with stakeholder participation. Appointing a representative of debt financing to the board provides a cautionary example. Are we surprised to find that when bankers are appointed to the board of directors, the firm starts leaning more heavily toward debt financing? Governance scholars David Larcker and Brian Tayan (2015, chap. 5) accurately noted that exhibiting such bias constitutes a violation of fiduciary duty; what is worse, such violations are very difficult to detect. Larcker and Tayan further noted that research results unfortunately suggest that when bankers serve on boards, they indeed tend to behave in ways that privilege the interests of their employers over those of the organization. This constitutes a breach of fiduciary duty.

The paradox of stakeholder participation on boards is effectively crystallized by the question, "Assuming board members represent their respective constituencies instead of the organization as a whole, how could they arrive at decisions that are in the best interest of the organization?" How does a car manufacturer's board of directors make a decision regarding plant closure if its board of directors consists of representatives of management, shareholders, banks, and employees, each advocating the interests of their respective constituencies? What, if any, is the common interest that all these stakeholders share?

Might an independent board of directors whose task is to incorporate stakeholder interests *without directly representing any of them* offer the comparatively efficient option? Posing this question effectively introduces the notion of director independence.

Independent Thinking in Oversight

Suppose a stakeholder group has two options. One is that it gets to appoint a representative who is directly incentivized to promote the interests of the specific stakeholder; the appointed board member would therefore effectively become the stakeholder's agent on the board. The other option is that the board consists of independent individuals whose fiduciary duty of loyalty and care is to consider what is best for the organization. In this second scenario, the board member would become a trustee of the organization.

Should the stakeholder prefer a tailored agent or a general trustee? This choice situation makes the distinction between the board consisting of stakeholder representatives and the board serving stakeholder interests salient.

Let us consider the question by examining shareholders. In many large corporations, board member compensation is significantly equity-based. In fact, this is not only common practice, but it is also a principle that the New York Stock Exchange Governance Guide endorses: "Currently, it is common to have equity represent a slight majority of regular annual compensation—such as a pay mix of equity compensation 55 percent and cash compensation 45 percent [. . .] The emphasis on equity compensation is also directionally consistent with the typical pay mix for senior executives."[9]

At first glance, equity-based director pay seems reasonable, as it aligns the interests of oversight and management toward increasing the value of shareholders' equity. In reality, this alignment may actually have just the opposite effect. Specifically, if both managers and directors are incentivized through equity, directors may be less inclined to exercise oversight over management. Counterintuitively enough, a more efficient way of incorporating shareholder interests into oversight is to make the board independent of shareholder interests; in short, populate the board with trustees of the organization, not agents of the shareholders. Finance scholars Harley Ryan and Roy Wiggins (2004, 500) elaborate: "[I]ndependence enhances shareholder welfare since board independence results in compensation contracts that provide directors with stronger incentives to monitor." In other words, independent directors are more efficient in monitoring top management precisely because their interests do not align with the interests of those whose actions they are expected to monitor. This observation reveals something essential about the value of independent judgment: All stakeholders should take seriously the possibility that the key to efficient oversight may be found in independence, not in representative participation.

Union representation on boards offers another example of the paradox of stakeholder participation. Suppose the workers' union appoints a union

---

[9] New York Stock Exchange Corporate Governance Guide chap. 21, p. 156.

representative to the car manufacturer's board of directors. Suppose then that the board must consider the choice of closing down a large assembly plant located in a small town. In formulating his or her position on the issue, will the union representative think of what is best for the organization or what is best for the workers? The law requires the former, but the union representative's own constituency would favor the latter. The resultant divided loyalty is so profoundly problematic that few organizations open the board of directors to employee participation. Instead, the relationships with high-specificity employees are addressed as a combination of targeted individual-level contracting and multiunit bargaining.

To be truly independent in judgment, a board member must be free of all other loyalties. Consequently, the bar is set at a very high level: Independent directors should be independent of not only the organization on whose board they serve but also those who appoint them. Only absolute independence secures independent judgment.

If absolute independence sounds idealistic, let us examine two examples. Consider first the organization of the judiciary. Even though members of the Supreme Court of the United States are appointed by the President, the Supreme Court does not represent the President's interests in any capacity. Article III, Section 1 of the Constitution of the United States declares that the Supreme Court wields the judicial power *of the United States*, and therefore serves the interests of the people. As a telltale sign of what we think comes fairly close to absolute independence in the governance sense, we witness time and again how Supreme Court Justices vote in a way that is completely at odds with the preferences of the President who appointed them.[10]

As another example, consider Neste, a Finnish oil company organized as a limited liability company with an annual revenue of €12 billion. Three aspects of Neste's board of directors merit attention here (Neste 2020): (1) all eight board members are independent of both the company and its largest shareholders; (2) only two of the eight board members have a nontrivial equity stake in the company (four board members own no shares at all); and (3) board compensation is limited to modest annual retainers that range

---

[10] In January 2022, the Supreme Court rejected former President Donald Trump's request to block the release of White House records to the select committee of the House of Representatives investigating the events of January 6, 2021. None of the three conservative Justices appointed by President Trump sided with Trump's request.

from €35,700 for regular board members to €67,900 for the chairperson; there is no equity-based pay.[11]

In the case of the Supreme Court, the idea that integrity must prevail over loyalty to any individual constituency is clear. But the fact that a for-profit oil company would appoint a completely independent board suggests that even in the for-profit setting, the idea of an exclusively fiduciary (as opposed to stakeholder or shareholder) duty is not an unreasonable proposition. We might therefore ask, "When does integrity *not* merit the designer's attention?" Applying this principle to board composition, it does not seem at all utopian to us that individual board members should never represent individual stakeholder interests but, rather, should have a fiduciary duty to the entire organization.

Summary: Returning to the Main Problem

Stakeholder conversations are simultaneously frustrating and indispensable. They are frustrating because they often regress to uncompromising advocacy of individual stakeholder interests. We share both Orts and Strudler's (2002, 218) criticism that stakeholder conversations tend to be "so broad as to be meaningless and so complex as to be useless" and Bebchuk and Tallarita's (2020, 91) concern that stakeholder governance may offer merely an "illusory promise." At the same time, stakeholder conversations are indispensable because designers must address the only partially overlapping and at times inconsistent interests of those who create value for the organization. We find overly optimistic pronouncements of compatible stakeholder interests intellectually dishonest, misleading, and potential sources of significant organizational waste. We must not let stakeholder governance regress to wishful thinking, appeasement, and mere rhetoric.

The problem, as we see it, is that many stakeholder conversations tend "to put the cart before the horse" and seek answers without being explicit about the questions. Why do organizations need stakeholder governance? If they do need it, should it be considered a matter of private ordering? If yes, why? If it is a matter of private ordering, how should it be implemented?

---

[11] In April 2022, Brand Finance (one of the leading independent brand valuation firms) ranked Neste as the second most valuable brand in Finland with a brand value of €2.2 billion, a 20 percent increase from 2021.

In their impressive and detailed review of the research literature on stakeholder management, Parmar and colleagues (2010) presented three different problem formulations for stakeholder management: (1) the problem of value creation and trade; (2) the problem of the ethics of capitalism; and (3) the problem of the managerial mindset. Even though all three are worth our attention and even though the three are interconnected, we find it infeasible to address all three in one tractable approach. Simultaneously trying to incorporate the managerial mindset, value creation, and the ethics of capitalism into the same conversation is bound to lead to confusion.

In this chapter, we have implicitly adopted the objective of value creation by asking, "How does the organization secure the voluntary cooperation of those constituencies who, by virtue of becoming contributors to the organization, are asked to become economically vulnerable?" Furthermore, we propose that it is useful to link vulnerability to voluntary, informed commitments to specificity.

We hope this chapter enables the designer to move toward rigorous, explicit, and transparent stakeholder analysis. Among other things, our approach can serve as a guide to prioritization: Which employment contracts require more of the designer's attention than others? Which supplier and customer relationships are more vulnerable than others? How are the relationships with the organization's financiers different from one another, and why does it matter? Our approach offers actionable tools for the analysis of specific constituency groups. Within each group, the designer is likely to identify contractual relationships that should be treated as stakeholder relationships in governance decisions. Awarding stakeholder status to a constituency that has nothing at stake is economically wasteful and distracts attention from the relationships that merit the designer's attention.

That some suppliers are more important than others is salient. How about comparisons across stakeholder groups? Are shareholders a more important constituency than suppliers? Frankly, we find such intergroup comparisons illogical, which is why we have not discussed them in this chapter. As we have shown, each constituency group exhibits within-group heterogeneity that is often sufficiently significant to have governance implications. Some employees are stakeholders, others are not; the same applies to suppliers, customers, and financiers. The only group where all members can justifiably be argued to be stakeholders are the providers of equity financing, because they are all, individually and collectively, vulnerable due to their status as residual claimants. It does not, however, follow that because all shareholders are stakeholders, their interests supersede the interests of those stakeholder groups where less than 100 percent of constituents are stakeholders.

Comparing shareholder interests to the interests of other stakeholder groups in the aggregate is ultimately a case of the *composition fallacy*. A composition fallacy occurs when one mistakenly attributes to a whole a characteristic that applies only to some of its individual members, and then draws conclusions from or acts based on this misattribution.

Designers who are unable to incorporate nuance into governance decisions may fall prey to the composition fallacy. A one-size-fits-all approach to stakeholder governance will result in excessive safeguards in some relationships and insufficient safeguards in others. Designers must understand that high-specificity employees require a different contracting approach than low-specificity employees, that fixed payments and residual payments cannot be handled by the same governance structures, and that although some suppliers should be considered stakeholders, the vast majority probably should not.

The approach proposed in this chapter hopefully offers a remedy to the composition fallacy. Instead of adopting a one-size-fits-all approach, designers should analyze each contractual relationship by identifying its critical characteristics (giving special attention to contractual hazards and vulnerabilities) and then seek discriminating alignment by devising tailored safeguards to secure the cooperation of the contracting party throughout the duration of the contract.

5

Nonprofit and Public Organizations

Nothing in the preceding chapters, or the subsequent ones, suggests that efficiency is an exclusive concern of organizations that seek profits. To make this argument clear, we devote an entire chapter to discussing efficiency in nonprofit and public organizations. We start this chapter by making two important distinctions: (1) for-profit versus nonprofit, and (2) public versus private. These distinctions are not as straightforward as one might think, and a closer look at how governance structures are designed is required. We then discuss the nonprofit theater as an example of governance in a nonprofit organization. Finally, the context of public organizations (or public-private partnerships) offers an opportunity to examine some of the crucial assumptions and boundary conditions of efficiency analysis. For example, the idea of net gains requires a number of assumptions that are not met in some public organizations. This insight links to the idea that the outcomes of governance decisions may not be commensurate, and consequently, an analysis of net gains is impossible. In such contexts, the idea of *governance as efficiency* may have to yield to *governance as integrity* (Williamson 1999, 340). Later in the chapter, we discuss the efficiency/integrity distinction in light of examples from contexts where efficiency analysis is infeasible or, at least, of secondary importance.

The Key Distinctions

Figure 5.1 shows a two-by-two matrix with four example organizations: (1) Finnair, the majority-state-owned Finnish commercial airline; (2) the University of Illinois, a public US university; (3) Caterpillar Inc., a private corporation incorporated in the state of Delaware; and (4) Real Madrid Club de Fútbol, a sports club in Madrid, Spain. We use these four examples as illustrations as we make distinctions between for-profit versus nonprofit and public versus private organizations.

Efficient Organization. Mikko Ketokivi and Joseph T. Mahoney, Oxford University Press. © Oxford University Press 2023.
DOI: 10.1093/oso/9780197610282.003.0005

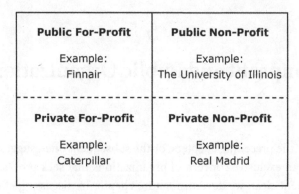

Public For-Profit	Public Non-Profit
Example: Finnair	Example: The University of Illinois
Private For-Profit	**Private Non-Profit**
Example: Caterpillar	Example: Real Madrid

Figure 5.1 Examples of for-profit, nonprofit, public, and private organizations

For-Profit vs. Nonprofit

Both for-profits and nonprofits often seek a surplus, only their motivations differ. The for-profit seeks a surplus to provide sufficient investment returns to the residual claimants to secure their continuing cooperation; the non-profit seeks "to provide a reasonable cushion or reserve against a rainy day or provide for future growth plans of the organization" (Gross, McCarthy, and Shelmon 2005, 15). In fact, even some of the motives for seeking profits are similar, as both for-profits and nonprofits may be interested in a surplus to provide for future growth.

As illustrations of nonprofit organizations, we intentionally selected two that show both a substantial economic surplus in their income statements and a significant net worth on their balance sheets: the University of Illinois (net worth of $4 billion), and Real Madrid Club de Fútbol (net worth of €533 million). In fact, nonprofits that produce a surplus and have net worth are easier to find than those that do not, which is consistent with legal and economic scholar Henry Hansmann's (1980, 838) observation that "[m]any nonprofits in fact consistently show an annual accounting surplus." What is central for governance purposes is how the surplus is governed.

Let us first examine the annual revenues and expenses of the University of Illinois, a public nonprofit organization. Revenues consist of student tuitions and fees, grants and contracts, state appropriations, investment in-come, and private gifts, among other sources. Expenses consist of payments to employees, employee benefits, payments to suppliers, scholarships, and fellowships, among others. In the fiscal year 2020, the University of Illinois' revenues exceeded expenses by $237 million, increasing the university's *net position* to about $4 billion. It is useful to think of the net position in balance-sheet terms as analogous to shareholders' equity. The University of Illinois's net position is held in the form of capital assets: treasury bonds and bills, asset-backed securities, equity funds, and money market funds. In sum, the University of Illinois is a public, nonprofit organization that has revenue, produces an economic surplus, and has net worth.

A private nonprofit organization is similar in many respects. Real Madrid Club de Fútbol is one of the largest sports organizations in the world. In 2019, it produced an after-tax surplus of €38 million from a revenue of €757 million. This annual surplus is added to the organization's net worth (or equity). In 2019, Real Madrid's net worth was €533 million. Because Real Madrid is a cooperative owned by its 91,000 members, or *socios*, this equity belongs to the organization—the *socios* are not residual claimants.

Despite seeking and producing an economic surplus and having net worth, both the University of Illinois and Real Madrid are nonprofit organizations: Their net worth belongs to the organization and cannot be appropriated by private actors. Indeed, one of the central tasks of oversight in a nonprofit organization is to prevent such appropriation.

Rules that regulate the governance of net worth have both public- and private-ordering properties. In the spirit of this book, our focus is on the latter, but since understanding the governance of net worth in its entirety is important, both merit attention. In the case of the University of Illinois, the $4 billion net position consists of three main categories of net assets: restricted nonexpendable, restricted expendable, and unrestricted (and expendable) net assets (see Gross et al. 2005). Expendable assets can be used for their intended purposes whereas nonexpendable assets must be held in perpetuity. Furthermore, restricted assets are subject to externally mandated restrictions. These constraints imply that only unrestricted assets effectively belong to the category of private ordering in the sense that they may be allocated to specific purposes at the discretion of management (by observing the rules set by oversight).

At the University of Illinois, both university management and oversight are responsible for "the university's reputation and strong financial position" (University of Illinois 2020, 12). No private appropriations can be made from the university's assets. Importantly, this restriction does not arise from the university being a public but a nonprofit organization, "barred from distributing its net earnings, if any, to individuals who exercise control over it, such as members, officers, directors, or trustees" (Hansmann 1980, 838).

The situation is appreciably similar for Real Madrid. Because the *socios* are not residual claimants, their only prerogative is that they are entitled to "enjoy the club's activities" (Real Madrid 2019, 10). Real Madrid is governed by the General Assembly, the President, and the Board of Directors, who collectively decide whether Real Madrid's annual surplus is entered into retained earnings, spent on the renovation of the Santiago Bernabéu stadium, used to finance Real Madrid youth teams, or some other uses. Real Madrid's €533 million net worth cannot be appropriated privately.

In sum, the essential governance aspect of the nonprofit organization stems from the fact that the organization has no residual claimants other than the organization itself. Consequently, the nonprofit's surplus must be properly governed and managed by the organization to prevent both inappropriate allocations and expropriations. Moreover, in the case where the nonprofit organization is awarded preferential tax treatment, efficient oversight of the nonprofit is no longer merely a matter of private ordering; it also becomes a matter of regulatory compliance.

For-profit and Nonprofit as Design Choices

The nonprofit form of organizing is more common in some contexts than others; education, healthcare, and publishing are examples of contexts where nonprofits are prevalent. However, we frame the question whether to organize as a for-profit or nonprofit ultimately as the designer's choice. Will the designer want to impose a distribution constraint on the surplus or not? This design choice is effectively illustrated by nonprofit entrepreneurs.

Why would a self-interested entrepreneur choose the nonprofit form of organizing? To be sure, the nonprofit form weakens the entrepreneur's profit-seeking incentive. However, economists Edward Glaeser and Andrei Shleifer (2001) suggested that deliberately lowering the entrepreneur's incentive intensity *is the whole point*. Specifically, by choosing the nonprofit form of organizing, the entrepreneur sends a strong signal to the organization's constituencies that the entrepreneur is not interested in profiting—indeed, cannot profit—from their contributions. Signaling a self-imposed low-powered incentive confers several benefits: "When customers, employees, or donors feel protected by the nonprofit status of the firm, the entrepreneur has a competitive advantage in the marketplace" (Glaeser and Shleifer 2001, 100).

Incorporating as a nonprofit can be directly linked to stakeholder governance (chapter 4). By lowering incentive intensity, the entrepreneur, as a designer, works toward securing the cooperation of the organization's stakeholders. When entrepreneurs self-impose a low incentive intensity, stakeholders may see their own commitments to specificity as less hazardous, because the economic holdup hazard is significantly reduced: "Employees may invest more in specific human capital at not-for-profit firms because these firms have less financial incentive to cut wages or perquisites *ex post*" (Glaeser and Shleifer 2001, 101).

Similarly, information asymmetry concerns are alleviated. Those who have comparatively limited access to information (e.g., employees or suppliers) need not be concerned about those with better access (e.g., managers and owners) exploiting the asymmetry.

In sum, commitment to weak incentives as a deliberate design choice may foster efficient governance (Williamson 1999). Low incentive intensity becomes a potential problem only if it emerges inadvertently or as an undesirable side effect of a governance decision in a situation in which high-powered incentives would be comparatively efficient. If this is the case, then the beneficial, intended consequences of the governance decision must be considered simultaneously with the inefficiency consequences of the undesirable loss of incentive intensity (see chapter 8 for a detailed discussion).

How does the self-interested entrepreneur benefit from low incentive intensity? If the nonprofit status of the organization indeed signals credibility, the organization increases its likelihood of attracting talented and committed employees, a broad customer base, and donors as financiers. The organization's customers may even be willing to pay more for the products and services of a nonprofit than a for-profit because they know that the surplus will not be appropriated by a profit-seeking entrepreneur. Furthermore, if the entrepreneur is also an employee of the organization, the organization can pay the entrepreneur a salary with reasonable perquisites.

Given the considerable failure rate of entrepreneurial firms (up to 90 percent by some estimates), organizing the entrepreneurial firm as a nonprofit may provide the self-interested entrepreneur with comparatively low-risk access to a steady income. In addition, the entrepreneur not only achieves this steady income in a reasonably comfortable and meaningful environment but may also gain the genuine respect and admiration of the organization's stakeholders.

The nonprofit entrepreneurial venture is, of course, subject to the familiar drawbacks of low incentive intensity. Indeed, the price is paid precisely in terms of the consequences of low incentive intensity: "[N]onprofit firms might be expected to be slower in meeting increased demand and to be less efficient in their use of inputs than for-profit firms" (Hansmann 1980, 844). However, organization scholars Akhil Bhardwaj and Anastasia Sergeeva (2022) challenge this line of reasoning by suggesting that a nonprofit cooperative does not necessarily forgo high-powered incentives, because residual claimancy is not the only means of achieving high-powered incentives. As always, it is the task of the designer to engage in an analysis of which feasible governance alternative is comparatively efficient.

How about Tax Minimization as the Main Problem?

Is the decision to incorporate as a nonprofit not driven primarily by the preferential tax treatment of nonprofits? This question merits a closer look.

In the United States, the nonprofit is exempt from federal income taxes, which provides "a particularly strong subsidy to the non-profit form" (Hansmann 1987, 79). As with all governance decisions, the situation must be considered in its entirety. To be sure, understanding tax implications is important, however, proposing tax considerations as the default explanation for the choice of the nonprofit organizational form is an oversimplification (see also Glaeser and Shleifer 2001). In fact, we suggest that from the governance point of view, choosing not to have a residual claimant because of tax benefits is misguided. What if there *are* constituencies with a legitimate residual interest, which should be incorporated into governance? Will the designer simply "trade in" their residual claimancy for the tax-exempt status? Are those asked to waive their residual claimancy still expected to bear residual risk? Will they accept their *de facto* transformation from a residual claimant to a donor?

It is of course possible that the designer chooses the nonprofit form with the intent of abusing it by providing private residual payments through expropriation. Designers who think such abuse of the non-profit form will pay off need to consider the potentially significant *ex post* transaction costs arising from the fact that when an organization is tax exempt, "the Internal Revenue Service may well take an interest in whether there is any distribution of profits" (Hansmann 1980, 874). How does the magnitude of the *ex post* transaction costs of having to conceal expropriation (and the consequences of potentially failing to do so) compare with the magnitude of the tax-exemption benefits? We propose that behaving opportunistically in choosing the organizational form is ultimately myopic.

Same Competitive Context, Different Choices

The world of competitive team sports offers a telling example of the notion that organizational form is not fully determined by the organization's environment but is indeed a matter of design choice. In contrast with the two Spanish football clubs Real Madrid and FC Barcelona, both organized as nonprofit cooperatives, many other European football clubs are incorporated as limited liability companies. The English football club Manchester United F.C. was founded as a *closed* (or *close*) limited liability company that went public (i.e., became *open*) in 2012. Manchester United Plc's stock is currently traded on the New York Stock Exchange, and in 2020, paid its shareholders $30 million in dividends. The French football club Paris Saint-Germain F.C. is organized as a closed limited liability company, fully owned by Qatar Sports Investments.[1]

Organizational form notwithstanding, the similarities between Real Madrid (a nonprofit) and Manchester United (a for-profit) are striking. Both (1) have income statements and balance sheets that are, for all practical purposes, identical in their structure; (2) have the same three sources of revenue (commercial, broadcasting, match day); (3) rely heavily on debt financing; (4) have a board of directors and a management team; (5) pay high salaries to their executives; (6) seek to maintain a healthy positive cash flow so as to generate an economic surplus; (7) attract the top football talent by offering them generous salaries, and (8) have the identical objective of winning championships, which includes beating one another in the European Champions League.

What, then, should we make of the fact that one is organized as a for-profit corporation and the other a nonprofit cooperative? As far as the two organizations are concerned, the material difference is that in one of these organizations, the owners are residual claimants who are entitled to a return on their investment; in the other, the owners are merely entitled "to enjoy" the organization's activities. This difference merits attention, but considering it simultaneously with all the similarities, it really does not seem like these two

---

[1] Discussing the key differences between Manchester United and Paris Saint-Germain effectively shows the value of using the words *open* and *closed* instead of *private* and *public*. Even though Manchester United's shares are publicly traded, it remains essentially a private firm because its owners are predominantly private investment companies and private individuals. Using the word *open* prevents confusion. Similarly, the essential characteristic of Paris Saint-Germain is that its shares are not publicly traded even though the organization itself is best described as public: PSG's owner Qatar Sports Investments is part of Qatar Investment Authority, a sovereign wealth fund. Using the word *closed* prevents confusion.

organizations are all that different. This brings us to the important conclusion that we should be cautious in drawing inferences about an organization simply based on the legal form it has adopted. The choice of the organizational form is an important design decision, but it is equally important to acknowledge the importance of governance microstructure. This consideration is important in the for-profit/nonprofit distinction but becomes even more crucial as we make the distinction between private and public organizations. In the public/private distinction, labels can be misleading, because whereas the designer can often choose between the for-profit and the nonprofit forms, the design choice is almost never between the public and the private forms. Instead, the governance decision is more fine-grained, because the key question is, "What are the roles of public and private actors in a partnership of the two?"

Private vs. Public

The public/private distinction is more challenging than the for-profit/nonprofit distinction because whereas the latter describes actual organizations, the former defines two ends of a continuum. Specifically, even though there are both exclusively public and exclusively private organizations, a vast number of organizations are best described as hybrids of the two, that is, public-private partnerships of sorts. For this reason, public and private are separated by a dashed line and for-profit and nonprofit with a solid line in figure 5.1. That the public/private distinction constitutes a continuum becomes salient in the context of limited liability companies. ·

Many limited liability companies, particularly smaller ones, are exclusively private in that all shares are owned by private entities holding the central decision rights and rights to the residual. Even large, open corporations are predominantly private even though public actors may hold an equity stake in them. For example, Norges Bank Investment Management, the investment fund of the Government of Norway, owns about one percent of shares in Apple.

There are also fully state-owned limited liability companies such as the federally owned electric utility corporation Tennessee Valley Authority (TVA) in the United States. However, fully state-owned corporations are uncommon. Most "state-owned" corporations are like Finnair, the flag carrier and the largest airline in Finland. Only 56 percent of Finnair's shares are owned by a public actor, the Republic of Finland. Securing the republic's interests as a shareholder is assigned to the Ownership Steering Department of the Prime Minister's Office. The remaining 44 percent of shares are owned by private institutions and individuals.

What Does It Mean for Finnair to Be a Public Organization?

The descriptively accurate term to describe Finnair would be a public-private partnership, but in case a definitive categorization is desirable for some purpose, most of us would probably categorize Finnair as a public organization because the state has a majority ownership stake. However, there are three reasons why classifying Finnair as a public organization may be misleading.

First, Finnair's employees are not civil servants; instead, they have private employment contracts with the organization. In Efficiency Lens terms, management consists exclusively of private actors with a private-law employment contracts with the organization.

Second, seven of eight board members are either private board professionals or executives of private firms; only one board member represents the Prime Minister's Office and, therefore, the public interest. In Efficiency Lens terms, those who exercise oversight are primarily private citizens with private-law employment contracts in private organizations.

Third, even though 56 percent of equity is state-owned, we propose that the majority of residual risk (when considered more broadly than just investment risk) is borne by private actors due to commitments to specificity. Pilots, maintenance technicians and engineers, and cabin crew all commit to specificity by completing training that is not only highly specialized but also highly specific. Even though a pilot certified to fly the Boeing 737-200 aircraft could in principle fly the aircraft for any commercial airline, the likelihood of a Finnair pilot finding employment in another commercial airline is low.[2] The same restriction applies to a maintenance technician specialized in component repair of the Airbus A350-900 aircraft. Consequently, the residual risk is borne not only by shareholders (44 percent of whom are private organizations and individuals) but also by employees (practically all of whom are private individuals with private-law employment contracts).

---

[2] About ten years ago, one of the authors had a pilot from the German airline Lufthansa as a student in his MBA seminar. The author asked the student how many Finnish nationals were employed by Lufthansa as pilots. The student promised to look into it and came back the next day with the answer: zero. Pilot mobility is severely constrained.

In sum, viewed through the Efficiency Lens, we see how Finnair, and many other organizations like it, are only ostensibly public. In fact, it would be perfectly justifiable to label Finnair "more private than public" even though in most categorizations (including fig. 5.1) Finnair is considered a public organization. A telltale sign that Finnair is indeed considered public is that one of the persistent topics in public discussions is Finnair's potential privatization, operationally defined as the state giving up its majority equity stake. In trying to follow these privatization conversations, it has been difficult to pinpoint an explicit, let alone agreed-upon, main problem that privatization would address. In what ways would the organization be more efficient if, say, 51 percent (instead of 44 percent) of Finnair's shares were privately held? What, if anything, would change in the management and oversight where the vast majority of actors are already private? Pilots would still fly the planes, cabin crew would serve the customers, technical experts would perform maintenance and repair duties (all under private-law employment contracts), and the board of directors would still serve as a fiduciary of the organization.

To be sure, Finnair has been at the center of many controversies. Like many other airlines, public and private alike, Finnair has had frequent and severe clashes with unions. Without going into detail on these clashes, we see commitments to specificity and debates over residual rights of control as the main drivers.[3] It is difficult to see how "privatization" would alleviate these problems; that the state owns a majority of the voting rights in the corporation seems like an ancillary issue. Consequently, we invite those promoting privatization of public organizations—both in the case of Finnair and more generally—not only to clearly define what they mean by the term *privatization* but also to explicate the main problem that privatization would address.

Let us return briefly to the Finnish oil company Neste (see chapter 4). The Republic of Finland owns 44 percent of the shares in Neste; the second largest shareholder is a private insurance company with a 1.3 percent equity stake. What purpose would be served in classifying Neste as a private and

---

[3] A recurring conflict between Finnair's management and the pilot's union concerns the rights to residual control over asset utilization: Can management contract with non-union pilots to fly the planes? This effectively raises the question who *de facto* owns Finnair's fleet of aircraft. In the conventional sense, the fleet is of course the property of the legal entity Finnair Plc. However, the question at hand is who owns them in the rights-to-residual-control sense, where the answer is not as clear.

Finnair as a public corporation? What aspects of governance would these classifications elucidate? To us, a much better option is to examine in detail the way these two companies incorporate into their governance decisions the fact that their residual claimants involve both private actors and the public interest. We find it plausible that shareholder demographics are not as relevant as one might think. Again, we must look beyond the form into the governance microstructure.

Caterpillar, the Archetypal Private For-Profit

Caterpillar Inc. is a categorically private organization, because the vast majority of its shares are held by private actors, most notably private institutional investors such as Vanguard, BlackRock, and Bill & Melinda Gates Foundation. Much as in the case of large publicly traded corporations, Caterpillar's ownership is highly fragmented across thousands of shareholders. Caterpillar is in many ways representative of the large, modern corporation. The compensation structure of Caterpillar's board of directors is also more representative of large open corporations in the United States: Nonemployee directors receive an annual cash retainer of $150,000 and an equal amount in restricted stock with a one-year vesting period. Directors are also required to own Caterpillar stock equal to five times their annual cash retainer (Caterpillar 2021). Caterpillar's board compensation is strikingly different in its structure compared to that of Neste and Finnair; the latter two neither incentivize board members with equity nor oblige them to become residual claimants through stock ownership.

Summary: Both Form and Microstructure Matter

The main conclusion from the preceding discussion is that the choice of organizational form, while foundational, establishes only broad guidelines for governance. The key message to the designer is that choosing the proper governance structure is a matter of both design choice and microanalytical detail. The latter becomes particularly relevant when attention turns to governance dynamics. Specifically, adaptation over time is seldom a matter of changing from one form to another but, rather, implementing finer-grained adaptations within the chosen form. Organization scholar Ilya Cuypers and colleagues (2021, 129) offer an example in the context of a joint venture:

[I]n response to contextual changes, firms might continue with a joint venture [joint equity limited liability company] rather than move to a wholly owned subsidiary [vertical integration], but they might increase the levels of hierarchical control within the joint venture by altering ownership stakes or reshaping the board of directors.

This example reveals the essence of governance adaptation: It is about changes *within* the form, not changes *of* the form.

In the spirit of analyzing governance microstructure, we examine in the following governance decisions in the context of a nonprofit performing arts organization. Our aim is to establish efficiency as a relevant topic in nonprofits as well. In the subsequent section, we take a closer look at organizations that involve a public interest of some kind. In these contexts, we propose that comparative efficiency analysis may not be central.

The Nonprofit Organization in the Performing Arts

How does a theater company organize itself? Should it choose a governance structure that includes a residual claimant? If the theater organizes as a nonprofit, how does it attract donors? Who is in charge of management and makes the most important decisions about repertoire? Who has the key oversight role? Is there residual risk? Who bears it and how?

In performing arts organizations, the artistic director has conventionally been the most important decision maker and, therefore, in charge of management. The artistic director is not only responsible for curating the season by choosing programming and content but also the person who, along with the artistic staff, has a key role in selecting artists with whom the theater contracts. The artistic director must also interact with the prospective financiers of the theater, that is, both prospective audiences (earned revenue) and donors (unearned revenue). In sum, the artistic director's role is central in the theater's relationship with its key constituencies: donors, audiences, artists, and staff. Nonprofit theaters are often in many ways expressions or extensions of one person's vision, especially in theaters where the artistic director is also the founder.

As the theater grows, its organization professionalizes in several ways. One sign of professionalization is that management is divided into "managing the art" and "managing the business" (cf. Bhardwaj and Sergeeva 2022). The artistic director is responsible for the former and a managing (or executive) director for the latter.

As the theater organization professionalizes, a number of constraints emerge on the artistic director's discretion. Instead of curating the season in a way that expresses the artistic director's vision, "the season planning process is determined by the needs of the theater, the community, and the artists" (Colburn 2007, v). The emergence of organizational constraints gives rise to oversight, which is exercised by the theater's board of directors.

Some nonprofit theaters succeed in covering their costs with earned and unearned revenue; others fail. Failure has variable consequences to donors, artists, audiences, and managers. Just like in other organizations, theater organizations have constituencies who, by virtue of their relationships with the organization, bear risk.

In sum, the professionalized nonprofit theater contains all three elements of the Efficiency Lens: management, oversight, and risk. We may thus apply the Efficiency Lens and conduct a stakeholder analysis to examine the governance ramifications.

A Stakeholder Analysis of the Nonprofit Theater

In the nonprofit, there are no residual claimants expecting residual payments, and some of the revenue is unearned as it originates in donations. These two idiosyncrasies make the nonprofit theater different from a for-profit commercial organization. At the same time, the general logic of stakeholder analysis is still equally applicable. Specifically, the designer can still evaluate each constituency for potential residual risk to determine whether the relationship between the constituency and the organization exhibits stakeholder characteristics. After having identified the stakeholders, the designer can seek the appropriate governance responses to safeguard the most important relationships.

Donors as Stakeholders
The absence of residual claims must not be interpreted as the absence of residual risk (Fama and Jensen 1983a). All that is required for residual risk to exist is a constituency that becomes vulnerable by virtue of its participation in the organization. In the nonprofit theater, the obvious bearers of residual risk are the donors, who are putting their wealth at stake.

At the same time, becoming a donor is not merely a matter of putting one's wealth at stake. There are also important reputation effects that further deepen the stakeholder relationship between the donors and the theater. Specifically, donors tend to offer not only their wealth but also their *identities* to the service of the theater. Furthermore, donors do not act independently of one another; instead, they are members of communities of donors. A well-known member of the community donating to a theater sends a signal to other members that the theater is a legitimate target for donations, which effectively ties not only the prominent donors' wealth but also their reputation to organizational outcomes. Therefore, even though donors are not residual claimants, they have a conspicuous residual interest in the theater organization and, consequently, a vested interest in efficient governance, oversight in particular.

The absence of residual claimancy does not make the agency problem irrelevant either. All that is required for an expropriation hazard (and an agency problem) to exist is the separation of management from risk. In fact, "agency problems between donors and decision agents in nonprofits are similar to those in other organizations where important decision managers do not bear a major share of the wealth effects of their decisions" (Fama and Jensen 1983a, 319). Because donations are inalienable (the donor cannot renege on a donation already made), the expropriation hazard is in some ways more acute in the nonprofit than it is in an open for-profit corporation where residual risk is freely alienable.[4]

Given that donors put both their wealth and their reputation at stake, it is understandable why board members of donor-dependent organizations often either represent donors or are in fact donors themselves (Fama and Jensen 1983a, 319). Donors exercise oversight to ensure their donations are used in the best interest of the organization and not expropriated as private benefits by powerful members of management.

That donors face residual risk is not novel (e.g., Turbide and Laurin 2014). In fact, the very idea of organizing as a nonprofit can be viewed as a deliberate signal to donors that their donations are safe (Glaeser and Shleifer 2001). Although the nonprofit form does not safeguard against expropriation of

---

[4] Even though recovering donations already made is not feasible, donors have efficient *ex post* remedies available in case donations are poorly managed by the organization. If a prominent donor concludes that the theater is mismanaging donations, one option is to refrain from future donations. The name of a prominent top-tier donor disappearing from the donor list sends a strong signal to the donor community that the theater is no longer a legitimate target for donations.

donor funds, it prevents their excessive appropriation. The difference between appropriation and expropriation is that appropriation can occur, even in excess, without breaking the rules. In contrast, expropriation tends to involve taking possession of wealth in ways that are not only inappropriate but possibly also illegal. The absence of a residual claimant creates a set of rules that mitigate excessive appropriation, but these rules are ineffective if they are not obeyed.[5]

Artists and Staff as Bearers of Residual Risk

The constituencies whose potential stakeholder status has received less attention are the artists and the staff. Just like donors, artists are not residual claimants. However, to the extent they commit to specificity or become vulnerable in other ways, they may bear residual risk.

Contracting relationships between a theater and its employees are subject to the fundamental transformation just like any other contracting relationship. In fact, this process was explicitly embedded in the governance of film studios in the early and mid-1900s. In what was known as the *studio system* (Gomery 2005), actors would sign long-term contracts with specific studios. For example, the child superstar Shirley Temple contracted in the 1930s primarily with 20th Century Fox and its predecessor Fox Film Corporation. Under the studio system, the names of specific actors became intertwined with the names of specific studios. The fundamental transformation would occur over time as the actors and the studios learned to contract and collaborate with one another.

Analogously with the Hollywood studio system, when artists and nonprofit theaters develop reciprocal relationships over time, stakeholder relationships emerge. Artists in the nonprofit theater context tend to develop long-term relationships with specific theater organizations by becoming *resident actors*. Specificity develops both inadvertently and through deliberate commitments and, as a result, switching costs becomes sufficiently high to merit the designer's attention. Importantly, dependency is bilateral, because

---

[5] The distinction between appropriation and expropriation is subtle but important. The organization's constituencies appropriate revenue in various legitimate ways: employees appropriate fixed salary payments, shareholders appropriate residual dividend payments, and so on. To the extent appropriation is excessive, it may become a cause for concern; excessive executive compensation is a representative example. In contrast, expropriation is always not only improper, but it may also be illegal. Insiders expropriating private benefits from a nonprofit organization is a representative example. Expropriation may result in the nonprofit organization losing its tax-exemption privileges for the fiscal year in which expropriation is discovered.

both artists and staff may possess idiosyncratic skills that become intertwined with the identity and the repertoire of the theater organization. The departure of one well-known actor cannot be addressed simply by contracting another well-known actor.

The relational process is a general phenomenon in the context of the arts and entertainment: The identities of individual directors, actors, producers, and studios matter. How would Gracie Films and 20th Television, the production companies of the animated television series The Simpsons, replace Nancy Cartwright, the actor who gives her unique voice not only to one of the central characters, Bart Simpson, but also to a half-dozen of others? Indeed, the world of arts and entertainment offers perhaps the most salient examples of specificity and high switching costs.

The idea that actors may bear significant residual risk has been incorporated into theater governance, but only very recently. In January 2022, after several years of internal conflicts and turmoil, American Shakespeare Center (ASC), a Virginia-based regional theater company, appointed Brandon Carter both as its artistic director and an *ex officio* member of its board of trustees. The interesting fact about Mr. Carter is that he is a resident actor at ASC. Moreover, at ASC, curating the season is not the exclusive prerogative of the artistic director; instead, it is based on a management structure described as "a coequal group of individuals."[6] This coequal group currently consists of the artistic director, director of creative planning, programming coordinator, digital projects coordinator, performance studies manager, and a community programs manager, all of whom are either artists or staff members. In many ways, ASC has embraced the idea that those in charge of management need not necessarily be managers (see chapter 2).

Audiences and Residual Risk

In chapter 4, we suggested that consumers are unlikely to bear sufficient residual risk to justify a stakeholder status. In the case of many consumer products and services, switching costs are low and the availability of alternative suppliers of products and services provides a sufficient safeguard. Interestingly, the nonprofit theater might constitute an exception to the rule: In the nonprofit theater context, audiences are not merely consumers of art but may also have a relationship that exhibits elements of residual risk.

---

[6] *Wash. Post* (Jan. 10, 2022). Retrieved at https://www.washingtonpost.com/theater-dance/2022/01/10/carter-american-shakespeare/

An analogous phenomenon is found in the world of professional team sports where spectators are not merely consumers of sports entertainment; over time, many become loyal, lifetime fans of specific teams.

The audience members with a clear residual interest are the donors who, in addition to funding the organization, are holders of season tickets. The residual interest of the nonprofit theater donor is found not in residual claims (there are not any) but in the effect the theater organization has on the surrounding community. Unlike Hollywood film studios and the for-profit world of Broadway theater, nonprofit theaters tend to be small, local organizations whose primary audiences reside in the local communities in which the theaters are located. Donors and actors are often residents of the local community as well. Local theaters are therefore not only commercial organizations but also social communities whose role extends beyond providing entertainment; they may become avenues of activism, social commentary, even instruments of social justice. In the research literature, these are sometimes labeled *hybrid organizations* in that they have both an economic and a social mission (e.g., Ebrahim, Battilana, and Mair 2014). To be sure, artistic expression can be intimately intertwined with social and political interests.

When a theater organization links to broader social objectives, we can see how not only donors and artists but also audiences may develop a residual interest. If the local nonprofit theater fails to curate the season in a way that meets the broader social objectives in the community, switching to another nonprofit theater in another community does not constitute a feasible remedy. Therefore, both the idea of switching and the associated switching cost seem inapplicable in this context.

What's Next?

Salma Qarnain, cofounder and executive producer of the New-York-based Black Man Films and former managing director and chief operating officer (COO) of Synetic Theater in Washington, DC, described (personal communication, March 1, 2021) an intriguing, emerging way of thinking about risk in theater organizations. Specifically, the conventional focus on donors and founding artistic directors as the sole stakeholders is being countered with the inclusion of artists. Artists have always been considered constituencies of the theater organization, but elevating them to a stakeholder status implies that their contractual relationships are now considered in broader governance terms that extend beyond employment contracts. Appointing Mr. Carter, a resident actor, as ASC's artistic director and member of the board of trustees is a representative example. Just like donors make a wager on organizational outcomes, so do artists and staff.

In the spirit of comparative analysis, the implications of this new governance thinking must be addressed in their entirety. Does the new model enhance organizational viability? Does a shared leadership model increase or stifle innovation? Does a broader consideration of stakeholder interests dilute the ability of the board to engage in efficient oversight of unearned revenue and therefore jeopardize the organization in the eyes of the donors? Does the new model lead to more diversity and inclusion? According to Ms. Qarnain, it is too early to tell whether the new governance models result in net gains for the organization—the unintended consequences are still largely unknown.

We see the situation as analogous to opening up the board of directors in for-profit corporations to broader stakeholder interests. Williamson (2008, 250) noted that "giving the board stakeholder responsibility dilutes its credible contracting support for equity." In the context of donor-based nonprofits, the concern translates to the question, "How will donors react when the organization elevates artists from a constituency to a stakeholder and incorporates their interest in board-level decisions?" We submit this to the designer as a central question to be addressed in thinking of board composition. In the following, we take a closer look at the nonprofit board in light of its fiduciary duty.

Fiduciary Duty of the Nonprofit Board

If we adopt the premise that the board has a fiduciary relationship with the organization, then the tasks of the nonprofit and the for-profit boards are essentially identical. In both contexts, there are those who bear residual risk. Whether those bearing residual risk are also residual claimants may be relevant but not central. More significant differences would emerge if we viewed only the shareholder, not the organization more broadly, as the beneficiary of the board's fiduciary duty in the for-profit setting. But as we established in chapter 4, such thinking is misguided.

Drawing on the insights of Fama and Jensen (1983a), we counsel the designer to view the fiduciary duty of the board in both for-profit and nonprofit organizations not in terms of residual claimancy but in terms of residual risk. Consequently, the board should incorporate into its decisions especially those constituencies that bear residual risk. In the nonprofit context, the sources of unearned revenue (the donors) are the obvious constituency with a stakeholder status. But to the extent that other constituencies (e.g., those with long-term employment relationships) bear residual risk, they should be considered stakeholders as well.

Unfortunately, there are reasons to believe that the boards of nonprofit performing arts organizations are inefficient in their oversight role (Galli 2011). It is also often the case that board members are beholden to the artistic director because they have been introduced to the board either by the artistic director or a fellow board member. When this relationship is combined with the principle of appointing donors to the board, the *de facto* targets of the board's attention are the donors and the artistic director. As we discussed in chapter 4, stakeholder representation on boards may jeopardize the board's independence.

Again, it is crucial to distinguish between stakeholder *representation* on the boards and incorporating stakeholder *interests* at the board level. Much as in the case of for-profit corporations where the CEO may be able to exercise excessive control over the board (Mace 1971), oversight in the nonprofit theater may be unduly influenced by the artistic director. Indeed, the artistic director may not only lead the board of directors but also choose its members. This influence leads to the undesirable outcome of insufficient separation of management and oversight, which may have adverse efficiency consequences. The proposition that incorporating employee interests into theater governance enhances governance efficiency merits attention. This consideration does not, however, necessarily imply artist representation on the board. Giving artists more prominent roles in managing the theater might offer a viable option. Again, appointing a resident actor as the artistic director is an illustrative example of a governance choice that might lead to an efficient outcome. Specifically, promoting artists to top managerial positions gives them more voice in the organization without running the risk of diluting donor interests at the board level.

The Boundaries of Efficient Governance

Throughout the preceding chapters of this book, we have promoted an efficiency approach to governance. However, efficiency is not always applicable in governance decisions; sometimes focusing on efficiency may be either premature or downright misguided. Whereas the boundaries of governance-as-efficiency thinking should be acknowledged in all contexts, we find that they become particularly salient in organizations that involve public actors and the public interest, which is why we find this chapter a suitable context for critically examining the boundary conditions and the limits of applicability of the comparative efficiency approach.

Let us start at a context in which a comparative efficiency analysis is conspicuously applicable: the make-or-buy decision in an industrial firm (chapter 3). In the make-or-buy decision, the trade-off is between production costs and transaction costs: Outsourcing the production of a component lowers production costs (because specialized suppliers are often more productive) but increases transaction costs (because transacting across a legal boundary complicates exchange). Applying the efficiency logic suggests that if the savings due to increased production efficiency offset the increased transaction costs associated with the outsourcing decision, using an external vendor to supply the component is comparatively efficient over in-house production.

In the following, we first explicate and then critically examine the assumptions underpinning an efficiency analysis of governance alternatives. Failing to understand the assumptions and the associated boundary conditions, the designer may apply the efficiency logic in contexts in which it is not applicable.

The Assumptions of Comparative Efficiency Analysis

A comparative efficiency analysis hinges on three implicit assumptions, summarized in table 5.1. One is that the transacting parties enter the transaction voluntarily. If there are power asymmetries, efficiency analysis of the transaction loses its relevance (Ketokivi and Mahoney 2020). In the case of power asymmetries, whether the component is produced in-house or purchased from an external vendor will be decided by the comparatively more powerful party who will likely base the decision on its own cost implications. A powerful buyer may simply impose the supply of a component to an external vendor and force the vendor to absorb as much of the cost of transacting as possible. However, this shifts focus from sustainable efficiency to myopic efficiency, and as we have established at the beginning of this book, the latter is not of interest to our exposition. Efficiency analysis

Table 5.1 The Three Assumptions Required for a Comparative Efficiency Analysis

Assumption	Description
Voluntary participation	The parties to the economic exchange enter the relationship voluntarily; participation is neither expected nor imposed.
Instrumental outcomes	Governance choice is guided by the common objective of organizing the relationship efficiently.
Commensurate outcomes	The trade-offs made in alternative governance choices can be assessed in efficiency terms; where a governance choice involves multiple outcomes, they must have a commensurate metric so that an analysis of net gains is possible.

starts with the premise that the exchange parties are interested in the efficiency of the relationship, not just their respective income statements and balance sheets.

The second assumption is that when the transacting parties evaluate alternative governance choices, neither the specific governance choices nor the outcomes of the choices have intrinsic value. A case in point, an efficiency analysis of the make-or-buy decision adopts the premise that there is nothing intrinsically valuable about lower production costs or lower transaction costs, both have only instrumental value. Indeed, this is the essence of the notion of *feasible alternatives*. Instrumentality of outcomes is the reason why the governance alternatives can be subjected to an explicit trade-off calculus.

The instrumentality assumption becomes challenged in contexts in which either the governance choices themselves or some of the outcomes of the choices have intrinsic value. For example, some business schools might endorse the principle that a respectable business school has its own faculty and, consequently, readily dismiss the extensive use of visiting and adjunct faculty as an option. If there are intrinsically valuable outcomes, comparative efficiency analysis loses its relevance.

The third premise is that efficiency analysis in general and the idea of net gains in particular assumes that the relevant outcome categories associated with each governance option are commensurate, and consequently, how they are traded off against one another becomes not only possible in principle (the second assumption) but also analytically tractable. In the case of the make-or-buy decision, the relevant cost categories are production costs and transaction costs. Even though the latter may be less salient than the former, the

Table 5.2 Examples of Governance Decisions That Challenge the Efficiency Approach

Governance decision	Efficiency assumptions violated or questioned
Inmate discretion in prisons	(a) Inmates' right to self-determination and the correctional staff's safety are both intrinsically valuable and incommensurate outcomes; and (b) inmates' participation in the organization is imposed.
Physical restraint of patients in psychiatric care	(a) The patient's physical integrity and the hospital staff's safety are both intrinsically valuable and incommensurate outcomes; and (b) patients object to being physically restrained.
Hybrid teaching in universities	(a) The outcomes for students in the classroom and for those attending online are not commensurate; and (b) faculty and administrators may value different objectives.

two remain commensurate cost categories that can be traded off against one another. Consequently, the idea of net gains becomes relevant: If savings in one cost category offset increases in another, net gains result.

It is straightforward to think of examples of contexts in which at least some of the assumptions are violated. Examples that involve public interest are the most conspicuous ones. Table 5.2 gives three different contexts in which governance-as-efficiency thinking is challenged. We discuss each briefly in the following sections.

Inmate Discretion in Prisons

One of the key design decisions in prison governance is the amount of discretion given to inmates regarding behavior, language, wardrobe, visitors, and so on. In governance terms, the question is about the inmates' residual rights of control. In his in-depth analysis of prisons in the states of California, Michigan, and Texas, political scientist John DiIulio (1987) elaborated on the organizational details of prison governance in important ways. DiIulio (1987, 99) started at the idea that "[w]hether a prison (or a prison system) is safe, humane, and treatment-oriented, on the one hand, or violent, harsh, and unproductive, on the other, may depend mainly on the character of its prison governance." Among other issues, DiIulio focused specifically on inmate discretion. Giving inmates more discretion and autonomy would privilege their rights to self-determination and possibly enhance their rehabilitation, but at the same time, it might increase safety hazards for prison staff. DiIulio (1987) observed that prisons in Texas gave comparatively less discretion to inmates than prisons in California and Michigan.

As table 5.2 shows, several assumptions of the efficiency approach are violated: Inmate participation in the organization is imposed, constituencies (inmates vs. staff) have strong *ex ante* preferences regarding specific governance options, and the constituency outcomes are both intrinsically valuable and incommensurate. Therefore, the question whether there is an amount of discretion that provides a comparatively efficient alternative is misguided. Consequently, as political scientist James Wilson (1989, 360) noted in his discussion of decision-making in such situations, "[h]owever thoughtful people decide these matters, I doubt they will decide them on economic grounds."

Physical Restraint of Psychiatric Patients

One of the most controversial topics in psychiatric care is the physical restraint of patients. In what is known as *five-point restraint*, the psychiatric patients' ability to move is all but completely eliminated by placing them on a gurney and physically restraining movement at all four limbs and the waist or the chest. Those in the five-point restraint cannot so much as scratch their noses—it is hard to think of a more serious invasion of a person's right to physical integrity. Just as in the context of prisons, the designers of restraint policies readily understand that a comparative analysis of net gains cannot possibly guide design decisions.

To be sure, efficiency is a relevant consideration in many design decisions regarding the governance of healthcare organizations. However, in discussions with a forensic psychiatrist who both made decisions regarding the restraint of psychiatric patients in her own organization and consulted her colleagues in other hospitals, it became clear to us that a comparative efficiency analysis had no role in the formulation of policies and procedures for physical restraint. Instead, ensuring system integrity was paramount. Considerations of integrity evolved largely around the question of patient rights, and one of the main objectives of both legislation and psychiatric care was to reduce the use of physical restraint as much as possible. The reason the issue is relevant in governance decisions is because legislation in and of itself has proved insufficient (Keski-Valkama et al. 2007). Both institutional and private-ordering measures are required.

In psychiatric care, staff safety is obviously an important concern, but it can usually be achieved by merely secluding the patient. Physical restraint is to be applied only in the extreme situation where the patient's own safety is in jeopardy due to an inadvertent or deliberate self-harm hazard.[7] Furthermore, in the event the patient is physically restrained, the process is made *deliberately inefficient* in the sense that not only is the patient under constant observation by a healthcare professional but also a formal report on the patient's condition must be submitted every hour. There are serious accountability consequences for prolonged restraint without cause, and the formal hourly reports are used in *ex post* evaluations of each restraint episode. Finally, all patients are systematically briefed after being restrained. All these principles and procedures are in place to ensure system integrity.

Hybrid Teaching at Universities

The COVID-19 pandemic forced all institutions of higher education to create policies and practices for organizing online instruction. As universities returned to the conventional in-class instruction in late 2021 and early 2022, they faced two options. One was to return exclusively to in-class, face-to-face instruction; the other was to adopt a hybrid format where some students would be in the physical classroom and others attended online. Can this choice be subjected to a comparative efficiency analysis?

As faculty members in higher education, we both observed that some constituencies answered in the affirmative and, accordingly, adopted an efficiency perspective in analyzing which option should be preferred. The premise was that instruction would be efficient when a maximal number of students could attend class. This premise led to the conclusion that the hybrid option would be preferred, as it would allow everyone, including those not physically present, to attend class.

We have reservations against subjecting hybrid teaching to a comparative efficiency analysis. This is because we do not think the outcomes for different constituencies are commensurate. Whereas those unable to attend class in person predictably value online participation, the hybrid format may lead to negative learning outcomes to those in the physical classroom. As faculty members who taught numerous hybrid classes in the 2020–2021 and 2021–2022 academic years, we found it a pedagogical impossibility to give equal attention to those in the classroom and to those attending online. The predictable, and unfortunate, adjustment that many faculty members made was that they switched from a conversational, dialectical approach to more

---

[7] In retrospective surveys and interviews, some restrained psychiatric patients expressed beliefs that the use of physical restraints ultimately protected their own safety; others expressed anger, fear, and distrust toward staff (Wynn 2004).

conventional lecturing. We submit that the two pedagogical approaches—dialectical versus lecturing—led to different kinds of learning outcomes that cannot be compared in efficiency terms. Consequently, the designer must use judgment (not efficiency analysis) to decide whether it is appropriate to forgo the benefits of interactive learning in favor of a large-scale lecture-like format.

Governance as Integrity and the Probity Hazard

How should the designer approach design decisions in situations in which the notion of comparative efficiency is inapplicable? How do designers facing decision situations illustrated in table 5.2 choose among the options available to them?

Since this book is about efficient organizing, the examples in table 5.2 fall outside the scope of any prescription that could be derived from the Efficiency Lens. Accordingly, the main purpose of the discussion here is not to make recommendations but, instead, to explicate the boundary conditions of the comparative efficiency approach. This said, organization economists may have something relevant to offer to the designer even in circumstances where comparative efficiency is no longer the central objective.[8]

In his discussion of public organizations, Williamson (1999, 340)—one of the main architects of the governance-as-efficiency approach—noted that there are contexts in which governance-as-efficiency must yield to governance-as-integrity. Instead of efficiency, the designer must place integrity, or *probity*, as the central objective. Accordingly, governance choices should be compared to one another not in terms of their comparative efficiency but in terms of their potential to avoid *probity hazards*. The prescription is to choose the governance option that leads to comparatively lower probity hazards.

---

[8] Some organization economists suggest that even in contexts where some of the assumptions required for efficiency analysis are not met, there may be governance decisions that can be subjected to an efficiency analysis. Even in the prison context, there are governance decisions in which the efficiency assumptions hold. For example, organization economists Oliver Hart, Andrei Shleifer, and Robert Vishny (1997) suggested that the question whether the operational privatization of a prison (delegating prison management to a private contractor while maintaining public oversight) can be subjected to an efficiency analysis. However, before such an analysis is conducted, the designer must ensure the assumptions of a comparative efficiency approach are indeed met.

That a comparative efficiency analysis is inapplicable does not mean that the Efficiency Lens and all its key concepts are irrelevant. Just the opposite: Nothing prevents the designer from analyzing, for example, the implications of separating (or not separating) management from oversight or management from risk in terms of system integrity. To be sure, efficiency is not the only reason why designers contemplate separation of powers. The designer merely has to acknowledge that the objective of separation (or nonseparation) is different in contexts that require high probity.

A case in point, in the context of polity, the separation of powers into the three coequal branches of government—the legislative, the judicial, and the executive—has more to do with the integrity of the system of government than its efficiency. In fact, polity represents a context in which some inefficiencies may be *deliberately designed* (Williamson 1999, 318) into the system to avoid the hazard that arises from, say, making hasty decisions. How bicameral legislatures pass legislation offers an illustrative example of deliberately slowing down the legislative process. The existence of not only trial courts but also appellate and supreme courts is an example of deliberately slowing down the judicial process. That the bicameral legislative process and the three-tiered judicial process are inefficient is obvious; however, this inefficiency is not a cause for concern, because in these contexts, probity is more important than its efficiency. There are contexts in which organizations should be *deliberately designed* to be economically inefficient.

At the same time, as we noted in chapter 3, there are aspects of the legislature where efficiency is a relevant concern. It is important to bear in mind that efficiency is not something that either is or is not relevant to an organization; it may be relevant to some transactions and relationships but not to others. Again, the unit of analysis in the efficiency approach is the relationship, not the organization in its entirety. Consequently, the designer should not discard the efficiency approach entirely simply because it does not apply in a specific decision situation. In fact, we propose that the ability to identify those decision situations where efficiency applies and when it has to yield to probity considerations is a very valuable skill for the designer.

The Importance of Analyzing Assumptions
The preceding discussion emphasizes the crucial role that various assumptions have in all decision-making. In general, making implicit assumptions explicit always enhances transparency. However, in addition to making the implicit explicit, we also counsel the designer to rigorously

analyze the assumptions to determine if they are applicable in the specific decision situation. The designer should neither accept nor reject an assumption without explicit analysis. This is an important reminder, because it may be tempting for a constituency to seek a privileged position or bargaining power by suggesting that a certain outcome has intrinsic value and, therefore, should not be subjected to an efficiency analysis. Yet after closer inspection, something that may seem like an intrinsically valuable outcome can be thought of in instrumental, efficiency terms. Also, sometimes even that which is intrinsically valuable can have instrumental antecedents.

A case in point, we might be tempted to suggest that personal safety is intrinsically valuable. This is a reasonable position, but at the same time, even a superficial look into contexts in which safety is relevant reveals that there are many aspects of safety that not only can be subjected to a comparative efficiency analysis but can also be addressed in contractual terms. Insurance is the obvious example. Purchasing an insurance policy is an economic transaction by which we exchange a portion of our economic wealth for peace of mind. Even though we might consider having peace of mind intrinsically valuable, it has contractual antecedents worth the designer's attention.

As another example of safety, consider job security. Employees, particularly those who commit to specificity, might understandably consider job security as intrinsically valuable. However, as we have hopefully established in the preceding chapters, employee commitments to specificity (and the resultant need for job security) can often be addressed in contractual, efficiency terms, and provisions for job security can be embedded in both individual employment contracts and governance structures more generally.

Summary

Examination of nonprofit and public organizations offers many insights into governance. We see the implications and conclusions as twofold.

One conclusion is that although the choice of the organizational form is a central decision, much of the governance action resides in the details and the dynamics within the chosen form. Therefore, even though the choice of form is consequential, the designer must not exaggerate its importance. Upon choosing the organizational form, much of the designers' work is still ahead of them. For example, the main difference between a for-profit and a nonprofit organization is that the former has a residual claimant but the latter does not. This is a relevant decision criterion, but its implications may not be as consequential as one might think. For example, the choice between having and not having a residual claimant is not a choice between seeking or not seeking a surplus, the main implications are how the surplus (the residual) is governed.

In general, due to the high variance observed within forms, we find the categorization of organizations into for-profit, nonprofit, public, and private less useful. To be clear, this does not mean the *concepts* are not useful. Just the opposite, *public* and *private* are essential concepts if we wish to explicate the general governance principles of, say, an operationally privatized prison: management is privatized, oversight remains public. It is therefore not the use of the concepts *public* and *private* but the notion of the *private prison* (categorizing an organization) that invites confusion. Discussions of privatization more generally tend to involve exaggerated claims about how privatizing a public organization increases efficiency. For these discussions to become more tractable, those who participate in them should be explicit about what they mean by privatization and what main problem privatization is aimed at addressing.

Organization scholars Barbara Levitt and James March (1988, 325) suggested that learning in organizations is *superstitious* "when the subjective experience of learning is compelling, but the connections between actions are outcomes are mis-specified." The problem with giving too much attention to the form may lead to superstitious learning. Specifically, because organizational forms are more salient to the observer than governance microstructures, the casual observer may incorrectly ascribe organizational outcomes to the organizational form instead of the characteristics of the governance microstructure that are always hidden from plain sight.

The second insight that arises from this chapter is that it brings clarity to the boundaries of efficiency thinking. To this end, we have in this chapter explicated the implicit assumptions that underpin the analysis of comparative efficiency. The goal of explicating the implicit is to provide the designer with the requisite tools to identify the contexts in which a comparative efficiency analysis is applicable. Here, it is crucial to maintain the proper level of analysis. Specifically, the notion that context matters is not to be understood as meaning that there are *organizations* where efficiency considerations are not applicable; the point is that there are specific *governance decisions* where this may be the case. Designers are faced with numerous design decisions both at the founding of the organization and over time. A central design skill is the ability to selectively apply comparative efficiency analysis to governance decisions in which it is warranted. To this end, making the assumptions underpinning comparative efficiency explicit is useful.

PART III

GOVERNANCE AND THE ORGANIZATIONAL LIFE CYCLE

Organizations face different challenges as they progress through different stages of their development and maturity. In this third part of the book, we examine the issues organizations face in the founding (chapter 6), growth (chapter 7), and mature (chapter 8) phases of their life cycles. We pinpoint unique challenges associated with each specific phase.

Chapter 6 focuses on the governance questions that an organization's founders face. The topic is important, because founders often assume that questions regarding organization design and governance can be addressed in the months and the years after the founding, when the organization has become more established. However, there are crucial questions that require the designer's attention even before the organization's founding. This chapter addresses both questions that can and should be addressed and are *ex ante* contractible (i.e., before the founding) and those that are subject to various *ex post* adjustments.

As organizations expand, their governance changes in fundamental ways. The most consequential changes have to do with the gradual separation of management, oversight, and risk. Chapter 7 focuses on the challenges and the dilemmas that separation creates for the designer. The separation dynamic tends to make the organization more vulnerable, which is pertinent particularly in situations in which the organization becomes the target of a takeover attempt. In chapter 7, we also examine the measures the designer can take to protect its stakeholder relationships.

As organizations mature, their designs and governance structures become institutionalized, and their modification becomes challenging. Chapter 8 focuses on the challenges that the persistence of governance choices presents to the designer. Persistence of governance structures is a potential cause for concern in intraorganizational relationships and transactions in particular. Accordingly, chapter 8 complements chapter 3 by a closer examination of the trade-offs associated with internal transactions.

6

The Startup Organization

Master's students in business administration who had just launched startup firms asked in class when they should start to think about organization design and governance in their firms. We gave them the only intellectually honest answer: It was probably already too late. The foundation of efficient organization is laid in the months and weeks before the founding, not after it.

The students' misconception likely arose from aspiring entrepreneurs thinking of organization design and governance in terms of organizational structures, reporting relationships, profit-and-loss structures, and so on. These aspects of design can indeed be addressed after the organization's founding. To be sure, a small startup need not contemplate whether to organize as a multidivisional firm or as a matrix; many decisions regarding the organization's macrostructure do not become relevant until months, perhaps even years, after the founding. Startup organizations tend to be fluid in their structures, which makes them efficient.

However, organization design and governance extend beyond structural choices, and there are many essential questions that merit the designer's early attention, because initial choices have far-reaching consequences. For example, once the designer of an industrial startup has decided that the form of the organization will be a limited liability company with restricted alienability of residual claims (see chapter 2), the organization is likely committed to this form for as long as it exists, or at the least, subsequent incremental governance decisions and adjustments will be constrained by the foundational decisions. Consequently, foundational decisions must be made with conscious foresight, which can work toward imprinting the organization with efficient governance principles and avoiding costly *ex post* adjustments.

Examining organization design and governance issues of the incipient organization is instructive in three distinct ways. One is that it helps the designer understand which aspects of governance are *ex ante* contractible and which must be addressed through *ex post* adjustment. For example, cofounders of a high-technology startup firm may be able to agree *ex ante* that the organization's objective is to seek growth, increase firm value, and

Efficient Organization. Mikko Ketokivi and Joseph T. Mahoney, Oxford University Press. © Oxford University Press 2023.
DOI: 10.1093/oso/9780197610282.003.0006

ultimately, go public through an IPO; what is not contractible is the time-line. The designer must carefully analyze contractibility and think of efficient safeguards for the noncontractible aspects of cooperation in particular. *Ex ante* contractible aspects are comparatively simpler because they can be addressed, by definition, by *ex ante* contractual safeguards. However, even there the designer must avoid a false sense of security: Not all *ex ante* agreements are enforceable and, consequently, may ultimately require *ex post* adjustment.

The second way in which examining startup organizations is useful is that it helps the designer understand what kinds of *ex ante* private-ordering measures are feasible in the first place. Feasibility is not merely a matter of contractibility but also one of understanding the limits the institutional environment imposes on private ordering. For example, most institutional environments uphold the principle that shareholders of limited liability companies have the right to sell their shares. Even though the law permits some private-ordering constraints, strict restrictions will likely be contested by the courts. In general, contracting parties cannot privately agree to something that jeopardizes someone's legal rights. However, what is considered illegal is not merely a matter of the letter of the law but more broadly its interpretation and application in specific cases. For example, strict restrictions on the transfer of shares would mean the contracting parties are effectively "contracting for market failure." In the case of a contractual dispute, the party arguing that the strict restriction should be enforced may have difficulty convincing the judge presiding over the dispute that the court should uphold a contract for an intentional market failure. The designer must be sufficiently informed to avoid introducing into contracts clauses that rest on a false sense of security about enforceability.

The third way in which an analysis of organizations at their founding is instructive is that it can help the designer better understand the relationship between the *ex ante* and *ex post* aspects of governance decisions. Even though the latter are always conditioned by the former, there are situations in which *ex post* decisions may not only modify but also sometimes even annul or reverse an *ex ante* condition. These situations do not present a problem as long as all parties to the contract agree. However, in many settings the decision to reverse an *ex ante* condition may be the prerogative of a subset of the contracting parties, which turns attention to residual rights of control. An enduring question in governance is how much discretion the board of directors should have in modifying corporate bylaws, and which modifications require shareholder approval. In Efficiency Lens terms, which aspects of *ex post* contracting are matters of oversight delegated to the board of directors?

We start this chapter with an example of a sports equipment industrial startup, in which one of the authors was both cofounder and chairperson of the board for the first three years. The purpose of the example is, on the one hand, to provide an illustration of the three benefits of analyzing startup organizations. On the other hand, we want to establish how fundamentally context-dependent startup governance is. Governance choices are not only dependent on how the designer formulates the main problem but also on how idiosyncratic institutional environments (most notably law) impose constraints on private ordering.

The Case of the Sports Equipment Startup

In August 2015, one of the authors of this book became a cofounder and chairperson of the board of an industrial startup that designed and manufactured sports equipment as well as developed and built the proprietary production technology used in production. In the two months preceding the founding, four prospective cofounders got together to discuss the central issues and challenges. A number of prospective product designs were complete, along with a few prototypes. The prototypes were handmade, and not even a rudimentary production system had been built. The prospective cofounders agreed that the common premise of not separating management, oversight, and risk would provide a useful starting point for thinking about governance (Figure 6.1).

The first challenge would be to build a production line and scale it up to a point where the firm could generate sales sufficient to secure a positive month-to-month cash flow. The prospective cofounders concluded that the firm would have the requisite technical expertise to build the production

The typical startup is founded on the principle of no separation of management, oversight, and risk: founders are in charge of management, populate the board of directors, and are the primary risk bearers.

Figure 6.1 The startup viewed through the Efficiency Lens

system, if needed. The greatest challenge for the startup was the financing of assets. Would they be financed through debt or equity?

We commonly think of decisions of debt versus equity financing and leverage as financial management decisions where the cost of capital is of central importance. But as Williamson noted, these decisions not only have governance implications, but they also *are* governance decisions: It is useful to regard "debt and equity as governance structures rather than as financial instruments" (Williamson 1988, 579).

The choice of debt versus equity financing has a number of important organizational ramifications that link to oversight in particular. In firms that rely on equity financing, the role of the board of directors is crucial in securing the rights of the providers of equity capital and the continuing supply of financing when needed. In a debt-financed firm, in contrast, the rights of the financier are stipulated in the formal contract (the loan agreement), effectively eliminating the need for additional governance interventions at the board level. If the organization defaults on its debt, the creditor has several options and safeguards available. More generally, firms that rely on debt financing tend to organize based on *formalization* (rule following); a stronger reliance on *discretion* is found in equity-financed firms (Williamson 1988, 581).

However, the financing of assets in and of itself was not construed as the main problem, because there was a more fundamental question that had to be addressed before the financing decision could be contemplated: What kind of production technology would be used? This question would, in turn, have to be considered simultaneously with the decision of whether the products would be produced in-house or by an external supplier—the question was fundamentally one of organizational boundaries. The prospective cofounders concluded that the main problem should be formulated as a *discriminating alignment* (see chapter 4) of the financial, the technological, and the organizational, the central question being, "How would the startup ensure that the three are in sync with one another?"

The cofounders weighed the different options and concluded that competitive advantage would be sought based on product differentiation. The aim of the startup would be to introduce a product with a drastically different structure than the incumbents' products. The cofounders figured that trying to compete in a highly consolidated market against large incumbents with massive scale and scope economies and market power would be challenging. Trying to enter such a market without significant product differentiation seemed like bad strategy. What must the startup offer that the established brands that dominated the market did not already offer? The strategic decision to introduce a drastically new product had immediate technological consequences, which in turn led to a number of fundamental governance decisions.

The immediate technological consequence was that the startup would have to develop not only the product but also the production system. Design and production of some parts and subsystems could be outsourced to external suppliers, but the startup would have to design and build other subsystems internally as well as integrate all subsystems—including those purchased from external vendors—into the overall production system; this would require considerable investments in engineering.

The upside of in-house production would be that the startup would maintain important residual rights of control with regard to production decisions (see chapter 2). In their attempt to be forward-looking, the cofounders concluded that in-house production would confer important advantages particularly in the growth phase of the startup. Specifically, if the firm designed and built the production system itself and was in charge of system integration, it would have control over the entire system. This control would make the scaling of production easier. The only thing the startup would have to ensure was the reliable supply of outsourced parts and subsystems. Achieving a reliable supply was deemed not to be a problem, because contractual relationships with technology suppliers were straightforward to formalize due to low specificity. As an example, consider the supply of aluminum or steel molds used to make some of the parts. All the startup would need to provide to the supplier were the technical specifications, which the supplier would feed into a general-purpose computerized-numerical-control (CNC) machine[1] to produce the mold. No long-term relationships would be required, and multiple suppliers would be available for each outsourced subsystem. It would make no sense for the startup to carry CNC machines on its balance sheet.

---

[1] The CNC machine is a general-purpose electromechanical device (e.g., a lathe) that can produce products for a variety of end uses using diverse materials, such as metals, plastics, or wood. All the CNC machine needs are instructions from a computer on the dimensions of the product to be produced. In many industries, an established, competitive network of large and small CNC machinists offers manufacturing services to a variety of buyers. In addition to there being a large number of CNC machinists, there are also many manufacturers of CNC machines, which ensures a competitive market throughout the value chain.

The downside of the decision to build a unique production system was that most of it would involve either internally developed or engineered-to-order, special-purpose technology that exhibited a high degree of physical asset specificity; the system would be a dedicated design, and thus the productive assets would have no redeployability. Unique, special-purpose assets are notoriously difficult to finance with debt, unless the firm can offer other, more liquid assets as collateral. Absent such assets, the cofounders concluded that if the startup was to be committed to a differentiated product, equity financing would be the only feasible option.

Given these initial conditions, what kinds of contractual arrangements would ensure an efficient startup organization? What kind of foresight would have to be incorporated? We discuss these issues in the following sections by comparing and contrasting what the law (the institutional pillar) stipulates and what the cofounders agreed privately (the contractual pillar).

The Institutional and the Contractual Pillars in the Case of the Sports Equipment Startup

Startup firms tend to incorporate as closed corporations (Fama and Jensen 1983a), that is, limited liability partnerships with an intentionally limited number of shareholders. Because there is no market for shares, it is considerably more difficult for cofounders to divest; often, the only feasible way to divest is to try to sell to another cofounder. There are usually not many outside investors willing to buy the cofounders' shares in the early stages of a startup in particular. Furthermore, it may be a bad idea for a startup to create an organization where new investors enter, and old investors exit, frequently. Consequently, cofounders may want to intentionally limit the alienability of residual rights.

Because ownership in a closed corporation is both unavoidably and deliberately "sticky," cofounders are well advised to agree on the specific rules by which equity will be governed, to make the organization credible in the eyes of risk and to ensure effective oversight. This gives rise to a common contractual pillar—the shareholders' agreement. Indeed, the shareholders' agreement constituted the most important contractual arrangement at the founding of the sports equipment startup.

Even though the shareholders' agreement is a matter of private ordering, the institutional pillar provides a useful starting point, because it establishes the broader context in which private ordering takes place. Cofounders should obviously be aware of the requirements that corporate law imposes on startup governance. However, two other issues that merit the designer's attention are less obvious: (1) Should some of the defaults in the law be modified or overridden? (2) What other governance issues not covered in the law should be incorporated into *ex ante* contracting?

The sports equipment company was incorporated in Finland; therefore, the central institutional pillar was the Finnish Limited Liability Companies Act of 2006. The cofounders used the shareholders' agreement both to override some of the defaults in the law and to agree on issues not covered by the law. Table 6.1 summarizes selected issues for illustration. The table does not constitute a complete list of all the issues contained in the shareholders' agreement; we have chosen for illustration a number of specific issues that either have more general appeal or that effectively illustrate important differences between the institutional and the contractual pillars.

Board Composition

Predictably enough, as the prospective chairperson of the board approached potential investors, several of them asked not only who would assume operational responsibility but also how the board of directors would be assembled. It became clear that the board would have to have a substantial equity stake in the startup, and that it would make little sense to appoint any outsiders to the board at the inception. Cofounders quickly converged to the idea that a board of directors of at least three members would be selected from among the cofounders, and that all board members would have to have at least a 10 percent equity stake in the startup. Expressed in the terminology of the Efficiency Lens, the cofounders wanted to avoid the excessive separation of oversight and risk. Having a board with only a minimal equity stake may work in a large corporation, but in a small startup, separating oversight from risk may immediately threaten the credibility of the organization in the eyes of both current and prospective providers of equity. Providers of equity constitute the most important stakeholder of a high-technology startup whose success hinges on the successful development and productive use of unique, high-specificity production technology. If the startup cannot secure the requisite funding, the startup fails, and discussion of all other stakeholder issues becomes a moot point.

Attention to board composition was relevant not only from the point of view of securing initial financing. The forward-looking cofounders knew

Table 6.1 The Institutional and the Contractual Pillars in the Sports Equipment Startup

Issue	The Institutional Pillar (Finnish Limited Liability Companies Act)	The Contractual Pillar (Shareholders' Agreement)
Composition of the board of directors	A minimum of two members at least one of whom resides in the European Economic Area (required); appointed by shareholders (default)	Three to five persons; a block of 30% of shares can appoint one member
Procedures for trading shares	Freely alienable (default); right of squeeze-out (default)	Freely alienable only among partners; tag-along and drag-along clauses regulate transfer of shares
Loyalty and care	Board members are subject to the fiduciary duty of loyalty and care to the organization (required)	All shareholders are subject to the fiduciary duty of loyalty but not care
Non-compete and confidentiality clauses	None	Strict non-compete and confidentiality clauses
Contributions clauses	None	None
Dividend policy	Shareholders have the right to minority dividend (default)	No minority dividend
Dispute settlement	None	Binding arbitration in Helsinki, in Finnish
Procedures for raising equity	Shareholders decide (default); regular issue requires simple majority (default); directed issue requires qualified majority (default)	No additional stipulations or overrides of defaults
Defining majority	1/2 for majority and 2/3 for qualified majority (default)	No additional stipulations or overrides of defaults

from the beginning that the startup would likely require multiple rounds of equity financing. For this to be successful, the firm would have to maintain credibility in the eyes of the providers of equity. It turned out the firm needed a total of five rounds of equity financing in the first three years.

Finnish law requires a limited liability company to have a board of directors. Further, the board must have as members a minimum of two natural persons at least one of whom resides in the European Economic Area (all EU countries, Norway, Iceland, and Liechtenstein). The law further stipulates that the decision to appoint board members belongs to shareholders. This legal requirement means that employees will have a formal oversight role in the corporation only if they either are also shareholders or if shareholders choose to appoint an employee representative to the board. Therefore, even in cases where employees have a *legitimate* reason for having board representation, they cannot make a *legal* claim for inclusion—legitimate and legal are not synonyms.

The cofounders decided that a two-person board would be too small and that a large board would be problematic. Consequently, in the shareholders' agreement they supplemented the requirement of a two-person minimum by requiring the board to have three to five members. They also supplemented the default that directors are elected by shareholders by allowing a block of 30 percent to appoint a board member. Without this override, all prospective board members would have to be supported by a simple shareholder majority.

Some organizations may delegate the selection of board members to the board itself; such boards are known as *self-perpetuating boards*. In a self-perpetuating board, boards are usually not allowed to increase board size by adding new members at their discretion; they are merely allowed to select replacements for outgoing members. Such autonomous boards are found in nonprofit settings (Hansmann 1980). In the sports equipment startup, a self-perpetuating board made no sense: All board members would always be selected in the annual shareholders' meeting, with the exception that a voting block of 30 percent could appoint a board member.

Procedures for Trading Shares

The law not only places no limitations on the ownership of shares, but the very spirit of the law is also to ensure unrestricted transfer of wealth. At the same time, unrestricted trading of shares may present a problem in a high-risk startup because it may invite instability and expose the startup to unwanted takeovers. The resulting hazard may discourage prospective shareholders from investing.

The shareholders' agreement of the sports equipment startup placed significant restrictions on the trading of shares, particularly if a trade would result in the introduction of a new shareholder. Consequently, the cofounders decided that existing shareholders could trade shares among themselves without restrictions; some cofounders accumulating more decision and voting power in the organization over time was not deemed problematic.

The cofounders further thought that categorically prohibiting the introduction of new shareholders would not be in the best interest of the organization. If one cofounder identified an attractive prospective shareholder but no additional equity financing was needed at the moment, why would existing shareholders be prohibited from selling some of their shares to the new entrant? The cofounders decided that this option should be made possible but that it would be done on a *pro rata* basis. This decision led to the introduction of a *tag-along clause* in the shareholders' agreement. The tag-along clause stated that if a shareholder identified a prospective buyer, all shareholders would be entitled to "tag along" into the sale based on their ownership share. For example, if a prospective buyer of one thousand shares was identified and the existing shareholders each owned 20 percent, each shareholder would be entitled to "tag along" by offering to sell a maximum of two hundred shares. Importantly, it is generally well advised to make "tagging along" optional; including a clause that could effectively force the dilution of ownership is thought to be bad governance. The tag-along clause effectively introduces a put option to existing shareholders.

Another set of rules for trading shares must be in place in the potential acquisition of the startup by another firm. Since many startups are interested in being acquired by a larger firm at some point, exit conditions must be stipulated. An exit usually means that the acquiring firm purchases all the target's outstanding shares. The law provides protection against involuntary sale of shares unless ownership is highly consolidated. For instance, Finnish law stipulates that a shareholder with more than 90 percent of all shares has the right "to squeeze out" the remaining minority shareholders at a fair price.

The default gives any shareholder with an equity stake of more than 10 percent the option to effectively block an acquisition. To provide a safeguard against such an economic holdup problem by a minority shareholder, shareholders' agreements often incorporate a *drag-along clause*. The drag-along clause states that in the event a third party makes a good-faith offer to acquire the firm, a majority (simple or qualified) of shareholders can "drag along" the rest to the sale. In the sports equipment startup, the shareholders' agreement contained a drag-along clause based on a simple majority. The drag-along mechanism effectively functions as a call option to purchase shares from existing shareholders.

Restrictions on the trading of shares can be viewed as a contractual mechanism that safeguards against one shareholder benefiting from the transfer of their shares at the expense of other shareholders. Without the tag-along clause, each shareholder would effectively face a unique market for the startup's shares; more powerful and better-informed shareholders might be able to use this to their advantage. Without the tag-along safeguard in place, more passive prospective shareholders might be reluctant to invest. Without the drag-along clause, shareholders would expose themselves to a holdup problem, as a minority shareholder could effectively block even an economically attractive acquisition offer.

Beyond Limited Liability

The question of who is expected to be loyal to the organization and why requires explicit attention in startups. The law assigns the legal fiduciary duty of loyalty and care only to the board of directors. In contrast, aside from the requirement to pay for their shares, shareholders do not have to work, attend meetings, make decisions, be loyal to the organization, or provide additional financing. This feature goes to the heart of the principle of *limited liability*: Purchasing shares must not be burdened by further obligations.

Shareholders' agreements can, and often do, impose additional obligations and restrictions on shareholders, effectively partially compromising the principle of limited liability. The designer must exercise caution here and craft all additional obligations carefully to secure the credibility of the organization in the eyes of both current and potential future shareholders. To the extent the organization's viability hinges on successfully raising equity in multiple financing rounds, all additional obligations pose a hazard as they limit the pool of prospective investors.

In the shareholders' agreement of the sports equipment startup, the cofounders agreed that the fiduciary duty of loyalty would be extended to all shareholders. This was achieved by requiring all shareholders to act in the best interest of the organization. Moreover, shareholders would be prohibited from entering into organizational arrangements in which they would be in competition with the startup.

How about the fiduciary duty of care? Should it be extended to all shareholders as well? This is a more complex question, because the duty of loyalty can largely be fulfilled by *passively refraining from doing something*. In contrast, fulfilling the duty of care requires *actively doing something*. Extending the duty of care to shareholders implies that all shareholders would be required to put in at least some work, if only to ensure that good decisions are made. This requirement would effectively lead to a *contributions clause* of some kind. Contributions clauses are some of the most contested issues in shareholders' agreements.

After careful deliberation, the cofounders decided neither to extend the duty of care to shareholders nor to include any contributions clauses, because these would likely not result in net gains. In fact, one central cofounder and another key investor who joined the firm in the fourth financing round would not have contributed to equity if the shareholders' agreement had included a contributions clause.

The designer must always consider the option that some investors only want to invest in equity with no role, formal or informal, in management or oversight. Consequently, embracing the democratic idea that "everyone also put in the work" may be misplaced. As always, an analysis of net gains must be conducted, although we are doubtful that a contributions clause would result in net gains in startups that rely heavily on equity financing.

Dividend Policy

Designers of startups that seek to become attractive targets for an acquisition must think carefully about how they manage a potential economic surplus. In many startups, cofounders agree that the startup should retain all its earnings and that the shareholders' payday would be the day the firm is acquired by another firm. Consequently, the startup might choose not to pay dividends at all. If this is the case, it may be best to write it into the shareholders' agreement.

The importance of an explicit dividend policy is particularly important in Finland, where the law contains an interesting idiosyncrasy not found in many other jurisdictions. Specifically, Finnish law goes further than many others in protecting the rights of minority shareholders. One of these rights is the principle of *minority dividend*, which states that a block of shareholders representing a minimum of 10 percent of all shares can force at least one half of the profits for the fiscal year to be distributed as dividend. In the sports equipment startup of eight cofounders with roughly equal equity stakes, the right to minority dividend would mean that any one shareholder could force a dividend.

The minority dividend is a default that can be overridden by an *ex ante* agreement of all shareholders. In the sports equipment startup, the cofounders unanimously agreed that all shareholders, current and future, would have to forgo the right to the minority dividend. The startup would have to be able to retain all its earnings to enable sufficient growth.

Settling Disputes

The law is silent on dispute resolution, which effectively means the contracting parties decide the most appropriate form of settling disputes. Most startups choose binding arbitration as the preferred method. Arbitration has three potential advantages over litigation: It is cheaper, faster, and has an expert presiding over the dispute. The cofounders of the sports equipment startup decided that disputes would be settled in arbitration. An additional stipulation was that arbitration would take place in Helsinki and that the language of the arbitration procedures would be Finnish.

In retrospect, the author who was one of the cofounders has concluded that the decision to default to the common practice of binding arbitration was ultimately ill informed. In a conversation with a legal expert about five years after the shareholders' agreement had been signed, the author learned that in Finland, arbitration is in fact often *much more expensive* than litigation. This point merits attention because this may not be merely an idiosyncrasy of the Finnish context. In his review of arbitration as a dispute-resolution mechanism, Stipanowich (2010, 1) noted that "[o]nce promoted as a means of avoiding the contention, cost and expense of court trial, binding arbitration is now described in similar terms—'judicialized,' formal, costly, time-consuming, and subject to hardball advocacy." Lord Michael Mustill, a British barrister and judge, expressed the concern in slightly more vivid terms by describing arbitration as having "all the elephantine laboriousness of an action in court, without the saving grace of the exacerbated judge's power to bang together the heads of recalcitrant parties" (cited in Stipanowich 2010, 23).

Minor Issues

There were a number of additional procedural and technical issues that the shareholders' agreement had to address. For example, the law protects the dilution of any shareholder's equity by permitting a *directed issue* of shares to new shareholders only in exceptional circumstances. By default, equity must be raised through a *regular issue* of shares where existing shareholders are entitled to buy the newly issued shares on a *pro rata* basis. Under Finnish law, a directed issue requires both a qualified majority of two-thirds of shareholders and a positive affirmation from the board that a regular issue is infeasible. The cofounders were satisfied with what the law stipulated and could not find any compelling reasons why the authority to raise equity should be delegated to the board of directors *as a general rule*. Instead, the cofounders decided that potential delegation would be deliberated in a shareholders' meeting on a case-by-case basis. Shareholders ultimately delegated the authority to raise equity to the board in every financing round.

Another technical issue was the definition of majority and qualified majority. The cofounders saw no reason to deviate from the default definition of majority as *fifty percent of shares plus one share* and qualified majority as *two thirds of shares plus one share*. The concern was that raising either threshold might cause delays in decision-making.

Summary of the Sports Equipment Startup

The preceding discussion and table 6.1 highlight the fact that the ability to raise equity financing was both foundational and critical to the sports equipment startup. Consequently, all the foundational governance decisions would have to be derived from and justified by this main problem. Let us briefly discuss three governance implications of this main problem formulation.

First, restricting alienability of residual claims signals stability and long-term commitment, and convinces the shareholders that they need not worry about the arbitrary introduction of new investors by one or a few shareholders. Note that this restriction is an *ex ante* decision where the objective is to establish credibility in the eyes of *prospective* cofounders: What kind of a governance structure will convince prospective investors to make a wager in the organization? It is understandable that an investor may not be interested in a "revolving-door startup" where individual investors can enter and exit without any oversight or joint decision-making, or where a minority shareholder can effectuate substantial changes to the ownership structure by unilaterally introducing new shareholders. Note that although neither tag-along nor drag-along clauses remove the residual rights from the shareholders, they do effectively transfer some of the residual rights of control from shareholders *as individuals* to shareholders *as a collective*.

Second, the company was founded with a total of eight cofounders, each with roughly an equal number of shares. The cofounders were aware that having an unusually large number of shareholders at the outset not only constituted a trade-off but that it also ran against conventional wisdom. The most obvious problem was that any decision that required shareholder approval would have to be supported by at least five of the eight cofounders. Furthermore, the larger the founder base, the more complex the coordination and the communication. At the same time, the cofounders agreed that a broad ownership base made sense given the main problem of securing the requisite equity financing both at the outset and in foreseeable future financing rounds. The startup could have had fewer founders, but this would have meant that it might not have been able to raise equity from its existing shareholders in future financing rounds. The cofounders decided to tackle the challenge of having to manage a relatively large number of shareholders already at the founding as an *ex ante* problem. This was successful in the sense that in the subsequent four rounds of financing, only one new shareholder was introduced.

The potential problem of cumbersome decision-making due to a large number of cofounders was alleviated by an active board of four members who collectively owned a majority of the shares. In fact, the four-member board was deliberately assembled from cofounders who had a somewhat higher equity stake than the others. This governance arrangement meant that the board could *de facto* make decisions that belonged to all shareholders. Instead of calling a shareholders' meeting, the board could simply reach out to all shareholders and propose a consensus decision. The board would inform the shareholders that it had reached a unanimous decision on an issue, which meant that the proposal had already secured majority approval. If all shareholders agreed to the proposal that everyone knew would pass anyway, the decision could be written and filed expediently as a unanimous shareholders' decision, without having to call a shareholders' meeting.

Third, governance decisions strongly echoed the idea of limited liability. Because all commitments above and beyond putting money at risk upfront and being loyal to the organization might alienate prospective investors, the shareholders' agreement did not contain contributions clauses or commitments to further financing. Moreover, the board of directors took shareholder interests as its primary objective. This priority did not mean that there were no other stakeholders; indeed, just the opposite. Many employees would be required to commit to developing firm-specific skills, which meant that they had a legitimate residual interest as well. However, this was not something that the cofounders considered so central that it would require the board's attention at the beginning. Again, the main problem was that the organization would have to secure a steady flow of equity financing until the firm could be financed by revenue. Had debt financing been possible, the board could have been given an altogether different primary task. As we mentioned earlier, in equity-financed firms, discretion in decision-making is central. Here, it is precisely the board of directors whose task is to use discretion by deliberating on the key financing issues. If financing were organized through debt, the board could direct its attention away from financing issues, which in debt-financed firms are more an issue of compliance and rule following. Understanding the intimate linkage between finance and governance is central (Williamson 1988).

Understanding Context Dependence

In the case of the sports equipment startup, the board attended primarily to shareholder interests because the main problem was defined in terms of raising equity. The main problem is always organization specific, and consequently, so are all the governance choices derived from it. In a setting where assets can be financed through debt or where the startup can quickly start to rely on revenue financing, there is no need to define the main problem in equity-financing terms. Consequently, the board of directors can be assigned a very different oversight role. In sum, context dependence enters into governance decisions through the contextually idiosyncratic main problem.

Another way in which context dependence enters governance decisions is through the institutional environment. Although many of the topics and issues in table 6.1 generalize to other settings, every environment exhibits idiosyncratic aspects as well. For example, not all jurisdictions require the limited liability company to have a board of directors. In Spain, one of the founding decisions the designer of a limited liability company (*sociedad limitada*) indeed faces is whether the company will have a board of directors. In Finland, the law requires limited liability companies to have a board of directors. Another idiosyncrasy of the Finnish legal environment is the principle of the minority dividend whereby a voting block of 10 percent can force a dividend for the fiscal year. The designer must incorporate the demands of the idiosyncratic institutional environment into governance decisions.

The General Case of Startup Governance

The sports equipment startup example presents one specific case of startup governance and offers an illustration of its context dependence. Even though all governance decisions are fundamentally context dependent, there are a number of broader issues that merit attention. In this section, we discuss three topics that we see as generally applicable: (1) *ex ante* contractibility,

(2) enforceability of private ordering, and (3) assignment of *ex post* decision rights.

Ex Ante Contractibility

Think back to your first summer job delivering newspapers, mowing lawns, or selling ice cream (see chapter 4). We venture to guess your contract with your employer required neither additional contractual safeguards nor *ex post* adjustments. More generally, many relationships the organization has with its constituencies are *ex ante* contractible and, therefore, can also often be safeguarded *ex ante*. The more the pertinent contracting issues can be addressed and formalized *ex ante*, the more the contract acquires the characteristics of a *complete contract*.

Not everything about a relationship is contractible. Noncontractibility typically arises when the desired outcomes of contracting are uncertain. For example, a high-technology firm can use employment contracts to hire R&D experts to work on various development projects. Whereas the firms' managers and the hired R&D experts can further formally agree on the scale and the scope of the R&D efforts, the outcomes of these uncertain innovation efforts tend to be noncontractible. For example, the contracting parties cannot (or at least probably should not try to) contract for the number of patents filed or the amount of revenue the new products and services developed will create. These are issues that must be addressed *ex post*. Similarly, a team of cofounders may agree that their startup will seek to be acquired by a large incumbent, but the exact timeline and the sale price are *ex ante* noncontractible.

Noncontractible does not mean nonaddressable. When an issue is noncontractible, it simply means that instead of approaching the governance of the relationship in terms of a formal *ex ante* contract, the designer must think of ways in which emergent issues will be addressed through *ex post* adjustment. In the following, we discuss two examples.

Ex Post Adjustment in Risky R&D Projects

In chapter 3, we presented R&D collaboration as an example of a situation in which efficient contracting is relevant. Specifically, to manage uncertain interfirm collaboration, the designer must determine whether a joint equity alliance offers a more efficient approach to adapting to uncertainty than collaborative contracting. This question effectively presents two governance options as alternatives: one emphasizes an *ex ante* contract and the other *ex post* adjustment.

That collaborative contracting presents the *ex ante* alternative is straightforward. Those engaging in R&D collaboration agree to an *ex ante* contract that stipulates the rights and the responsibilities of both parties. In case something unexpected that is not covered by the contract emerges, the contracting parties must adjust the contract through *ex post* negotiation. The *ex post* adjustments effectively create a new *ex ante* contract to be enforced in the future. Even though adjustments are made *ex post*, the general idea is to address problems by *ex ante* specification.

Adjusting formal contracts becomes cumbersome in collaborations beset with high uncertainty and ambiguity. Instead of seeking "to contract the noncontractible," the collaborating parties may decide to choose a governance structure that assigns the decision rights over *ex post* adjustments to a separate legal entity. In R&D collaboration, a joint equity alliance constitutes such an entity. In a joint equity alliance, considerations that are *ex ante* contractible are embedded in the alliance's founding documents. However, instead of trying to anticipate the potentially numerous *ex post* adjustments *ex ante*, the designer assigns the decision rights over the requisite adjustments to the alliance, more specifically, to its board of directors. The board will convene whenever an issue requires attention and then either addresses the issues directly or delegates them to the alliance's management. Under conditions of high uncertainty, this governance arrangement can be more efficient than collaborative contracting.

Ex Post Adjustments in Determining Share Prices in Unlisted Companies

How do shareholders of unlisted companies determine the price at which shares are bought and sold? In contrast with publicly traded companies where shares have an unambiguous market price, determining the share price of a closed corporation requires an explicit valuation procedure. Even though the share price at any future date is *ex ante* noncontractible, there are ways in which a forward-looking designer can address noncontractibility *ex ante*. This merits attention, because as legal scholar John Ghinger (1974, 225) noted, the way shareholders' agreements approach noncontractibility leaves much to be desired:

It is ironic that lawyers who are extremely careful in the conception and drafting of transfer restrictions and death buy-out provisions are content to permit the most significant provisions of the agreement, those dealing with purchase price and payment thereof, to speak loosely in terms of "book value," "annual installments," and the like.

When the buyer and the seller enter the transaction voluntarily, the requisite *ex post* adjustment will occur autonomously as the buying and the selling parties negotiate the price—no additional safeguards are required. But how should the organization safeguard situations in which transfer of shares is involuntary? For example, a shareholders' agreement may stipulate that shareholders who violate the shareholders' agreement must relinquish their shares. However, instead of adopting purchase price provisions based on potentially vague terms such as *fair value*, an informed shareholders' agreement might stipulate the procedure by which shares will be valued in the case of an involuntary transfer. Agreeing on the procedures would likely not solve all problems, but it would make the *ex post* decision of share price determination easier compared to a situation in which the shareholders' agreement stipulated purchase "at fair value." The valuation of young firms is particularly challenging because cash flows are uncertain, and the book value of assets is likely not a useful measure. Agreeing on the basic rules by which the value of the underlying business would be calculated paves the way toward an informed analysis.

Even though all *ex post* adjustments are ultimately a matter of reacting to unexpected events as they occur, giving them *ex ante* attention by agreeing on the procedures that will be followed in the case an adjustment is required has one substantial advantage. Specifically, when the contracting parties address potential *ex post* adjustments *ex ante*, they share a common interest of defining what is fair from the point of view of the organization. Once an actual dispute occurs, entrenched positions quickly emerge as the disputing parties feel compelled to defend their own positions. It is more efficient to agree on the rules of conflict resolution before disputes occur, that is, when the transacting parties view potential (not actual) disputes from behind what philosopher John Rawls (1999) called the *veil of ignorance*. When the contracting parties do not know how they themselves might be affected, "they are obliged to evaluate principles solely on the basis of general considerations" (Rawls 1999, 118).

Enforceability of Private Ordering

Overzealous and uninformed reliance on private ordering may lead to unenforceable contracts. To be sure, safeguards that provide a false sense of security can be significant sources of inefficiency. The contractual hazard is pronounced in situations in which young, inexperienced entrepreneurs launch their first startup. Strapped for cash, the cofounders may choose to work out the foundational contractual arrangements without the assistance and expertise of legal counsel. However, the decision to avoid *ex ante* transaction costs may be myopic and, consequently, result in considerable *ex post* transaction costs.

Whenever contracting parties agree to do something that is inconsistent with the law, the law prevails. Although this point may seem self-evident, sometimes determining what is and what is not consistent with the law is not straightforward. Misguided entrepreneurs may think that all they need do is ensure that they know "what the law says." In reality, the letter of the law often provides merely broad guidelines, which will then be interpreted in specific cases.

The designer must exercise caution whenever private ordering seeks to adjust or to override either the legal rights or the legal obligations of the contracting parties. Uninformed designers may engage in excessive (and wasteful) private ordering that ultimately infringes on the legal rights of the contracting parties. A common misconception is to think that as long as all contracting parties enter into the agreement voluntarily, the contract will be enforced by the courts as well. Two examples illustrate that this assumption may not hold.

Contracting for Market Failure? Limits on the Right to Buy and Sell Property

It is understandable that the cofounders of a high-risk startup firm will want to safeguard against the intrusion of unwanted new shareholders. The designer may also want to decide whether individual shareholders can exit the firm by taking advantage of private information and selling all shares to a third party, leaving other shareholders "stuck" with the new investor. Although some restrictions may be desirable, the designer must tread carefully not to excessively limit the transferability of stock. Ghinger (1974, 215) noted that when courts are asked to assess the reasonableness of restrictions placed on the transfer of shares, "it is certain that any absolute prohibition against transfer will fail." Indeed, absolute prohibition would effectively be the equivalent of contracting for market failure: There might be a situation in which a buyer and a seller have agreed on a price at which the shares would be transferred from the seller to the buyer, but a contractual restriction prevented the transaction, effectively inducing a market failure.

In the case of limiting transferability of shares, limitations based on the principle of equal treatment of all shareholders are usually not only legally sanctioned but also efficient, forward-looking governance. Equal treatment is at the heart of tag-along and drag-along clauses described earlier. Tag-along clauses ensure that no shareholder is allowed to benefit from private information at the expense of the others; drag-along clauses prevent an individual shareholder from holding the others hostage. Tag-along and drag-along clauses help build startup credibility in the eyes of particularly those who join the firm simply as investors, that is, residual claimants who seek no role in management or oversight. Courts tend to view both tag-along and drag-along clauses as reasonable and justified restrictions on the transfer of shares.

Can the Parties Privately Contract Not to Sue One Another?

Many shareholders' agreements contain a clause that requires disputes to be resolved through private ordering, most commonly by binding arbitration. The sentiment is salient, but the implications are not. Does this mean the contracting parties have abdicated their right to sue one another no matter what? What if there is a reason to suspect one contracting party has acted illegally? The issue is complex because making a promise not to sue and, symmetrically, receiving assurances that one will not be sued, are both legally problematic. If one party decides not to honor the agreement not to sue, will the courts enforce the mutual commitment to private ordering? They may not.

A shareholders' agreement by which shareholders commit to alternative dispute resolution should not be viewed as a legally binding obligation to use private ordering in all disputes. For example, by signing a shareholders' agreement with an arbitration clause, shareholders do not relinquish their right to sue the board of directors for violations of their fiduciary duty, nor do they preempt shareholders from filing a police report if they have a reason to believe that the board has committed a criminal act. In the United States for instance, the First Amendment to the Constitution protects "the right to petition the Government for a redress of grievances." Any private contract that limits this right is profoundly problematic.

On the issue of what can be privately contracted, we counsel the designer to avoid optimism and to err on the side of caution: If in doubt, assume the safeguard is *less* effective than intended. For example, agreeing on binding arbitration should be viewed as a sincere wish to settle conflicts privately, not as a legally binding contract that the courts will uphold. Whether a specific clause in a contract is enforceable is not up to the contracting parties, or sometimes even an arbitrator, to decide: "[A]rbitrators cannot arbitrate disputes where shareholders seek the rescission of the very shareholders' agreement which empowers the arbitrators to intervene" (Brownlee 1994, 309).

Finally, legal scholar Owen Fiss (1984) offers an intriguing angle to private-ordering approaches that merits attention. Fiss (1984, 1085) argued against alternative dispute resolution because it exhibited the same shortcomings as plea bargaining:

> Settlement is for me the civil analogue of plea bargaining: Consent is often coerced; the bargain may be struck by someone without authority; the absence of a trial and judgment renders subsequent judicial involvement troublesome; and although dockets are trimmed, justice may not be done. Like plea bargaining, settlement is a capitulation to the conditions of mass society and should be neither encouraged nor praised.

The proposition that there are situations in which justice may be more important than peace is worth the designer's consideration.

Assignment of *Ex Post* Decision Rights

Whenever the future is uncertain and contracts materially incomplete, the need for *ex post* adjustments arises. When an issue is not *ex ante* contractible, the designer must decide how to allocate the residual rights of control efficiently (Grossman and Hart 1986, 696). For example, who should have the authority to make the following adjustment decisions?

1. Increase the size of the board of directors.
2. Appoint a board member.
3. Change the way by which disputes are resolved.
4. Adopt antitakeover provisions (see chapter 7).
5. Adjust the way by which fair value of equity is determined in a closed corporation.

All these *ex post* adjustment decisions, and scores of others, require the designer's attention at the founding of the organization. Even though the specific adjustment decisions are made *ex post*, the designer must create the requisite *ex ante* rules that govern how these decisions will be made and by whom. In Efficiency Lens terms, principles of oversight regarding adjustments must be delineated *ex ante* to guide *ex post* management decisions.

Which Residual Rights Are the Board's Prerogative?

In limited liability companies, *ex ante* decisions regarding residual rights of control commonly involve deciding which issues require shareholder approval and which are the prerogative of the board of directors. Giving the board too little, or too much, power can lead to significant inefficiencies. On the one hand, if boards have too little power, decision-making becomes cumbersome. Stringent limits on the board's ability to act unilaterally also send a mixed signal to board members: Why does the designer grant a group of persons a central fiduciary role only to strip them of the authority to make decisions? Does the designer trust the board or not? Moreover, if the board has only limited discretion, will it ultimately be held responsible for something over which it has no control? Here, understanding the essentially fiduciary (not contractual) role of the board is crucial—the board cannot privately contract out of its legal duties to the organization. On the other hand, if the board has too much power, entrenchment and agency problems may pose serious hazards. We return to the topic of entrenchment when we discuss antitakeover provisions in chapter 7.

Summary: Understanding Governance by Contract

This chapter on incipient organizations complements chapter 3, which addressed contractual relationships within and across organizations. In this chapter, we emphasize the importance of viewing the incipient organization through the lens of "governance by contract" (Fisch 2018). To this end, the designer has three tasks:

1. identify which issues are *ex ante* contractible and for which efficient *ex ante* safeguards can be implemented;

2. identify which issues are not *ex ante* contractible but require *ex post* adjustment; and

3. allocate the residual rights of control regarding potential *ex post* adjustments.

We caution against excessive optimism regarding the efficiency of *ex ante* contracting. A significant hazard arises from mistakenly thinking that the *ex ante* contractible is also *ex post* enforceable. Not falling prey to a false sense of security requires an understanding of the limits that the institutional environment sets on private ordering. This issue likely requires legal expertise and experience in the specific jurisdiction in which the organization is embedded. Even though spending precious shareholders' equity on lawyer's fees at the founding of a startup sounds unappealing, these fees likely pale in comparison with the *ex post* adjustment costs that arise when the contracting parties realize that their contracts are materially unenforceable.

We similarly counsel against overlooking the importance of conscious foresight regarding *ex post* adjustments. Specifically, the general principles by which *ex post* adjustments are made should be considered matters of *ex ante* agreement. Although designers cannot provide *ex ante* solutions to *ex post* problems, they can, and should, agree on which procedures will be followed and who exercises the residual rights of control in these procedures. When residual rights of control are poorly defined, a common problem we have witnessed is that shareholders adopt the attitude that the board of directors is directly responsible only to them and that they can give the board advice with the expectation that the advice is always to be followed. However, the idea that the board (the fiduciary of the organization) is accountable only to shareholders (merely one of the stakeholders of the organization) is problematic. This notion further becomes untenable when ownership is fragmented, and consequently, shareholder interests are not only heterogeneous but also potentially conflicting. In addressing the potentially volatile situation of conflicting interests, both the designer and the board can take comfort in the fact that there is nothing in corporate law that establishes the board's exclusive accountability to shareholders. The board is well advised to give attention to shareholders, but this must be done without compromising the two essential characteristics of the fiduciary role: independent judgment and responsibility jointly to *all* residual claimants (Blair and Stout 2001).

7

The Expanding Organization

As organizations expand, they experience two dynamics, which can both be described using the Efficiency Lens. The more intuitive of the two is what we label the *growth dynamic*, which refers to the increasing scale and scope of management, oversight, and risk:

1. When the organization grows, planning and coordination challenges become more complex. To adapt to the expanding scale and scope, the organization decentralizes, adds vertical layers to its structure, establishes lateral cross-unit linkages to enhance collaboration, and so on. Furthermore, international expansion and product diversification may prompt the organization to adopt a multidimensional matrix structure with complex reporting relationships. These are examples of the expanding scale and scope of management.

2. As the organization grows, it needs both to deepen and to broaden the mechanisms by which it exercises oversight over management. The organization adds more members to its board of directors, amends its bylaws, and implements oversight functions at all levels of the organization: The board of directors exercises oversight over the top management team, top management team over divisional management, divisional management over functional management, and so on. As Jensen and Meckling (1976, 309) aptly noted, principal-agent relationships exist *at every level of management in all organizations*, which also gives rise to the need for oversight at all levels. Finally, as a closed corporation goes public through an IPO, the institutional environment starts to impose more elaborate disclosure requirements on the organization. These are examples of the expanding scale and scope of oversight.

3. As a limited liability company raises more equity to finance its operations, the scale of its investor risk increases. Scope of risk expands as well through various fundamental transformations that convert some employee groups, key suppliers, and large customers into stakeholders

Efficient Organization. Mikko Ketokivi and Joseph T. Mahoney, Oxford University Press. © Oxford University Press 2023.
DOI: 10.1093/oso/9780197610282.003.0007

over time (see chapter 4). Commitments to specificity through relation-specific investments lead to bilateral dependency that broadens the pool of constituencies with a residual interest. These are examples of the expanding scale and scope of risk.

The growth dynamic has been thoroughly covered in the published literature on organization design, most notably under the rubric of *organizational redesign*. Since we have little to add to the conversations on the general challenges of the expanding scale and scope of organizations, we direct the reader to excellent treatments of this topic in the published literature.[1]

In this chapter, we focus on the more elusive *separation dynamic*. An expanding limited liability company offers an illustration. As the company expands, the scale of its oversight increases, which is manifested by the addition of members to the board of directors. However, because the new members are increasingly likely to be outsiders (particularly if the firm is heading toward an IPO), the expansion of oversight tends to be associated with the separation of oversight from management. An obvious manifestation of separation is the declining proportion of insiders on the board of directors. Moreover, as the number of individuals and collectives who bear risk increases, not everyone can be afforded (or even wants) an oversight role. This effectively separates oversight from risk. Finally, as those who make the most important strategic decisions bear a smaller portion of the wealth consequences of their decisions, management and risk become separated as well. Figure 7.1 illustrates the mutually reinforcing role of the growth and the separation dynamics. Specifically, expansion of management, oversight, and risk occurs in directions that leads to increasing separation.

The reason we focus in this chapter on the separation dynamic is twofold. One is that it has received less attention than the growth dynamic in the organization design and governance literature. The other reason is that we find the separation dynamic to be in many ways more foundational to governance than the growth dynamic. Indeed, the separation of ownership and control has stood at the very foundation of corporate governance for nearly a century. In their classic *The Modern Corporation and Private Property*, legal scholar

---

[1] Excellent practitioner-oriented texts on the managerial challenges of organizational growth are organization design scholar Jay Galbraith's two books *Designing Matrix Organizations That Really Work* (Galbraith 2009) and *Designing Organizations* (Galbraith 2014). The rich literature on scaling up organizations is also relevant; we recommend in particular *The Founder's Dilemmas* (Wasserman 2012). More academically oriented works include the 1959 classic *The Theory of the Growth of the Firm* (Penrose [1959] 1995) and *Scale and Scope* (Chandler 1990).

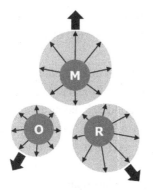

As the organization expands, management, oversight, and risk not only expand in scale and scope (the growth dynamic) but also tend to start to separate from one another (the separation dynamic).

Management, oversight, and risk tend to expand in directions that enhance their separation.

Figure 7.1 The growth dynamic and the separation dynamic of the expanding organization

Adolf Berle and economist Gardiner Means (1932, 7) noted that "[t]he separation of ownership from control produces a condition where the interests of owner and of ultimate manager may, and often do, diverge, and where many of the checks which formerly operated to limit the use of power disappear."

The separation dynamic continues to be essential to governance because it presents the designer with a dilemma, succinctly expressed by Grossman and Hart (1980, 42): "In all but the smallest groups social choice takes place via the delegation of power from many to few. A fundamental problem with this delegation is that no individual has a large enough incentive to devote resources to ensuring that the representatives are acting in the interest of the represented." The reason this fundamental problem constitutes a dilemma is that although separation of powers and delegation are necessary, monitoring the actions of those to whom decision-making is delegated becomes cumbersome with increasing separation. A case in point, when those who make the most important decisions no longer bear the wealth consequences of their decisions (management separates from risk), how can those who bear risk ensure adequate oversight? Furthermore, how do those who bear risk ensure that those to whom oversight is delegated genuinely adopt a fiduciary role? We unfortunately have plenty of evidence that the separation of powers gives rise to various hazards.

Understanding separation as a dynamic phenomenon is crucial because separation of powers is not how organizations are born. In an incipient organization, the small group of individuals who make the most important decisions tend to exercise oversight over their decisions and be the principal risk-bearers. Even the largest of organizations started small:

> Cofounders Larry Page and Sergey Brin started in their Stanford dorm rooms by building an internet search engine that they brought to market as Google. The "two Steves"—Jobs and Wozniak—started by building a computer circuit board, Apple I, and selling Jobs' VW microbus and Wozniak's calculator to begin funding its production. (Pollman 2019, 166)

The separation dilemma emerges over time as the organization expands and delegation becomes necessary. Importantly, the necessity for separation emerges not only due to the increasing scale and scope of the organization but also as something that is mandated by the organization's environment. For example, before a closed corporation can be listed on a stock exchange, it must clearly separate oversight from management by having the majority of board members be independent. The separation dynamic therefore offers further insight into the interplay of the contractual and the institutional pillars.

Addressing the Separation Dilemma

In the seven-year period spanning from the founding to the IPO, Tesla Motors raised a total of $200 million of equity in a total of six funding events (Series A through F). In the later financing rounds, Tesla's ownership was opened to external investors. Concurrently with the broadening ownership base, the composition of Tesla's board of directors expanded from a board of three cofounders—Marc Eberhard, Elon Musk, and Marc Tarpenning—to a board with nine members. Predictably, the addition of board members occurred in lockstep with the addition of shareholders. For example, in Series B, Valor Equity became a shareholder and its owner Antonio Gracias a board member; in Series C, Draper Fisher and VantagePoint became shareholders, both appointing a board member. The first independent board member was not appointed until Series F. Concomitantly with Series F, Tesla also established an audit committee, a compensation committee, and a nomination committee to its board. Various board committees were established in preparation for the IPO.[2]

---

[2] Nasdaq corporate governance guidelines require that a corporation listed on the Nasdaq stock exchange have audit and compensation committees that consist of exclusively independent directors. Having a nomination committee is optional.

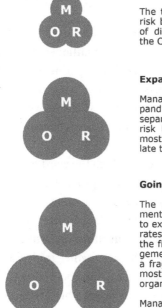

Founding (2003)

The three founders are the primary risk bearers and populate the board of directors; one founder becomes the CEO.

Expansion (2003-2009)

Management, oversight, and risk expand in scale and scope, but no separation of the three emerges: risk bearers continue to make the most important decisions and populate the board of directors.

Going Public (2010)

The scale and scope of management, oversight, and risk continue to expand, but in the IPO, risk separates materially from management: the financial consequences of management decisions are now borne by a fragmented group of shareholders most of whom have no role in the organization.

Management may continue its participation in oversight, but is demoted to a minority role.

Figure 7.2 Tesla's expansion viewed through the Efficiency Lens

Viewing Tesla's expansion through the Efficiency Lens is straightforward. As Tesla expanded, it followed a simple rule: Gradually separate management, oversight, and risk from one another. There was no material separation of the three either during Tesla's founding or during the first years of its expansion. To be sure, the scale and the scope of management, oversight, and risk increased: The scale and the scope of Tesla's operations were increased, more board members were added, and more equity was raised. At the same time, a close examination of the Series A through F issues and the concomitant changes in Tesla's governance show that during the early years of Tesla's expansion, management, oversight, and risk remained concentrated around a small number of individuals and investors. Separation did not become necessary until Tesla headed to its IPO in 2009. Figure 7.2 summarizes Tesla's path from the founding to the IPO, viewed through the Efficiency Lens.

Why Going Public Requires Separation

When a limited liability company goes public, it starts to offer its shares to anyone willing to pay the market price. As we have mentioned earlier, the word *public* is a misnomer in the sense that limited liability companies remain privately owned even when shares are publicly traded. It seems misdirected to use the word *public* to describe an organization when the word is merely a characteristic of the institutional context (the stock exchange) in which private transactions are executed.

At the same time, there are two senses in which the word *public*, although not strictly speaking descriptively accurate, does provide a useful label. One is that publicly traded securities are no longer an exclusively private concern. For one, although the exchange of publicly traded securities involves private actors, trading takes place in a centralized institutional setting—the stock exchange. In the stock exchange, securities are further traded at a market price. The task of the stock exchange, as an organization, is to ensure price integrity. A common threat to price integrity arises from asymmetric information, that is, corporate insiders being better informed about the future prospects than outsiders. Asymmetric information should give the stock exchange an incentive to regulate, monitor, and disclose to the public especially those transactions that involve organizational insiders. Regulation, monitoring, and disclosure can aptly be described as activities that benefit the public. Asymmetric information is not a problem in a closed corporation where those who trade shares are insiders and where a tag-along clause in the shareholders' agreement (see chapter 6) offers a safeguard to the comparatively less-informed shareholders. The word *public* is useful also in the sense that publicly traded corporations are subject to more public scrutiny than closed corporations. For example, legislation places significantly more stringent disclosure requirements on publicly traded firms.

For the stock exchange, as an organization, probity (see chapter 5) is essential. It is one thing for an individual corporation to lose credibility by failing to maintain its integrity as an organization, but it is quite another if this happens to an organization such as a stock exchange. The stock market is an indispensable source of risky financing to companies seeking funding for highly specific assets and projects. Its failure can have devastating ripple effects on industries, even entire societies. Proper functioning of the stock exchange is not only a matter of getting the prices of the traded securities right, but also a matter of the integrity of the organization. The Supreme

Court described the importance of probity of the stock exchange: "It requires but little appreciation of the extent of the Exchange's economic power and of what happened in this country during the 1920's and 1930's to realize how essential it is that the highest ethical standards prevail as to every aspect of the Exchange's activities."[3]

Establishing and maintaining integrity activates both the contractual and the institutional pillars. Stock exchanges must not only be sufficiently regulated by the authorities (the institutional pillar), but they also have to engage in self-regulation (the contractual pillar) by monitoring those whose shares are traded on the exchange. To this end, stock exchanges have explicit, elaborate rules that listed companies must follow. Many of these rules address the characteristics of the securities themselves, but for our purposes, the rules regarding corporate governance are the most relevant. Some of the rules warrant attention here because they shed light on the changes that must occur in corporate governance at an IPO.

The Importance of Independent Oversight

When management, oversight, and risk expand in scale and scope, there is a natural drift toward greater separation of the three. In addition, the organization's environment starts to impose various independence and separation-of-powers requirements. For example, Nasdaq and New York Stock Exchange (NYSE) require that the majority of board members be independent. Independence involves a number of both formal and informal requirements. Not having an employment relationship is a good example of a formal, "bright-line" requirement of independence. To qualify as independent, neither the board member nor his or her family members can have had an employment relationship with the company within the last three years.[4]

However, establishing independence is not simply a matter of ticking the proper boxes to establish formal independence; the essence of independence resides in directors using independent *judgment*. The main concern is that the

---

[3] Silver v. N.Y. Stock Exch., 373 U.S. 341 (1963).

[4] Just to show how detailed the requirements are, Nasdaq Rule 5605 provides an exhaustive list of people who are considered family members: "a person's spouse, parents, children, siblings, mothers- and fathers-in-law, sons- and daughters-in-law, brothers- and sisters-in-law, and anyone (other than domestic employees) who shares the person's home."

nonindependence of a director may interfere with the exercise of independent judgment. Yet, independent judgment is so foundational that we promote it as the most important tool in addressing the separation dilemma: Those exercising oversight in the organization must genuinely embrace their fiduciary role.

The importance of implementing a sound process for selecting board members cannot be overstated. In his pioneering analysis of boards of directors, legal and management scholar Myles Mace (1971) made a number of observations that should give us pause. Mace's central conclusion was that boards were often unduly influenced and controlled by CEOs, which raised the concern that oversight and management might not be sufficiently separated. For example, CEOs might be able to exert influence on the selection of board members and often also set the board's agenda, particularly if the CEO also chaired the board. Mace's (1971, 205–06) conclusion regarding board members' ability to monitor management was equally disconcerting: "A few board members ask discerning questions. Most do not."

The issues Mace identified may not pose a hazard in closed corporations, but they can be toxic to the credibility of an open, publicly traded corporation. Many of the corporate scandals at the turn of the millennium—Enron, Tyco, WorldCom, and many others—had the common denominator of insufficient *de facto* separation of powers and inadequate oversight. Insufficient separation of management and oversight is untenable in situations where the majority of risk-bearers are members of neither management nor oversight and yet, bear the brunt of the financial consequences of bad management decisions.[5]

An alternative would be to ensure that the largest shareholders have representation on the board, thus keeping oversight and risk in lockstep as the organization expands. This was indeed the case in Tesla's expansion where each financing round prior to the IPO occurred with the simultaneous addition of new board members representing the incoming investors. However, whereas keeping risk and oversight in lockstep is feasible prior to the IPO, it is no longer an option for open corporations whose ownership becomes unavoidably fragmented. With the exception of Elon Musk who owns about 20 percent of Tesla's shares, the largest individual shareholders own just a few percent stake.

---

[5] At Tesla, this concern is alleviated because CEO Elon Musk is Tesla's largest shareholder with 23.1 percent of all outstanding shares (as of June 30, 2021). This means that at Tesla, management and risk are not as clearly separated as they are, say, at Apple, whose CEO Tim Cook owns only 0.02 percent of all shares (as of December 28, 2020), which is more typical of large, open corporations. Due to a lower separation of management and risk, Tesla is an organizationally exceptional open corporation.

Why should someone with, say, a 5 percent stake in the corporation get to appoint a board member? This issue leads to what we view as the most fundamental question in board composition: Does stakeholder representation on boards enhance efficiency? We have covered this issue in chapter 4 in the discussion of the *dilemma of stakeholder participation*. In the following, we extend this discussion by introducing another complicating factor—the separation hazard.

The Separation Hazard

Consider a small startup firm where five cofounders contribute the requisite equity, three form the board of directors, and one board member becomes a full-time employee. The startup, as an organization, is best described as a cooperative agreement among a small group of individuals all of whom have a residual interest and bear residual risk. The concern for agency problems is negligible, because for all practical governance purposes, principals act as their own agents. If the board holds the voting majority of shares, every board meeting is *de facto* a shareholders' meeting. Concerns for asymmetric information are further alleviated by the tag-along clause and potential economic holdup problems are preempted by the drag-along clause in the shareholders' agreement.

When management, oversight, and risk are not materially separated, everyone involved in the organization is readily incentivized to do what is best for the organization. This alignment does not mean that everyone wants exactly the same thing; indeed, cofounders often disagree on issues. But conflicts among known individuals with everyone committed to risk are more likely to be manifestations of honest disagreements than opportunistic attempts at seeking private benefits at the expense of other cofounders.

The separation of management, oversight, and risk involves a number of fundamental changes to the organization. One immediate consequence of separation is that principal-agent relationships emerge throughout the organization. Consequently, those in charge of oversight at various levels of the organization find themselves monitoring individuals who have merely an employment relationship with the organization; the fraction of employees who are also residual claimants rapidly declines. As the organization expands further, the board finds itself no longer controlling the majority of votes at the shareholders' meeting. Finally, before a private limited liability company can go public, the majority of its board members must be independent. These phenomena are familiar in expanding organizations.

When an organization expands, it no longer exhibits many of the characteristics of what we colloquially ascribe to an organization: unity of purpose, stable and unambiguous participation, and, most importantly, a clear distinction of what is "inside" versus "outside" the organization. As the organization expands, organizational boundaries become elusive as individuals and collectives participate in the organization's activities in various roles and in varying degrees. Some are merely passive investors entitled to residual payments; others are full-time employees who are guaranteed fixed payments. Here, it is useful to think of the organization as the interconnection of diverse contracting relationships the organization has with its constituencies, that is, as a *nexus of contracts*. In the nexus-of-contracts thinking, the organization itself is viewed merely as a "fictional entity" that consists of "a complex process in which the conflicting objectives of individuals (some of whom may 'represent' other organizations) are brought into equilibrium within a framework of contractual relations" (Jensen and Meckling 1976, 311).

Invoking the nexus-of-contracts analogy can be instructive in developing an understanding of the contractual aspects of the organization in general and the separation dynamic in particular. The nexus-of-contracts analogy invites the designer to view the organization and its constituencies as a collection of diverse contractual relationships where distinct rights and responsibilities are defined for the transacting parties (fig. 7.3). The heterogeneity observed in these rights and responsibilities is a direct consequence of the separation dynamic. More generally, the nexus-of-contracts analogy invites us to think of the organization not in terms of entities but in terms of contractual relationships.

Some of the contracts in the nexus are written, formal, *ex ante* contracts; buyer-supplier contracts, employment contracts, and loan agreements are representative examples of formal contracts based on private ordering. Other relationships should be considered contractual even in the absence of a formal contract; the residual claimancy of shareholders is the most salient example. Finally, some contracts in the nexus are more accurately described as obligations that originate in the institutional environment; tax liabilities are a good example. All these examples describe relationships between the organization and one of its constituencies, which can all be usefully examined in terms of the rights and the obligations they bestow on the exchange parties.

Note that the board of directors does not appear explicitly in figure 7.3. This deliberate omission is consistent with our premise that the relationship

Figure 7.3 The organization as a nexus of contracts

between the organization and those in charge of central oversight should not be viewed in contractual terms. In the nexus-of-contracts analogy, the main task of the board of directors is to ensure that the nexus *in its entirety* is efficient. Accordingly, it is useful to think of the board of directors as a trustee of the nexus itself: The board's role is to engage in "other-regarding behavior" (Blair and Stout 2001, 404) to ensure the efficiency of all contracts the legal entity has with its constituencies. Given this fiduciary role, it is straightforward to see why the board of directors should remain independent and not become a stakeholder in the organization.[6]

When decision-making powers, monitoring, and risk-bearing are concentrated in a small number of actors, the nexus is comparatively simple.

---

[6] The idea that the board of directors should be considered a fiduciary of the entire organization as opposed to being merely a representative or an agent of shareholders is not novel. Already in 1932, legal scholar Merrick Dodd (1932) argued that in specializing in various organization-specific tasks, employees may *de facto* invest in the organization in a way that is analogous with the investments made by shareholders. Commitments to specificity create a residual interest that requires the designer's attention. Dodd's ideas have been further expanded and elaborated by Clark (1985) and Blair and Stout (1999, 2001), among many others.

Delegation is trivial as those involved in the organization are entitled to participate in the central decisions and bear the economic consequences of their choices. But when the organization grows and powers start to separate, some delegation of decision rights becomes necessary. Especially when risk becomes materially separated from management, executives will be able to make decisions on behalf of the risk-bearers without their explicit approval. Without the requisite safeguards, this can give rise to organizational hazards.

Another issue that adds to the separation hazard has to do with asymmetric information arising from the separation of management and oversight. What are the chances that a very busy director who spends roughly one day a month attending to the organization's issues is able to effectively monitor the decisions of a manager who, in stark contrast, spends all the days in the month managing the organization? Mace's (1971, 205–06) observations regarding the reality of boards are just as relevant today as they were in 1971: Board members are very busy executives whose motivation and time to serve as directors of other companies is highly limited. Because of this limitation, many of those tasked with oversight lack even the basic competence of being able to ask management discerning questions.

In sum, when the organization expands its scale and scope, its members specialize in different roles, decision-making powers are delegated, and diverse principal-agent relationships emerge throughout the organization. Consequently, the organization becomes fragmented in a number of ways. In the following section, we examine the implications of such fragmentation in the context of ownership changes. Whereas changes in ownership may occur in all organizations, they are particularly relevant in expanding organizations that are more likely to experience recurring, both incremental and radical, changes in ownership. Furthermore, although most changes in ownership are desirable and benefit all constituencies, others involve various degrees of "hostility" that affect the participants of the nexus in drastically different ways. A forward-looking designer must think of proper safeguards in case there are "hostile" buyers in the market for organizations.

Changes in Ownership in the Market for Organizations

Just like contracting parties exchange products and services with one another in markets for products, organizations can be bought and sold in the market for organizations. Mergers, acquisitions, takeovers, and leveraged buyouts are examples of exchange where the object of the exchange is an organization, or a part of it.

It is useful to think of the acquisition of an organization by another as the acquisition not of assets but of central decision rights. This way of thinking is particularly fitting in contexts in which the target is an organization where fixed assets are not central; a professional service firm is a representative example. When a large law firm acquires a smaller firm, it does not acquire ownership of the smaller firm's lawyers but does obtain the rights to plan and coordinate their activities. However, as we discussed in chapter 1, even in the case of organizations with fixed assets, the essence of ownership resides not in the title to the assets but in the rights to make decisions regarding their use; both decision rights and residual rights of control. Furthermore, because the market for organizations tends to be especially relevant in the context of limited liability companies, we typically speak not of the market for organizations, but of the *market for corporate control* (Manne 1965; Jensen and Ruback 1983).

Expansion is often a sign of success, or at least, potential for success. Firms with a promising future are more likely to attract potential buyers. Moreover, because expansion is also associated with increasing organizational fragmentation and hazards, the potential buyer may also be able to take over the organization without the approval of some of its stakeholders. The designer's task is to ensure that the decision to be acquired is made by the explicit approval of the organization's key fiduciary, its board of directors. The designer's task is therefore to ensure that in the event of an acquisition, the fiduciary has the requisite bargaining power to negotiate with the buyer to act in the best interest of the organization.

Wanted vs. Unwanted Acquisitions

To be sure, the market for corporate control can serve a useful purpose (Manne 1965). If organizations are traded between voluntary participants on an open market, the ownership and control of organizations are more likely to end up in the hands of those who value them the most. For example, the leadership of one firm may look at a smaller competitor and conclude that its value-creating activities can be improved or that economies of scope can be realized by the merger of the two companies.

In discussing changes in ownership, we often make the distinction between "friendly" and "hostile" takeovers. A takeover is "friendly" when the acquirer approaches the target's board of directors in good faith; in a "hostile" takeover, the acquirer bypasses the target's board of directors and makes offers to purchase shares directly to the target's shareholders. If the "hostile" buyer is successful in purchasing a majority of the shares, it can proceed to replace the target's board of directors (and subsequently management) without the target's approval.

We submit that directing attention only to the buyer's motivations and actions results in an understanding of acquisitions that is partial at best and misguided at worst. To understand an acquisition in its entirety, we must also incorporate the motivations and the actions of those who negotiate on behalf of the target. Just like the representatives of the acquirer, the representatives of the target may or may not act in good faith. Instead of making its decisions by incorporating the interests of the entire nexus of contracts, the target's board may engage in self-serving and entrenched behaviors. To incorporate both the target and the acquirer side to the analysis, we propose that the friendly/hostile distinction be replaced by the wanted/unwanted distinction (table 7.1). A takeover is wanted when both the acquirer and the target negotiate voluntarily and in good faith; if either party is an unwilling participant or either side acts in bad faith, the takeover is unwanted.

We present the wanted/unwanted distinction with an important caveat. The designer should not think of takeovers as categorically being either wanted or unwanted. No matter how unwanted an acquisition is, at least 50 percent of the target's voting shareholders must deem it wanted, otherwise the acquisition will not take place. Similarly, no wanted acquisition enjoys the unconditional approval of all the target's and the acquirer's constituencies; Tesla's acquisition of SolarCity (see chapter 2) is a perfect example. The same caveat applies to the friendly/hostile distinction. In a hostile takeover, the acquirer exhibits hostility primarily toward the target's board of directors, not its shareholders, employees, or any other constituency. Furthermore, *disregard* might be descriptively a better word than *hostility* to describe the buyer's behavior toward the target's board.[7]

---

[7] We do not know where and how the word *hostile* entered into the antitakeover lexicon, although Orts (1992, 24) offered one plausible account in the US context. According to Orts, political constituents in the so-called rustbelt states (e.g., Pennsylvania, Ohio, and Illinois) believed that corporate takeovers posed a threat to the jobs in their states. These perceived threats fueled public measures to address takeovers, most notably antitakeover legislation in the form of *corporate constituency statutes*. Perhaps not surprisingly, Pennsylvania—not, say, Florida or Hawaii—was the first US state to adopt a constituency statute. However, protection against takeovers is for all practical purposes a matter of private ordering because constituency statutes permit *but do not obligate* directors to consider broader stakeholder interests. Incorporating a constituency statute into corporate governance is ultimately a matter of board discretion (Bebchuk and Tallarita 2020).

Table 7.1   A Comparison of Wanted and Unwanted Takeovers

Issue	Wanted takeover	Unwanted takeover
Mutual interest	Both the acquirer and the target act voluntarily	The target is an unwilling participant
Whom does the acquirer approach?	The target's board of directors	The target's shareholders
Bargaining power	The target's board of directors has sufficient bargaining power	The target's board of directors lacks bargaining power or is bypassed altogether
Whom does the target's board represent?	The target's entire nexus of contracts, those with a residual interest in particular	The target board's and management's entrenched interests
Reason for accepting an offer	The target's board concludes the offer is beneficial to those with a residual interest and the board's justification is supported by a shareholder majority	The acquirer secures a voting majority of shares without the target board's approval
Reason for rejecting an offer	The target's board concludes the offer is not in the best interest of those with a residual interest	Either the target's board is entrenched and rejects the offer out of self-interest, or the acquirer fails to acquire a voting majority of shares

The wanted/unwanted distinction elaborates the friendly/hostile distinction in two important ways. Specifically, whether a friendly or a hostile takeover attempt should be considered wanted or unwanted depends on the motivations on the target's side. A hostile takeover attempt may well be wanted if the target's board has entrenched itself and rejects all offers, including ones that would be beneficial to its residual claimants. The target's board might resist a takeover attempt simply because board membership may be a significant source of income to the board members. In a takeover, the target's board is often dismissed in its entirety, which means loss of income to its members. Similarly, a friendly takeover attempt may exhibit characteristics of an unwanted takeover if the target's board lacks bargaining power and, consequently, has trouble negotiating on behalf of the target's residual claimants.

Protection against Unwanted Takeover Attempts

We counsel the forward-looking designer to address the hazard of unwanted acquisitions already at the founding of the organization. To this end, the designer has two related objectives. One is ensuring that those exercising primary oversight in the organization authentically internalize their fiduciary role. The importance of independent judgment becomes pronounced in situations in which the organization becomes the target of unwanted acquisition attempts. Safeguards aimed at forcing all potential acquirers to negotiate with the target's board of directors provide protection against unwanted acquisitions.

The second objective is to ensure that when oversight and risk are separated, the board of directors maintains credibility in the eyes of the organization's residual claimants. In the case of takeovers, the importance of those residual claimants with decision and control rights—the shareholders—is paramount. Unwanted takeovers become impossible in situations in which a simple shareholder majority refuses to consider purchase offers that have not been approved by the target's board of directors.

Formulating the Main Problem

Just like all governance decisions, protection against unwanted takeovers requires the formulation of a main problem. Let us start at the general premise that the designer should safeguard those contractual relationships where vulnerability is present and suggest that this premise applies to changes in ownership as well. The key question therefore becomes, "Which relationships in the nexus become vulnerable in the event of an unwanted takeover attempt?"

Formal contracts are more likely to survive acquisitions. When one firm purchases another, it commonly purchases all the contracts in the nexus: buyer-supplier contracts, employment contracts, loan agreements, and so on. There is no immediate reason to assume that these formal contractual relationships will become jeopardized when ownership changes. In fact, the effect may be just the opposite, particularly in situations in which a comparatively smaller growing firm is purchased by a large incumbent. The acquisition may lead to better job security for employees, larger order volumes for suppliers, and lower probabilities of defaults on loans. Unless those with a formal contractual relationship also have a residual interest in the target, no additional safeguards are needed.

The situation is more complex with constituencies that have a residual interest in the target. In the event of an acquisition, this residual interest is either eliminated altogether or transformed into a residual interest in the acquiring organization. For example, in an all-stock acquisition, the target's shareholders exchange their shares in the target firm for shares in the acquiring firm. For this exchange to be in the best interest of the target's shareholders, the target's board must have sufficient bargaining power to negotiate on behalf of the target's shareholders. Not surprisingly, the main problem in protection against takeovers has conventionally been framed in shareholder terms: The organization should implement those antitakeover provisions that enhance the shareholders' bargaining power in the event of a takeover attempt.

Addressing the Main Problem

Suppose the designer decides that protection against unwanted takeovers is desirable. What are the design tools available to implement protection in the case of unwanted takeover attempts? In the following, we discuss two examples used to safeguard against hostile takeovers: staggered boards and the poison pill.[8]

Staggered Boards

The hostile acquirer's central objective is to replace the target's board of directors as rapidly as possible. The longer it takes to replace the board after an acquisition, the less economically attractive the target becomes to the hostile buyer. Consequently, an intuitive delay tactic for the target is to make the replacement of the board more difficult. This impediment can be achieved by adopting a *staggered board*. In a staggered board, only a certain portion

---

[8] There are numerous other antitakeover measures, such as dual class shares, supermajority merger approval provisions, fair-price amendments, reduction in cumulative voting provisions, and anti-greenmail provisions. Since covering all these in detail is outside the scope of this book, we recommend the following scholarly work on the topic (in chronological order): Grossman and Hart (1980), DeAngelo and Rice (1983), Jensen (1986), Hirshleifer and Sheridan (1992), Sundaramurthy, Mahoney, and Mahoney (1997), Bebchuk, Coates, and Subramanian (2002), Bebchuk (2003), Liu and Mulherin (2019). To complement these academically oriented texts, Larcker and Tayan (2015) offer an excellent text to practitioners.

of board seats are opened for reelection at the annual shareholders' meeting. Staggered boards are a common and effective form of protection adopted in the pre-IPO stage. In their empirical study of hostile bids, Bebchuk, Coates, and Subramanian (2002) found that not a single hostile bid was successful against well-structured staggered boards in the five-year period examined.[9]

The way staggering provides antitakeover protection is straightforward. However, whether any governance measure is ultimately efficient requires a broader consideration of the net impact. An undesirable consequence of staggering is that it effectively protects board members from being rapidly replaced. This protection is problematic, because any measure that makes a person, or a group of persons, more difficult to replace facilitates entrenchment. A staggered board may have the unintended consequence that the board may be reluctant to reject all acquisition offers, including ones that might be beneficial to shareholders.

The dilemma that staggering presents effectively highlights the importance of having an independent board that fully embraces its fiduciary duty. Anything that leads to the board developing a stakeholder relationship with the organization presents a hazard because the board may start acting in ways that is beneficial to the board as a stakeholder, not to the entire nexus of contracts. In their study of antitakeover provisions and shareholder wealth, Sundaramurthy, Mahoney, and Mahoney (1997, 239) found that "the market reacts less negatively to antitakeover provisions adopted by boards with a chairperson who is not the CEO than to antitakeover provisions adopted by boards chaired by the CEO." Expressed in Efficiency Lens terms, the less management is separated from oversight, the more skeptically those bearing risk will interpret the board's actions to engage in protection. We also know from research on board litigation that boards chaired by the CEO are sued more often by shareholders than boards that are not chaired by the CEO (Kesner and Johnson 1990). Entrenchment becomes particularly hazardous when the prerogative to adopt antitakeover measures is delegated to the board of directors, which is the case in the poison pill defense.

---

[9] The principle of staggering is not limited to corporations; it is employed in many contexts in which rapid replacement of a decision-making body is undesirable. For example, only one-third of the seats in the US Senate are up for election in a given election year; senators have a six-year term, with one-third of the seats up for election every two years.

The Poison Pill

A common antitakeover provision available at the discretion of the target's board of directors is that of making the target's shares less attractive in the eyes of prospective hostile buyers. The mechanism is known as the *poison pill*. The name is misleading because the poison pill acts more like a dilutor than a toxin; the poison pill dilutes the acquirer's equity in the event of a hostile takeover attempt. The target's board may activate the poison pill whenever an acquirer purchases a threshold stake of the target's stock (usually between 10 and 20 percent of outstanding shares) without the target board's approval (Sundaramurthy et al. 1997).

There are two variants of the poison pill. A *flip-in poison pill* gives the shareholders of the target firm the right to purchase additional shares in the target firm at a deep discount after a hostile acquirer purchases a threshold stake. This effectively floods the market with the target's shares, thus diluting the acquirer's stake in the target. A *flip-over poison* pill gives the shareholders of the target firm the right to purchase shares in the acquiring firm at a discount. Both variants have the same effect of diluting the acquirer's post-acquisition equity either in the acquirer (flip-over) or the target (flip-in) firm.

The poison pill constitutes a strong form of protection because it effectively blocks hostile bids completely. We are not aware of any instances of the acquirer "swallowing the pill"—purchasing a threshold stake in the target, triggering the pill, absorbing the dilution, and then continuing to buy shares until a voting majority has been attained.

A Broader View of Residual Interest

As both staggered boards and the poison pill illustrate, residual interest in antitakeover conversations is usually considered only from the point of view of shareholders: An antitakeover provision should be adopted if it benefits the shareholders.

Defining residual interest in shareholder terms may be contrived in contexts where other stakeholders have a legitimate residual interest due to their commitment to organization-specific skills (in the case of employees) or relation-specific investments (in the case of suppliers and customers). As we suggested in chapter 4, commitments to specificity should be considered analogous with investments in equity, and therefore, deserve to be supported by credible commitments from the organization. We thus propose that the focus in antitakeover conversations and designer's decisions should not be limited to shareholder wealth but should incorporate residual interests more broadly.

To address the broader implications of takeover defense from the point of view of those committing to specificity, let us turn to the *ex ante* challenge the designer faces: How does the designer ensure that the organization's stakeholders are willing to put something at stake in the organization by committing to specificity? How will employees, suppliers, and customers who are asked to commit to specificity react if they find that the organization has not adopted safeguards against unwanted takeovers?

Consider the case of the employees who are asked to commit to specificity by learning and further developing organization-specific skills, for example, by engaging in firm-specific R&D and innovation activities. These employees may understandably view *all* takeovers as potentially hazardous to their careers. A potential consequence of insufficient antitakeover provisions is that it lowers the employees' willingness to commit to specificity. In the case of a growing high-technology firm, this may further lead to an underinvestment in innovation, which can have devastating consequences if the firm's competitive strategy is innovation-based. Decisions regarding the extent to which one is willing to commit to specificity are understandably affected by uncertainty regarding postacquisition employment and compensation (Dey and White 2021).

If the ability of the organization to create value hinges on sufficient levels of commitment to human capital specificity, the designer can consider antitakeover provisions as a way of signaling credible commitments toward high-specificity employees. In this signaling function, antitakeover provisions could lead to important economic bonding effects with high-specificity employees and, consequently, secure adequate levels of investment in human capital specificity by employees.

More generally, mergers and acquisitions tend to be more disruptive, and a greater cause for concern, to those constituencies with long-term relationships with the organization. To the extent these relationships are crucial for organizational viability (as they often are), the designer should think of antitakeover provisions as credibility instruments toward all those stakeholders with a residual interest. In competitive markets and contexts in which switching costs are low, the concern is alleviated (Cremers, Nair, and Peyer 2008).

The nexus-of-contracts analogy is useful in exploring the broader ramifications of takeover hazards. Because different constituencies have different kinds of contractual relationships with the organization, they tend to be affected differently by changes in ownership. Management scholars Andrei Shleifer and Lawrence Summers (1988) pointed out that making choices regarding antitakeover provisions by focusing exclusively on shareholder wealth does not necessarily result in a comparatively efficient solution for the organization. Furthermore, Shleifer and Summers's suggestion that shareholder gains may come at the cost of breaching some of the organization's long-term contracts with its constituencies should give the designer pause; the trade-off gives rise to both an *ex post* and an *ex ante* problem. If the constituencies whose contracts are breached have committed to specificity, takeovers may lead to serious *ex post* disruptions; the organization's failure to signal credible commitments to long-term relationships may in turn lead to the *ex ante* problem of underinvestment in specificity.

The more recent literature on takeover defenses has highlighted the importance of their *bonding effect*. Finance scholars William Johnson, Jonathan Karpoff, and Sangho Yi (2015, 329) empirically corroborate the hypothesis that "takeover defenses can help to bond the IPO firms explicit and implicit commitments to its stakeholders, including customers, suppliers, and strategic partners." The researchers specifically found that having large customers, dependent suppliers, and strategic partners was not only associated with a more extensive deployment of takeover defenses but also with longevity of post-IPO relationships.

Summary: Expanding Organizations, Changing Governance

Most theories and models of governance are, if only implicitly, aimed at large, established organizations (Pollman 2019). The purpose of this chapter on expanding organizations and the previous chapter on incipient organizations has been to shed light on the idiosyncratic governance aspects of young and expanding organizations.

Research literature on organizational expansion tends to focus on the managerial (as opposed to governance) challenges that growth poses for the organization. For example, what did it take for Tesla to go from an annual production of 50,000 automobiles in 2015 to 500,000 in 2020? Even though questions of scaling are plainly essential in all organizations, we posit that it is ultimately not growth but the associated separation of management, oversight, and risk that requires the designer's attention. This is because the separation dynamic presents the designer with a more profound governance challenge than the growth dynamic. To be sure, international expansion, product diversification, and scaling of organizations are far from straightforward. At the same time, the managerial challenges of organizational growth are broadly and deeply covered in the published literature, and we have little to add to these conversations. The challenges that the separation dynamic presents are in our view both more challenging and less discussed.

We present the separation dynamic as an inevitable consequence of the growth dynamic. As the organization expands, the number of organizational subunits and vertical levels increases. This increase gives rise to multiple principal-agent relationships within the organization, effectively separating management from oversight throughout the organization, not merely at the top. Just like the board of directors exercises oversight over the top management team, so does the top management team over division management, division management over functional management, functional management over functional subunits, and so on.

Viewing the organization as a nexus of contracts brings the governance challenges associated with the separation dynamic effectively into focus. In this chapter we have chosen corporate takeovers as an illustration of the challenges associated with the separation dynamic. Corporate takeovers constitute a salient example of situations in which different stakeholders are affected in different ways, and when focusing on the interests of just one of them runs the risk of diverting attention from efficient organizing. Yet, we propose that efficient organizing is ultimately in the best interest of both the target and the acquirer. In general, because shareholder returns are postappropriation measures of performance, they tend to be poor proxies for organizational efficiency and value creation. As Shleifer and Summers (1988, 37) importantly pointed out, sometimes takeovers can create value for the shareholders but simultaneously destroy value for the organization due to their disruptions to efficient contracting with other stakeholders. The disruptions pose a hazard in situations in which commitments to specificity are crucial for the organization's viability. Underinvestment in specificity often means underinvestment in R&D and innovation.

Consistent with the general approach taken in this book, we emphasize the context dependence of the challenges associated with expanding organizations. As always, we counsel the designer to start at defining the main problem. If the main problem in the context of antitakeover provisions is defined in terms of all residual claimants (not just shareholders), the designer must conduct an explicit analysis to determine which constituencies have a residual interest. If employee commitments to specificity are negligible and relationships with suppliers and customers largely transactional arm's-length relationships, then shareholders can be viewed as the sole constituency with a residual interest. Consequently, decisions regarding takeover defenses can be structured around the effect on shareholder wealth. However, to the extent that constituencies other than shareholders have a legitimate residual interest, the designer should incorporate these interests into the analysis. If it is indeed the case that privileging shareholders means breaching implicit or explicit contracts with those who have committed to specificity, the inefficiency implications of takeovers may offset shareholder gains. As always, the designer must analyze the ramifications of all governance alternatives in their entirety.

The bonding effects of takeover defenses are more difficult to quantify, which is a likely reason academics have preferred the more easily measured outcome of shareholder wealth. Here, we might observe that we academics live in a world where it is both possible and permissible to simplify problems by abstracting out that which is not quantifiable, seek an exact answer, and then finish by noting that real-life organizations are more complex than what our models assume.[10]

In stark contrast with academics, designers live in a world where not being able to address the problem in its entirety has real consequences and in which offering caveats and excuses of intractability or immeasurability is ineffective. Readily measurable or not, breach of contract with those who have committed to specificity can have serious *ex ante* and *ex post* efficiency consequences in the organization. We are, however, encouraged by the more recent research literature that addresses outcomes more broadly than just

---

[10] In fact, the use of words such as *optimization* or *maximization* is a telltale sign that the academic is drawing conclusions based on a simplified model. Optimization and maximization are infeasible in just about any real-life decision situation. When was the last time a discussion of "maximizing shareholder wealth" led to any practically relevant insight? Also, it is important to debunk the notion that the law requires maximization of shareholder wealth; we are not aware of a single instance of the word *maximization* (or any of its variants) appearing in corporate law. We further concur with Jensen (2001, 11) who noted that whenever academics use the word *maximization*, they are actually referring to the more general (and realistic) objective of *value seeking*: "It is not necessary that we be able to maximize, only that we can tell when we are getting better—that is moving in the right direction." Jensen's position is consistent with the pursuit of comparative efficiency.

in terms of shareholder wealth (see the excellent and thorough review by Mulherin, Netter, and Poulsen 2017 for more details).

In situations where residual interest is not limited to shareholders, the board's role as the organization's fiduciary becomes pronounced. In an organization where the board acts as a representative of shareholders or has itself been made a residual claimant through equity-based compensation, the organization may adopt antitakeover provisions that are inefficient.

8

The Institutionalized Organization

In the early 2000s, one of the authors consulted a large multinational corporation whose division managers had long been critical of the bloated corporate headquarters and the annual corporate management fees imposed on their divisions. The situation finally came to a head when one division manager analyzed the corporate fees in detail and found, among other things, that his division was effectively paying the corporation $2/page for the centrally organized photocopying services. The competitive rate would have been somewhere around $0.05/page. How can paying a 4,000 percent premium for a service possibly go unnoticed in an organization?

There are several plausible explanations for the persistence of the manifestly inefficient organization of photocopying services. One is complacency. Just like humans are creatures of habit and become set in their ways, organizations develop established ways of structuring and managing their contractual relationships. The multinational in question had always contracted with the providers of photocopying services centrally, and the cost had been allocated to the divisions. At the time the centralized service was introduced, the chances are it served an efficiency purpose. Whatever led to the exorbitantly high cost must have occurred incrementally over time through a series of progressive distortions (Williamson 1975, 118). Furthermore, if in particular the cost at the outset was acceptable, the progressive distortions never garnered further attention from the designer, even when there was a reason to believe a better option might be available. As sociologist Everett Hughes (1939, 283) put it, a "once technically useful means of achieving some known end persists as an accepted and even sacred practice after better technical devices have been invented."

A second plausible explanation is that the high cost of photocopying services was known but nobody had the incentive to do something about it. Indeed, one of the primary drawbacks of organizing activities internally is that incentive intensity is comparatively lower than in interorganizational transactions. We venture to guess that division managers were not

Efficient Organization. Mikko Ketokivi and Joseph T. Mahoney, Oxford University Press. © Oxford University Press 2023.
DOI: 10.1093/oso/9780197610282.003.0008

incentivized to improve the efficiency of photocopying services within their divisions, they had more important issues on their agenda.

A third possibility is that even if a division manager did identify the inefficiency problem, conducted a comparative efficiency analysis, and voiced the inefficiency concern to corporate management, suggestions for improvement might simply have been ignored. Organizing shared services is often one of the central functions of the corporate headquarters, and division heads calling into question the efficiency of centralized services implicitly undermines the corporation's value-adding role. Consequently, even if improving efficiency of shared services did enter the division managers' agenda, it might not necessarily have entered that of corporate management.[1]

A fourth and final possibility is that the problem was one of collective action. In order to challenge the centralized provision of photocopying services, it would not be sufficient for just one division manager to challenge the *status quo*. Instead, there would have to be a division manager who is sufficiently motivated to rally support from all divisions. The idea of the division heads in a large multinational joining forces to challenge corporate headquarters on the issue of overpriced photocopying services sounds almost comical.

No matter what the root cause of the problem was, all plausible accounts are variations on the familiar theme of "organizations assuming a life of their own." Due to cognitive, economic, organizational, and political factors, governance structures tend to persist over time even if they no longer serve an efficiency purpose. Even when a more efficient alternative emerges, it may not be implemented due to various inertial forces. The designer must understand that in large, established organizations, intraorganizational transacting in particular may be subject to inefficiencies that are difficult to overcome. This unearths the dark side of institutions and institutionalization, the main topic in this chapter.

---

[1] We find it plausible that the excessively high cost of $2/page was in large part caused by the photocopying services fee including cost categories that had little to do with the services provided. Corporations are known for sometimes engaging in various "creative" accounting practices when they allocate costs to divisions. In the specific case of the multinational, the corporate headquarters had about four times as many employees as corporations of similar size with a similar corporate parenting role would have (see Goold and Campbell 2002a, chapter 6). Since the headquarters did not generate any revenue, all its costs had to be allocated to the divisions. The chances are the vast majority of photocopying costs was simply corporate overhead.

Institutions and Institutionalization

The word *institution* is like the word *strategy* or *culture* in that it can mean different things in different contexts. At the same time, the word *institution* is unlike the word *strategy* or *culture* in the sense that it can invoke both positive and negative connotations; that something *has been institutionalized* can be both a source of comfort and a cause for concern.

The positive connotation of institutions stems from the order and the stability they confer. This positive view is succinctly expressed by the definition of institutionalization as "the emergence of orderly, stable, socially integrating patterns out of unstable, loosely organized, or narrowly technical activities" (Broom and Selznick 1955, 238). In the spirit of this definition, we might offer the New York Stock Exchange and the Securities and Exchange Commission as two central economic institutions both of which have an indispensable role in the functioning of the US economic system. Their role becomes evident during times of conflict when adversaries seek to undermine one another's central institutions.

We can, however, think of institutions in the more abstract sense as well. The limited liability company (an organizational form), an independent board of directors (a governance principle), and the employment contract (a formal agreement) are three central institutions that work toward supporting economic business activities. The taxi ride example in chapter 1 is also replete with "social microinstitutions" of all kinds. For example, how does the taxi driver know that a person waving one's hand at a passing taxi indicates that the person needs transportation? How does the person in need of transportation in Madrid know that the green light on the taxi's roof sign means that the taxi is neither busy nor off duty? We know because there are institutionalized ways of nonverbal communication in the specific context. In the most general sense, we can define *institution* as any commonly agreed-upon way of organizing an activity.

In all these examples, the word *institution* acquires an exclusively positive meaning; institutions contribute to the efficient functioning of the economic system. Efficiency arises from the fact that institutions make behaviors predictable, they facilitate communication, and so on. In fact, many institutions have been deliberately designed with such efficiency in mind. Just imagine how hopelessly inefficient it would be to buy and sell shares of the General Motors Company if the New York Stock Exchange and the Securities and Exchange Commission did not organize and exercise key oversight over the trading of GM's nearly *one and a half billion* shares. In this sense, institutions breed efficiency.

At the same time, institutions may also be sources of inefficiency. Sociologist and legal scholar Philip Selznick (1957, 16–17) noted that the institutionalization of an activity, structure, or routine involves an "infusion of value beyond the technical requirements of the task at hand." We suggest that there are two distinct ways of interpreting the notion of "infusion of value."[2] The positive interpretation suggests that as an activity or an organization institutionalizes, it is no longer an instrument toward some technical end but, instead, becomes considered intrinsically valuable in its own right. Importantly, the positive interpretation suggests that institutionalization is largely beneficial to the organization; Selznick (1996, 271) noted that institutionalization is the very process by which organizations develop their distinct characters and distinctive competences.

Both acknowledging and embracing the positive interpretation, we also wish to give voice to an alternative, less flattering interpretation of institutionalization. The negative interpretation holds that over time, institutions may become a source of inefficiency. This is because "infusion of value" may also mean that governance choices are either no longer called into question or simply have become embedded in the organization in ways that make changes prohibitively costly. If in particular the objective is to maintain an organization that adapts to changes in its environment, it is easy to see how embeddedness hinders adaptation and constitutes a threat to efficiency. For example, if the organization has adopted a functional structure that has become infused with value over time, there is a probability it will not be replaced by a divisional structure even if the latter were deemed comparatively efficient.

The institutionalization of governance structures is in many ways antithetic to the prescription of remaining relentlessly comparative. In chapter 6, we sought to establish that the relentlessly comparative designer should take nothing for granted; the governance needs of a small startup organization are very different from those of an expanding or a mature organization. In their insightful article on organization redesign, management scholars Christopher Worley and Edward Lawler (2006, 19 [emphasis added]) noted

---

[2] It did not occur to us until the writing of this chapter that we, the two authors of this book, read this passage from Selznick in more or less opposite ways. One of us interprets the "infusion of value" as positive and desirable, and the other, as negative and undesirable. Both interpretations warrant the designer's attention.

that even though designers often speak of the importance of adaptation, "the truth is that most businesses have organized themselves in ways that *inherently discourage change*." In our view, the discouragement stems from the persistence of governance structures.

The challenge that institutionalization presents to organizational efficiency is succinctly presented and summarized by sociologists John Meyer and Brian Rowan (1977). In their classic analysis of organizational structures, Meyer and Rowan suggested that formal organizational structures tend not to serve the purpose of efficiency; instead, they are meant to signal *legitimacy* to the organization's key constituencies. When Meyer and Rowan (1977, 340) looked at the structure of an organization, they saw "myth and ceremony," not efficiency. Although myths and ceremonies may serve important purposes, efficiency tends not to be one of these purposes.[3] Two examples illustrate the point.

The Manager as an Institution

When the first author of this book chaired the board of directors of an industrial startup, he quickly learned that the CEO is an institution not only in established firms but also in startups. As he reached out to a number of external investors to raise equity, one of the first questions many prospective investors asked was, "Who is your CEO?" Note that the question was not whether the startup had a CEO or not—that the firm had a CEO was something prospective investors took for granted.

During the first two rounds of financing, the company did not have a CEO, because the board saw no immediate efficiency reasons for appointing one, and the law did not require it. But the board soon realized that without a CEO, attempts at raising equity would be impossible. Therefore, although the board did not see any efficiency reasons for appointing a CEO, it had no option but to appoint one in order to appear legitimate in the eyes of external investors. In sum, it might not have been efficient for the startup to have a CEO, but it certainly seemed appropriate.

---

[3] The position that the objective of formal organizational structures is not efficiency (as defined in this book) but legitimacy is both well established and compelling. There is a rich research tradition on the topic in the sociology literature, starting with the foundational works of the German sociologist Max Weber. In the organization research literature, the edited volumes by Powell and DiMaggio (1991) and Greenwood et al. (2008) provide excellent summaries of this research and the key arguments. Selznick's (1957) classic book *Leadership in Administration* also merits reading.

More generally, we tend to take it for granted that firms have managers. Indeed, that the startup must have a CEO is an instance of the more general notion of the institutionalization of the manager as an organizational role. At the same time, as we suggested in chapter 2, whether managerial work is performed by individuals whose formal position is that of a manager is not something to be taken for granted but, instead, something to be analyzed. We have on multiple occasions observed how rigorous discussions on management are hamstrung by the fact that the formal organizational position of the manager has been institutionalized. Discussions on the future of management (and managers) seldom lead to actionable insights. In the provocatively titled article "First, Let's Fire All the Managers," strategy scholar Gary Hamel (2011, 51) aptly noted that "we are all prisoners of the familiar."

The idea that a startup firm must have a CEO ultimately suggests that the *de facto* foundation of an organization is both technical and ideological. A case in point, the founding of a startup exhibits many features of a ritual where many ideas are taken for granted. For example, one common assumption embedded in many shareholders' agreements is that arbitration is preferable to litigation because the former is cheaper and less time-consuming. Consequently, cofounders ritualistically introduce to the shareholders' agreement a clause of binding arbitration as the preferred method of dispute resolution. At the same time, experience has shown that the taken-for-granted assumptions of less costly and less time-consuming arbitration are contestable (Stipanowich 2010).

To sociologists, the institutionalization of both organizations and our thinking about them is a familiar phenomenon. Meyer and Rowan (1977, 344) elaborate:

> Ideologies define the functions appropriate to a business—such as sales, production, advertising, or accounting; to a university—such as instruction and research in history, engineering, and literature; and to a hospital—such as surgery, internal medicine, and obstetrics. Such classifications of organizational functions, and the specifications for conducting each function, are prefabricated formulae available for use by any given organization.

Fully acknowledging Meyer and Rowan's position as understandable and well argued, we alert the designer to the potential inefficiencies embedded in the "prefabricated formulae," particularly when the assumptions embedded in them may be either incorrect or become obsolete over time. Taken-for-grantedness may ultimately transform into a liability.

R&D Spending as an Institution

The second example of institutionalization concerns R&D spending and innovation. For over two decades, politicians and policymakers in the European Union have lamented the low levels of innovation in European firms. The aim of the so-called Lisbon Strategy, launched in 2000, was to make Europe "the most competitive and dynamic knowledge-based economy in the world."[4] The strategy called, among other things, for more investment in knowledge and innovation. A key metric for gauging investment in innovation is Gross Domestic Expenditure on R&D (GERD), defined by OECD as "the total expenditure (current and capital) on R&D carried out by all resident companies, research institutes, university and government laboratories, etc., in a country."[5] The objective of the Lisbon Strategy was to raise R&D spending in the European Union to 4 percent of the gross domestic product (GDP). The implicit one-size-fits-all prescription was that all EU member countries, regardless of their industrial structures and histories, should raise their R&D spending to 4 percent of their national GDP.[6]

Even though the ways in which organizations can innovate are numerous, equating innovation with R&D is a long-standing institution both among policymakers and strategy researchers (Sawhney, Wolcott, and Arroniz 2006). The reason R&D spending is appealing is that it provides a general, unambiguous accounting metric for an elusive, multidimensional concept. Furthermore, because R&D spending is something companies must disclose in their annual reports, the metric is also publicly available information, which makes the it easy to monitor not only at the country level but also at the level of industries and even individual organizations.

---

[4] Lisbon European Council, Presidency Conclusions, March 23–24, 2000 (www.europarl.europa.eu/summits/lis1_en.htm), accessed August 11, 2021.

[5] OECD Data (data.oecd.org/rd/gross-domestic-spending-on-r-d.htm), accessed August 11, 2021.

[6] By all accounts, the Lisbon Strategy has failed. While GERD in the EU has increased from 1.7 percent in 2000 to 2.1 percent in 2020, it is not only nowhere near the 4.0 percent target, but it is also considerably below the OECD average of 2.5 percent (source: OECD Data, data.oecd.org/rd/gross-domestic-spending-on-r-d.htm, accessed August 11, 2021). One contributing factor to the problem may be that most executives in Europe we have talked to have never heard of the Lisbon Strategy. If the objective is to encourage R&D investment in firms, a policy that is invisible to corporate managers has little hope of being effective.

Not surprisingly, R&D spending as a proxy for innovation receives less support from executives and practitioners. In an interview with *Fortune* magazine in November 1998, Steve Jobs gave what is perhaps the best-known, and most scathing, evaluation: "Innovation has nothing to do with how many dollars you have. When Apple came up with the Mac, IBM was spending at least 100 times more on R&D. It's not about money. It's about the people you have, how you're led, and how much you get it" (Kirkpatrick and Maroney, 1998, 90).

It is hard to disagree with Mr. Jobs. At the same time, critique from even arguably the most prominent corporate executive of all time has done next to nothing to dissuade the use of *R&D intensity*—annual R&D spending divided by annual revenue—as the most common metric of innovativeness in economic research on innovation. In some contexts, the very definition of a *high-technology company* is based on R&D intensity: To qualify as a high-technology company, one must have an R&D intensity of at least 10 percent.

The R&D intensity example unveils a central characteristic of institutions. As taken-for-granted ways of thinking, they are incredibly resilient in the face of even the most rational and justified critique. We encourage the designer to challenge such resilience whenever it threatens efficient organization, no matter how appropriate the principle or action that is protected may be regarded.

Remediableness and Adjustment Costs

The general prescription in comparative efficiency analysis is to modify a given governance structure when a superior alternative emerges. However, in determining whether the new alternative can be implemented with net gains, one must incorporate various adjustment costs into the efficiency analysis. Even though the new alternative might offer a comparatively efficient governance structure, the benefits it offers may not always offset the adjustment costs associated with its implementation. The QWERTY keyboard layout offers perhaps the best-known example.

The QWERTY layout was designed in the 1800s for mechanical typewriters. One of the problems was that the mechanical arms on which the keys were mounted would jam if typing was too fast (David 1985). In an attempt to slow down typing, the layout of the keyboard was intentionally designed to be inefficient. To this end, the letters would be positioned such that the person typing would have to use the comparatively weaker little and ring fingers on the commonly used letters, and the comparatively stronger index and middle fingers on the less commonly used letters.

The advent of computers effectively eliminated the problem of typing too fast. Yet, the efforts to develop and adopt more efficient keyboard layouts have been, for all practical purposes, nonexistent. Most of us think that the QWERTY layout is good enough, and consequently, simply do not see the point of searching for better alternatives. Many of us simply take the QWERTY keyboard for granted and are not compelled to search for better alternatives.

However, there is another angle to the QWERTY story that tends to receive less attention. Specifically, what is the adjustment cost associated with switching to another keyboard layout, and can this cost be recovered through improved efficiency? Williamson (1999, 316) elaborated: "[I]mplementation costs need to be included in the efficiency calculus. It is fanciful to treat two modes 'as if' they were de novo entrants if, in fact, one has incurred initial setup costs and has durable, nonredeployable assets in place while the other has not." Consequently, a seemingly inefficient governance choice may persist because even though a more efficient alternative exists, it cannot be implemented with net gains.[7]

Whether driven by taken-for-grantedness, complacency, convenience, or lack of high-powered incentives to make internal inefficiencies agenda items for management or oversight, it behooves the designer to understand the consequences of various efficiency distortions present in intraorganizational relationships in particular. In the following sections, we examine the implications of institutionalization for organizational efficiency by taking a closer look at two biases: (1) persistence bias and (2) internal transaction bias.

In chapter 3, we approached the question of contracting within and across organization in terms of the costs of transacting. For example, in contemplating the make-or-buy decision, the designer should incorporate

---

[7] Whether alternative keyboard layouts offer efficiency advantages that offset the adjustment cost is debatable. David (1985, 332) cited experimental studies conducted in the US Navy in the 1940s that suggested the Dvorak keyboard layout to provide a superior alternative even after accounting for adjustment costs. In a strong rejection of David's argument, economists Stan Liebowitz and Stephen Margolis (1990) challenged Dvorak's superiority on two grounds. One was that experiments other than the Navy study suggested that the Dvorak keyboard's comparative efficiency in typing speed was either marginal or nonexistent. The other was that the idea of a new dominant design taking over an incumbent based on technical efficiency considerations alone was based on "a sterile model of competition" (Liebowitz and Margolis 1990, 22). Echoing the second point, we propose that ignoring adjustment costs results in a sterile analysis of comparative efficiency.

both production costs and transaction costs into the analysis. In the following, we revisit the issue by taking a closer look at the advantages and the disadvantages of specifically *internal* transactions. We further focus on the advantages and disadvantages of internal transactions in the context of established organizations where governance structures have institutionalized over time. The general advantage of intraorganizational transacting is that it has various informational benefits over interorganizational transacting; the general disadvantage is that persistence of internal governance structures may give rise to efficiency distortions over time. The disadvantages shed light on some of the more elusive aspects of transaction costs found in institutionalized organizations.

Persistence Bias

Organizational macrostructures tend to persist over time, and redesign is challenging. One source of the challenge is resistance to change: Organizational redesigns are politically volatile as they tend to create winners and losers as some subunits and individuals gain and others lose power (Goold and Campbell 2002b). However, another reason structures persist is because they simply become taken for granted or adjustment costs grow large. Here, we highlight this more elusive source of persistence: The problem in taken-for-grantedness is not *resistance* but the designer's *inability* either to see that redesign is needed or that a new structure with net gains can be implemented. To explore this idea in detail, let us examine the four stages through which growing corporations go as they expand in their scale and scope: (1) ad hoc structure; (2) functional structure; (3) divisional structure; and (4) matrix structure (e.g., Bernstein and Nohria 2016). Each stage is supported by a central taken-for-granted assumption about its efficiency. Table 8.1 summarizes the four stages, their taken-for-granted assumptions, and their sources of inefficiency.

Most companies start small, and although some governance issues require attention already at the outset, a formal organizational structure for the division and coordination of tasks tends to be viewed as unnecessary. Instead, the organization's overall design is best described as an *ad hoc structure*: There are no formal organizational positions and reporting relationships either do not exist or are managed informally. Organizational members are assigned to their respective tasks based on either the members' own preferences or

Table 8.1 Taken-for-Grantedness in Organizational Structures

Structure	Taken-for-granted efficiency premise	Source of inefficiency
Ad hoc	Small organizations should remain flexible instead of adopting unnecessary formal structures	Low routinization and lack of prioritization
Functional	Creating organizational subunits by pooling similar tasks economizes on specialization	Functions have low-powered incentives and prioritization of projects and products is cumbersome
Divisional	Creating organizational subunits with self-contained assets and outputs promotes accountability and enables high-powered incentives	Replication of similar tasks in multiple subunits (e.g., each division has its own R&D function)
Matrix	Lateral structures and cross-unit sharing leads to economies of scope	Compromises high-powered incentives of the divisional structure

ad hoc rules. The taken-for-granted efficiency premise is that small organizations must remain flexible and that adopting formal structures would be unnecessary (and therefore wasteful). In the incipient organization, this assumption is often reasonable.

As the organization grows, similar tasks must be repeated, and prioritization of projects and activities becomes essential. Consequently, the inefficiencies of the ad hoc structure become amplified to the point that they exceed the benefits that flexibility has to offer; the ad hoc structure is no longer comparatively efficient.

In their first attempt at implementing a formalized structure, designers often find themselves grouping together tasks that are similar in content and that require similar expertise (Galbraith 1971). Accordingly, employees who create revenue are assigned to the sales/marketing department, those who convert raw materials into final products to the operations department, and those who create new products to the R&D department. Grouping similar tasks to form organizational subunits gives rise to the familiar *functional structure*. Functional tasks tend to be self-contained (e.g., operations can largely be run without inputs from marketing or R&D) and grouping organizational members with similar functional skills into the same department has many informational advantages. The key concept is *economies of specialization*, which confers many benefits. The taken-for-granted assumption is that pooling a "critical mass" of like-minded employees into the same organizational subunit facilitates economies of specialization.

The drawback of the functional structure is that functions tend to have low-powered incentives. This problem stems from the fact that although functional tasks are self-contained, value creation is not; it is generally impossible to organize individual business functions as profit centers. For example, running a production unit as a profit center would require that both the revenue and the cost of the unit are salient. Although costs may be salient, profit is not. The revenue of the production unit would depend on the price at which finished products are transferred to the sales/marketing department. Because transfer prices are often arbitrary, so is the production unit's revenue. The solution is to organize the production unit as a cost center, but the trade-off is that the incentive intensity of a cost center is lower than that of a profit center (see chapter 2).

Another problem with the functional structure, which often emerges over time when the organization begins to expand not only in scale (volume) but also in scope (number of products), is that prioritization of outputs becomes cumbersome. How does the functional structure incorporate the fact that some products are strategically more important than others? In the functional structure, those in charge of products or product groups (the product managers) must negotiate separately with all functional departments for their contributions.

Just as in the case of the ad hoc structure, the drawbacks of the functional structure intensify over time. With the broadening scope, low-powered incentives and lack of prioritization may become so significant that the organization's structure must be redesigned to implement high-powered incentives and clear accountability for those in charge of the organization's outputs. The structural solution that achieves this is the *divisional structure*, where the grouping of individuals is no longer based on tasks but on outputs. In the divisional structure, high-powered incentives are created for division management by assigning profit-and-loss (P&L) responsibility to the divisions.

Switching to a divisional structure does not mean the functional structure is eliminated, as each division within the divisional structure may create a functional substructure within their divisions. The task of the divisional functions is to serve the needs of the division and its products. The central assumption in the divisional structure is that creating subunits that are

self-contained in terms of their tasks, assets, and outputs enhances accountability and creates high-powered incentives for divisions to create value.

Divisional structure has the disadvantage of redundancy and replication,
which becomes an efficiency liability in organizations where the outputs of
different divisions share many similarities. Reconsider briefly Volkswagen
Group's divisional structure (chapter 3). The functional needs of Volkswagen,
Audi, Seat, and Škoda (four of the largest divisions) are appreciably similar. Specifically, each division must design, produce, and sell passenger
automobiles. Due to this significant overlap, it would make little sense to
have all four divisions manage their unique and isolated business functions,
product development in particular. The need to share resources and to leverage competences across divisions gives rise to the *matrix structure*.

In the matrix structure, there is no single overarching dimension that
defines the macrostructure of the organization; instead, there are multiple
dimensions of strategic importance. The dimensions commonly found in
matrix organizations are product, function, and geography; in some contexts,
there may also be a separate customer dimension (Galbraith 2009). The matrix structure has the advantage of capitalizing on economies of scope by
enhancing collaboration and the transfer of competences and information.

The problem with the matrix structure is that it compromises the high-
powered incentives of the divisional structure and adds administrative complexity. To the extent that complexity and lower-powered incentives become
sources of significant inefficiencies, the matrix structure may not be comparatively efficient.

Why Persistence Causes Delayed Responses

The four structural solutions and their respective strengths and weaknesses
are well known and documented in the organization design literature. Our
focus in this chapter is on why they tend to persist and what the designer
can do about it. In this context, by *persistence* we mean a situation in which
a macrostructure other than the one currently in place presents a comparatively efficient alternative, but the designer fails to recognize this. The transi-
tion from a functional to a divisional structure provides an example.

It is well established that the functional structure works well if the scope of
the organization's outputs is narrow and there is no compelling need to prioritize products. But at what point has the scope become sufficiently broad

for the divisional structure to provide a comparatively efficient alternative to the functional structure? Insofar as persistence is concerned, we propose this question as the designer's primary challenge. Furthermore, an inability to address the question due to complacency becomes a liability.

Suppose the organization has been expanding the scope of its outputs but has held on to a functional macrostructure for ten years. Seeing the divisional structure as potentially more efficient may elude the designer who, quite simply, views the now-familiar functional structure as appropriate. Again, we do not refer here to the common phenomenon of the functionally "siloed" organization in which functional managers develop entrenched positions and become protective of their own functions. Instead, we refer to a situation in which the designer takes the functional macrostructure for granted, effectively forgoing a continuous and relentless comparison of alternative macrostructures. The problem is inadvertent complacency, not deliberate subgoal pursuit. To be sure, the failure of a functionally structured organization to divisionalize may also be caused by the entrenchment of functional management, which may make adjustment costs so high that the divisional structure cannot be implemented with net gains. The only feasible (and decidedly costly) remedy to entrenchment might be the dismissal and replacement of functional managers by new managers who are willing to enter a divisionally structured corporation.

Persistence of the Internal Organization

To be sure, exchange relationships and cooperative value-creation activities both within and across organizations develop taken-for-granted characteristics over time, making persistence a potential source of inefficiency in all exchange relationships. However, persistence likely presents a comparatively more significant challenge to internal organization where taken-for-grantedness may be more prevalent and adjustment costs high. As management scholar Peter Drucker (1973) famously noted, no organization wants to abandon anything. In contrast, cross-organizational relationships tend to be subjected to periodic evaluation and active renewal decisions. Many notable economists such as Friedrich Hayek (1945) have noted that the fundamental advantage that markets (i.e., interorganizational transactions) have over firms (i.e., intraorganizational transactions) is their ability to adapt autonomously over time.

Consider the decision whether a company should have an internal legal department or whether it should contract with an external law firm. Legal scholar David Wilkins (2012) suggested that three different factors explain the increasing use of in-house counsel in US corporations: (1) the economic argument suggests that in-house counsel lowers legal costs; (2) the substantive argument suggests that internal lawyers give better guidance because they have more intimate knowledge of the organization; and (3) the professional argument suggests that as company employees, inside lawyers are more likely to take the organization's long-term interests into account. Wilkins (2012, 260) further suggested that these three arguments have become embedded in "the *ideology* of the in-house counsel movement [that] is now broadly accepted throughout the US legal profession."

The drawback of internal counsel is that internal lawyers are employees whose contracts are more difficult to terminate than those of outside counsel. To invest in internal counsel is to commit to a fixed amount of legal expertise within the organization. Much like having an internal division that produces and supplies parts to another division, having an internal counsel becomes a sunk cost. Moreover, the incentive intensity of the internal counsel will be lower than that of the external lawyer. The billable-hour method and billable targets used in law firms tend to create high-powered incentives to use the lawyer's time as efficiently as possible.

With internal counsel, billable targets are not as relevant (if at all), which reduces incentive intensity. With lowering incentive intensity, "corporate counsel may feel pressure to accentuate their legal capabilities in order to be seen as valuable and non-redundant" (Jenoff 2012, 733). Furthermore, when in-house lawyers work for just one client (i.e., their employers), there may be added pressure to broaden the lawyer's role from an advocate and a legal advisor to mediator, compliance officer, even a business team member (Jenoff 2012, 732). This broadening scope of activities may confer benefits on the one hand, but on the other hand, the comparatively high levels of specialization of the legal profession may become a liability. When lawyers work as compliance officers or business team members, their skills are not likely in their best or even next-best use, and yet, the cost to the organization remains the same. Given the organization has decided to hire internal lawyers, it must find them something to do.

The in-house counsel example is useful because it highlights the problem of persistence in relationships that involve contractual relationships with human capital. In the case of technological assets, persistence tends to be less problematic due to depreciation. Designers need not worry to the same degree about technological assets persisting, because technological assets become obsolete over time as they lose their value through depreciation. The persistence of fixed assets does not occur inadvertently but, instead, requires active reinvestment decisions. In these reinvestment decisions, the designer can engage in an explicit deliberation over whether reinvestment serves an efficiency purpose. In stark contrast, organizational subunits, structures, and employment contracts do not depreciate in the accounting sense and, consequently, can persist without explicit attention, deliberation, and active reinvestment decisions. At the same time, subunits, structures, and contracts can depreciate in the sense that their ability to create value declines over time. What makes such organizational (as opposed to technological) efficiencies particularly vexing is that complacency on the part of the designer may cause them to persist for long periods of time.

The use of in-house counsel is an illustration of the general challenge that persistence bias causes specifically *within* organizations. In the following section, we discuss the general topic of trade-offs in internal transactions. Just as it is important for the designer to engage in a comparative analysis of intra- versus interorganizational contracting (see chapter 3), understanding the trade-offs associated with intraorganizational transacting is essential.

The Trade-Off of Internal Transactions

Further building on the premise that the problem is one of complacency, taken-for-grantedness, and adjustment costs, we turn to governance problems that are in the economics literature discussed under the rubric of *transactional distortions* (Williamson 1975, 118). Here, we adopt the label *efficiency distortion*, as it is a descriptively better title for our purposes: We are specifically interested in how, over time, some aspects of the organization's governance may become "distorted" in that what once was comparatively efficient no longer is so. We further highlight the largely inadvertent drivers of distortions; they occur as governance choices gradually shift out of alignment with the characteristics of the relationship and the environment in which the relationship is embedded.

To examine the trade-off associated with internal transactions, consider the situation in which an organization consists of multiple subunits (e.g., divisions) that transact with one another. For example, organization design scholar Jay Galbraith (2002a, chapter 8) described the *front/back model*, an organizational structure found in many large technology corporations that provide solutions of large scale and scope to their corporate clients. The front/back hybrid is a special case of the multidivisional firm that consists of market-facing divisions (the front structure) that host the customer operations, and technology-facing divisions (the back structure) where individual products and services are developed and maintained. Galbraith (2002b, 201) discussed the networking and telecommunications equipment company Nokia Networks as an example of the front/back hybrid. The task of the front structure at Nokia Networks was to provide network solutions to massive cellular network operators such as AT&T, Vodafone, and France Télécom (now Orange). The back structure, in contrast, was responsible for developing the individual technologies (e.g., IP networks, data center infrastructure, cyber security, and operations support systems) that the front assembled into network solutions. The central organizational challenge in the front/back hybrid is how to connect the front with the back.

Why are the components developed and the solutions assembled by internal units of the same organization? What advantages does the integrated front/back hybrid offer over the alternative where one firm creates customer solutions by purchasing the requisite components and subsystems from external vendors? In the following, we discuss the advantages and the disadvantages of transacting internally.

The Advantages of Transacting Internally

What is the price of a gallon of milk? A smartphone? A flight from Madrid to Chicago? In many instances, acquiring information on prices is a simple matter of discovering the market price. If a product or a service can be bought at an unambiguous market price, the advantages of internal transacting become elusive. Indeed, why would an organization choose to internalize an activity it could easily contract an external supplier to execute at a specific, predetermined market price?

There are two general situations in which prices are not a simple matter of discovery. One is when the object of exchange is unique, and consequently, there simply is no market; the other is when the object of exchange creates value only when it is integrated into a broader product or service to create value. For example, how do the automotive seating manufacturer Adient and the final assembler of automobiles (e.g., Volkswagen) determine the price at which Adient supplies car seats to Volkswagen's final assembly? Even though Adient's seats may not be unique, there really is no competitive market that provides salient market prices. What is more, car seats do not provide value independently of other components, instead, they must be embedded within a broader system of the automobile. When the value an individual product or service provides is fundamentally contingent on other products and services, its price cannot be based on the value it provides; cost-based pricing offers the obvious alternative. In such contexts, transacting internally may provide an informational advantage over transacting in the market.

In cost-plus pricing, the exchange takes place at a price that consists of the seller's cost and the seller's margin. But what is the seller's cost, and how is the margin determined? If the object of the exchange is a component that is to be integrated into a broader system, what is the cost of integration? Will the buyer absorb the cost of integration, or should it be taken into consideration when the seller's margin is determined? Are the buyer and the seller aware of one another's costs, or are there information asymmetries? How are disputes resolved?

Unique products or intermediate products that must be integrated into final products obviously have a price. But these prices are not so much *discovered* in the market as they are *constructed* by the transacting parties (Eccles and White 1988). This process of constructing prices is facilitated if the transacting parties are parts of the same parent organization. A corporate parent that has access to the cost information of both parties is in a unique position to mediate the process as an impartial facilitator. In economic terms, when the transaction is intraorganizational, management may fulfill an important quasijudicial function (Williamson 1975, 30) and mediate potential disputes. If the transaction were interorganizational, the dispute might escalate more easily to a point where it strains the relationship. When transacting internally, "the parties are more inclined to adapt cooperatively" (Williamson 1975, 30). In addition, cooperative adaptation is mandated in the sense that internal disputes must be handled internally—the courts will not settle such disputes.

In sum, the advantages of transacting internally arise from two related sources. One is that informational asymmetries cause comparatively fewer problems due to the presence of a parent that has access to information on both sides of the transaction. The other advantage is that the organization facilitates *ex post* adaptation when disputes arise.

The Disadvantages of Transacting Internally

In the front/back hybrid, what are the technologies the front purchases through internal transactions from the back, and where can it use its discretion and purchase from the market? Symmetrically, which products and solutions does the back sell exclusively to the front, and when can it sell to external customers? Should the parent organization mandate internal transactions whenever they are possible? Are internal transfer prices set unilaterally by the parent or are the internal buyer and seller allowed to negotiate?

The designer must understand that all policies that limit the internal buyer's and the internal seller's discretion tend to lower incentive intensity. When the internal buyer has a captive internal supplier, and vice versa, the incentive intensities of both parties inadvertently and unavoidably decline. Unlike in the case of deliberately designed low-powered incentives (see chapter 5), internal transactions tend to be associated with unintentionally lower incentive intensities. In the front/back hybrid, if those responsible for the back know that their outputs are always guaranteed to receive demand from the front, their declining incentive intensity may have adverse consequences such as underinvestment in R&D. Specifically, if the back has a captive buyer who is required to purchase technologies for customer solutions from the back, the latter is immediately disincentivized to invest in R&D.[8] Symmetrically, if the front is guaranteed an internal supply of components from the back, its incentive to maintain its own purchasing competences declines.

Even though mandating internal transactions may be sensible at the outset, it may result in internal cross-subsidization that ultimately protects nonviable capabilities. The phenomenon is sometimes called *internal procurement bias* (Williamson 1975, 119).

Internal transactions become even more problematic if the inefficiencies become salient to the transacting parties. For example, the problem of internal procurement bias is further exacerbated if an internal supplier realizes

---

[8] If the back is grouped into profit centers and executive compensation is linked to the unit's profitability, there is an immediate disincentive to invest in R&D, especially if demand from the front is guaranteed by the parent organization. But why would a front/back hybrid assign P&L responsibility to the back instead of the front? If solutions are modular and consist of interchangeable components that have a market price (e.g., routers and switches in the telecommunications equipment context), it may well make sense to assign primary P&L responsibility to components or products (the back) and only secondary P&L to solutions and customer accounts (the front). Some front/back hybrids calculate revenue in both the product and the customer dimensions and implement a hierarchy of P&L structures.

it could receive a higher price for its outputs if it sold them to an external customer, but at the same time, is required by the corporate parent to trade only internally. Symmetrically, an internal customer may realize it could obtain a component at a lower price from an external supplier. Efficiency distortions that arise from mandated internal transacting are a cause for concern, but when these inefficiencies become salient to the transacting parties and are not addressed, the viability of the entire organization is threatened.

Importantly, the problem is more fundamental than that of getting the transfer prices right. If internal procurement bias has led to a situation in which an organization is maintaining a nonviable competence through cross-subsidization, the obvious solution is to seek a viable competence in the market and terminate cross-subsidization.

Summary: Institutions as a Liability

Well-defined institutions are the bedrock of all functioning societies and economic systems; their importance cannot, and must not, be understated. At the same time, the informed designer is well advised to give attention to problems that arise from taken-for-grantedness that may follow from the "infusion of value beyond the technical requirements of the task at hand" (Selznick 1957, 16–17).

To be sure, losing sight of "the technical requirements at hand" due to taken-for-grantedness of an institutionalized governance structure may become a liability in all exchange relationships. However, institutionalization poses a hazard particularly in situations in which the relationship is not relentlessly monitored for efficiency. This can occur especially in those internal exchange relationships where depreciation does not provide the requisite mechanism for eliminating obsolete, non-value-adding activities. Whenever the exchange relationship is subjected to periodic review and evaluation, the designer has the opportunity to be relentlessly comparative. Capital reinvestment decisions and regular contract renewal present such opportunities, but in the case of internal organizational structures and processes, these opportunities tend to be absent. This may give rise to various efficiency distortions.

In chapter 3, we compared intra- and interorganizational transactions in an attempt at specifying the conditions under which each is comparatively efficient. In this chapter, the objective has been to complement chapter 3 by examining the trade-offs associated with internal transactions. The well-established advantage of intraorganizational transactions is that they offer various informational benefits. In situations where prices cannot be simply discovered but must instead be constructed, the internal organization offers several advantages. One is the existence of impartial general management that can alleviate problems that stem from asymmetric information. Not only is cooperation and adaptation easier within organizations, but internally transacting parties have also an incentive to cooperate, because disputes must be resolved as matters of private ordering. To this end, the internal organization has central quasijudicial functions for internal dispute resolution.

The disadvantages of the internal organization are more elusive, which is why we have devoted explicit attention to them here. The disadvantages become pronounced in established organizations that have a broader set of institutionalized structures, activities, and exchange relationships within their boundaries. To the extent that institutionalization within organizations leads to inadvertent outcomes such as gradually declining incentive intensity, internal governance structures start to exhibit efficiency distortions.

Efficiency distortions alone do not imply that intraorganizational relationships are comparatively inefficient and inferior to interorganizational relationships. As in all governance decisions, our prescription to the designer is to analyze the issue in its entirety. In the case of internal transactions, the designer should consider the advantages jointly with the potential efficiency distortions due to internal organization. The problem with the failure to incorporate efficiency distortions into the comparative analysis is that it makes the designer complacent. Considering the benefits of internal transactions while ignoring the drawbacks leads to bias specifically toward internal transactions. Complacency may ultimately prove costly, as in the case of division managers discovering that their divisions were paying a 4,000 percent premium for centralized photocopying services. If an efficiency distortion of this magnitude can persist for years, one cannot help but wonder what kinds of remediable inefficiencies are embedded in the taken-for-granted practices of established organizations.

Epilogue

Economist Frank Knight (1941, 252) prescribed to those interested in behaving economically to "make their activities and their organization *efficient* rather than wasteful," and that "[t]his fact deserves the utmost emphasis." Building on this idea, the pioneering organization economist Oliver Williamson (1988, 571) suggested that the resultant "organizational imperative" is to design governance structures that align with the characteristics of the relationships the organization has with its constituencies. The ultimate objective of all the chapters and illustrations in this book has been to explore the ramifications of this imperative.

Although we might not go as far as to suggest that efficiency deserves the "utmost emphasis," we maintain that it certainly deserves the designer's attention. In chapter 1, we described efficient organization as analogous with a healthy blood pressure: certainly a worthy objective, but hardly the most important aspect of one's health, let alone the reason for one's existence. We believe this analogy creates a useful connotation of how the designer can, and should, think of efficient organization.

Since all organizations involve a multitude of diverse relationships, they also involve a multitude of governance structures; indeed, *each relationship* in which the organization is involved has its own governance structure. For example, the organization has a relationship with all its employees, and each relationship may exhibit both general and idiosyncratic features. Similarly, governance structures with providers of capital must be structured in a way that secures mutual credibility and continuing cooperation. Relationships with those entitled to fixed payments (debt financing) must be structured differently than relationships with those entitled to residual payments (equity financing). Governance, as a general term, refers to the totality of all these structures that support and secure the organization's relationships with its constituencies.

The reason we refrained from using the term *corporate governance* in this book is because we have sought to bring the level of analysis to the relationship. Consequently, we highlight the notion of *governance of contractual relationships*, a term that is well established in the contemporary literature on organization economics. The distinction between corporate governance and governance of a contractual relationship is not merely semantic; it has profound implications for designers of organizations. One is that since the totality of contractual relationships tends to be context-specific and idiosyncratic, so are governance structures. Therefore, mimicry and benchmarking of other organizations may be misguided. Instead, the designer must rigorously analyze the key relationships and choose governance structures accordingly. A common misconception is that the institutional environment determines governance structures and that those facing a similar institutional environment should have identical governance structures.

That all organizations have a multitude of contractual relationships (and a multitude of governance structures) has another profound implication: Efficiency will always be relevant in one way or another. We are hard-pressed to think of an organization where *not a single* relationship in which the organization is involved would not benefit from a comparative efficiency analysis. Consequently, it behooves all designers to identify and carefully analyze relationships where seeking efficient governance is relevant. Efficiency arises from making trade-offs in a way that results in a positive net effect, or net gains, for the parties in the relationship.

Symmetrically, the designer must be mindful of relationships in which comparative efficiency does not apply. Critically, there are relationships in which the objective of positive net gains becomes infeasible, and the governance-as-efficiency approach no longer applies. Even in these relationships, the designer must still make a governance choice; however, the choice can no longer be justified in efficiency terms.

The applicability of comparative efficiency analysis is not a question of whether the organization is for-profit or nonprofit, or whether it is public or private. What is relevant is not the organizational form but the context and the characteristics of the specific relationships. Comparative efficiency analysis loses its relevance in relationships where the alternative governance choices involve outcomes that cannot (or must not) be traded off against one another in the conventional economic sense. The informed designer will be able to identify such situations and supplant an economic analysis with other forms of deliberation and judgment to determine what is appropriate, not what is efficient. In many relationships in which comparative efficiency is no longer operational, governance-as-integrity takes precedence over governance-as-efficiency.

Importantly, that integrity takes precedence over efficiency does not imply rejection of the latter. Once integrity of a relationship has been secured, an efficiency analysis may well be applicable to the same relationship in a way that not only fosters efficiency but simultaneously further bolsters integrity. A case in point, in most contexts the separation of management and oversight—separation of powers—tends to promote both integrity and efficiency.

Problems arise when the quest for efficiency compromises integrity, which can happen in two ways. One is that efficiency is considered in short-term, myopic terms; the other is that efficiency analysis is used outside its boundaries of applicability. In both cases, the problem is not efficiency but its uninformed application. We hope that this book has established that such misapplication is remediable, and that comparative efficiency analysis, properly applied, can always either provide the foundation or a complement to other organizational objectives. To this end, we emphasize two principles to guide the way. One is the idea of *other-regarding behavior* proposed by legal scholars Margaret Blair and Lynn Stout. The other principle is adopting the kind of an *analytical mindset* that organization economist Oliver Williamson endorsed throughout his career: Have an active mind, be disciplined, and be interdisciplinary.

We hope this book can serve as a catalyst in the proliferation of analytical, other-regarding designers.

Glossary of Terms

This glossary of terms contains the definitions and the descriptions of the central terms used in this book. However, instead of presenting conventional formal definitions, our objective is to establish the relevance of each term in the context of organization design and governance. To this end, this glossary is constructed according to two principles.

The first principle is that for a concept to be relevant to organization design and governance, it must be explicitly contextualized. Consequently, the definitions offered in the following are not meant as formal, universal definitions; rather, they are presented specifically in the context of the efficiency approach adopted in this book. The definition of *governance* is an illustrative example of context dependence. Our definition reflects the contractual, private-ordering aspects of governance. In contrast, those adopting an institutional perspective (organizations such as the OECD, for instance) might define governance from the point of view of compliance, not contracting. Different definitions serve different purposes.

The second principle is inspired by the concept of *nomological validity* in quantitative psychology: A concept does not acquire its full meaning until it is considered in conjunction with other concepts with which it is related. Consequently, in discussing the definition of a given concept, we may invoke several other concepts simultaneously. These other concepts are either intimately related to the focal concept, crystallize its meaning, or provide a useful contrast. Discussing *residual claimant* in conjunction with *residual* is a good example. Specifically, the concept of the economic residual remains merely a measure of net income until we ask whether someone can present a legitimate claim for it. Introducing the residual claimant makes the concept of residual relevant to governance.

As an example of one concept providing a contrast to another, *transactional contracting* provides a useful contrast to *relational contracting*, as does *hazard* to *risk*.

Terms Included in This Glossary

Alignment (and Adjustment)
Contracting (Transactional vs. Relational, Complete vs. Incomplete)
Credibility (and Credible Commitments)
Dependency (Unilateral vs. Bilateral)
Design (and Designer)
Efficiency
Efficiency Distortion
Ex Ante vs. *Ex Post*
Failure
Feasibility (and Remediableness)
Fiduciary (and Fiduciary Duty)
Forbearance (and Quasijudicial Functions)
Fundamental Transformation
Governance
Hazard
Incentive Intensity
Institution
Main Problem
Management
Myopia
Organization
Oversight
Ownership
Private Ordering (vs. Legal Centralism)
Probity (and Probity Hazard, Sovereign Transaction)
Profit-seeking vs. Nonprofit Organizations
Public vs. Private Organizations
Rationality (and Bounded Rationality, Self-Interest vs. Opportunism)
Residual (and Residual Claimant, Residual Interest)
Risk (and Switching Cost)
Safeguard
Specificity (and Temporality, Dedicated Assets)
Stakeholder (and Stakeholder Analysis)
Transaction Cost

Value Creation vs. Value Capture (and Preappropriation vs.
    Postappropriation)
Viability

Alignment (and Adjustment)

Some environments are more uncertain and change more rapidly than
others; some contracts are subject to more transactional hazards and risk
than others; some contracts are short term, others are long term. The contexts
in which organizations operate and in which contractual relationships are
embedded are highly diverse.

The foundational idea in efficient organization is that governance choices
must align with the context. It is incumbent upon the designer to discriminate, that is, to derive the efficiency implications of different alternatives,
and then choose the one that is comparatively efficient. Williamson (1991,
277) used the term *discriminating alignment* to describe the outcome in
terms of aligning transaction characteristics with governance choice.
Importantly, because an organization has a multitude of relationships with
diverse constituents, discriminating alignment must be applied separately to
all relationships.

For example, if the purchasing manager of an industrial firm faces the
governance choice of either making a component in-house or outsourcing it
to an external supplier, discriminating alignment calls for an analysis of the
efficiency implications of the two alternatives. If the part is something the
firm buys frequently, if its availability is subject to high uncertainty, and if
the exchange relationship involves relation-specific investments, then a discriminating alignment analysis likely leads the manager to a conclusion that
it is more efficient to produce the component in-house to better safeguard
against transactional hazards.

Due to various inertial forces, organizations tend to be more stable than
their environments. The inability to adjust instantaneously without cost
means that over time, governance choices may drift out of alignment with the
demands of the organization's environment. In the case of the industrial firm,
perhaps technological developments eliminate the need of relation-specific
investments, and consequently, the use of an internal supplier becomes
less efficient than outsourcing. In this case, maintaining discriminating

alignment prescribes governance adjustment, which is always associated with a cost. Adjustment cost is a special case of an *ex post* transaction cost.

In considering adjustments due to misalignment, the designer must exercise discrimination as well. Some misalignments are inconsequential in the sense that even though realignment might enhance efficiency, the improvement is so small that the organization may not even be able to recover the associated adjustment cost. Use of discrimination must always involve the analysis of *net gains*.

Contracting (Transactional vs. Relational, Complete vs. Incomplete)

We distinguish between the formal/legalistic and the informal/collaborative domains of contracting. A written contract that stipulates the responsibilities of the contracting parties is a good example of the former. The formal domain links to law in the sense that disputes over formal contracts are often settled in the context of jurisprudence.

Even though formal contracts are plainly essential, this book seeks balance by incorporating also the informal and the collaborative side of contracting. By making the formal/informal distinction, we want to point to the *ex ante* and *ex post* features of contracting. The notion of a formal contract implies that the key aspects of contracting are determined *ex ante* (before the contract is in force). Consider a simple employment contract: The formal *ex ante* contract specifies the rights and the responsibilities of the contracting parties. In case of a dispute, the most important document to which the parties will refer is the formal contract (as well as the applicable laws, which of course are in force *ex ante* as well).

Most employment contracts are transactional in the sense that the formal contract is sufficient to safeguard the relationship. Employer-employee relationships become more complex when employees become bearers of residual risk and develop a legitimate residual interest. These relationships are no longer merely transactional but also exhibit relational characteristics. The formal contract is still relevant but may no longer be sufficient in and of itself.

The relationship between a limited liability company and its shareholders is a good example of a relationship in which a formal contract is inconsequential. Even though the relationship can still be considered contractual, there is no *formal* contract that stipulates the responsibilities of the contractual parties, the duties of the corporation in particular. In the contractual relationship between the corporation and the shareholder, the shareholder is given nothing but a nebulous promise that the organization's board of directors will incorporate shareholder interests into its decisions. Unlike in the case of the employment contract, there is no formal *ex ante* contract that specifies in detail what incorporating shareholder interests means. Furthermore, if the board fails in its attempts at producing returns to the shareholder, the shareholder may have no recourse.

The formal and the informal are not mutually exclusive. Indeed, informal contracting can sometimes complement formal contracts. Goldberg (1976, 428) elaborates:

> While the [contracting parties] might want to go into considerable detail at the formation stage concerning the rights and obligations of each party given various contingencies, it will often prove too costly to specify the precise terms of the contract and it will be desirable instead to use rough formulae or mutual agreement to adjust the contract to current situations. As the relational aspects of the contract become more significant, emphasis will shift from a detailed specification of the terms of the agreement to a more general statement of the process of adjusting the terms of the agreement over time.

Consequently, the contract becomes more a general *framework* than an explicit *agreement* (Williamson 2002b).

The notion of a *complete contract* pertains to contracting situations in which the responsibilities of the contracting parties can be specified and codified into the formal contract in a way that renders *ex post* adjustments immaterial. In contrast, relational contracting characterizes situations where the contracting parties must rely on the mutual agreement to adjust *ex post*. Relational contracting is often found in transactions involving bilateral dependency and specificity that require various additional safeguards to address contractual risk.

Williamson (1996, 378) offered an extensive list of reasons why a complete *ex ante* contract may be infeasible:

> (1) not all the relevant future contingencies can be imagined, (2) the details of some of the future contingencies are obscure, (3) a common understanding of the nature of the future contingencies cannot be reached, (4) a

common and complete understanding of the appropriate adaptations to future contingencies cannot be reached, (5) the parties are unable to agree on what contingent event has materialized, (6) the parties are unable to agree on whether actual adaptations to realized contingencies correspond to those specified in the contract, and (7) even though both the parties may be fully apprised of the realized contingency and the actual adaptations that have been made, third parties (e.g., the courts) may be fully apprised of neither.

Credibility (and Credible Commitments)

Entering into exchange relationships involves various degrees of transactional risk. The relationship is credible when the contracting parties voluntarily "make a wager" by committing to the exchange despite the risk involved. Note that the question is not whether one party finds the other credible but, rather, whether the conditions of the contract are such that they secure the requisite cooperation of all exchange parties—credibility is a property of the arrangement, not the parties themselves. These conditions are met when all parties have made sufficient mutual credible commitments, described by Williamson (1983, 519) as "reciprocal acts to safeguard a relationship."

Even though credibility is, for all practical purposes, synonymous with trust, using a common term as a label for what is ultimately a complex issue may be misleading:

> [U]ser-friendly terms [such as *trust*] do not encourage us to examine the deep structure of the organization. Rather, we need to understand when credible commitments add value and how to create them, when reputation effects work well, when poorly, and why. Trust glosses over, rather than helps unpack, the relevant micro-analytic features and mechanisms. (Williamson 1996, 216)

We agree with Williamson that the term *mutual credible commitments* may be more conducive than *trust* in inviting the designer to explicate the principles, structures, and actions necessary for securing collaboration under transactional risk. This said, we ultimately find that what is essential is elaborating the mechanisms by which risky relationships are safeguarded—choosing which labels to use to describe the mechanisms is of secondary importance.

Dependency (Unilateral vs. Bilateral)

Two exchange parties are bilaterally dependent if the consequences of the termination of the relationship are so significant that they require the designer's *ex ante* and *ex post* attention in both organizations. For example, supplier switching costs on the buyer's side and buyer switching costs on the supplier's side may both be sufficiently high for the parties to be motivated to implement the proper safeguards against an unwanted termination of the relationship.

If switching costs are high for one party and negligible for the other, dependency is unilateral. Contracting under unilateral dependency is fundamentally different from contracting under bilateral dependency, because additional safeguards would be redundant for the party that faces a negligible switching cost. Unilateral dependency is often found in contracting situations in which one of the parties is significantly larger and more powerful than the other. In this book, we have little to say about transacting under unilateral (or strongly asymmetric) dependency, other than perhaps making the unsurprising observation that under unilateral dependency, the comparatively more powerful exchange party sets the rules which the comparatively less powerful party either accepts or rejects. In a one-time exchange, accepting unilateral dependency would be myopic, but with frequent exchanges, there can be interproject and intertemporal spillovers. Under such conditions, the dependent party, say, an original equipment manufacturer to Dell, could gain reputational effects that increase its chances of striking deals outside the dyadic exchange. Over time, the supplier may become more valuable to Dell, which transforms the relationship to bilateral dependency.

Design (and Designer)

The most intuitive way of thinking about organization design is to think of the organization's structure. Is the organization structured by function (functional organization)? Is the corporation a single-business or a multibusiness firm? If the organization is a matrix, what are its central dimensions? It is also straightforward to think that organizations are structured the way they are because that is how they were deliberately designed. To be sure, multibusiness firms do not simply emerge over time without deliberate design decisions.

In this book, we embrace the premise that organizations are deliberately designed. We use the common label *designer* to refer to all those involved in the design decisions of an organization. For example, in a limited liability company, the three central designers are shareholders (who design by voting in shareholder meetings), the board of directors (who design by making decisions in board meetings), and top executives (who design by making executive decisions). That there is a designer also carries the assumption that the designer seeks to be rational in its decisions. In our exposition, rationality of the designer is aimed at building and maintaining an efficient organization.

Efficiency

If there are two ways of organizing an activity, one should choose the one that uses a smaller number of inputs to produce the output. Throughout this book, efficiency is a comparative notion that invokes the known alternatives: Of all the known and available options, the one that produces the least amount of waste is *comparatively efficient*. All feasible options (the comparatively efficient option included) are flawed in the sense that they produce at least some waste.

The most salient example of waste is physical waste produced by a production line. However, for the purposes of this book, various forms of *organizational* waste are central. The free-riding problem is a good example. In an environment where individuals can minimize their effort without sanctions, productivity (efficiency) is comparatively lower compared to an environment where free-riding is "metered well" and free-riding sanctioned: "If the economic organization meters poorly, with rewards and productivity only loosely coupled, then productivity will be smaller; but if the economic organization meters well productivity will be greater" (Alchian and Demsetz 1972, 779).

Ineffective communication can also sometimes constitute a form of significant waste. This may be due to opportunistic behavior and the deliberate dissemination of false or misleading information. However, there are also benign sources. For example, consider the buyer-supplier relationship of a final assembler and a component supplier of a smartphone. Suppose that in this relationship, the buyer and the supplier must engage in continuous collaboration and problem-solving to ensure continuous innovation of products.

These processes involve various forms of communication: emails, video-conferencing, phone calls, product team meetings, and the like. It is easy to see how the requisite communication is more challenging (and potentially wasteful) in situations in which the buyer and the supplier represent different firms. An obvious reason is that within firms, classified information travels with less friction and many problems can be solved using business judgment and authority. In contrast, problem-solving in cross-firm relationships requires (more time-consuming) negotiation. Finally, the use of language and various coding procedures (e.g., accounting practices) tend to be more standardized within organizations, which facilitates intraorganizational communication.

Efficiency Distortion

In established organizations, internal structures, processes, and principles may give rise to inefficiency. For example, a production unit in an industrial firm may use an internal supplier for some of the components needed in final assembly. Over time, this arrangement may lead to *internal procurement bias* in which "the existence of an internal source of supply tends to distort procurement decisions [. . .] A norm of reciprocity easily develops, [for example], I buy from your division, you support my project proposal or job promotion" (Williamson 1975, 119, 120).

Another manifestation of efficiency distortion is *internal expansion bias*, where the organization adopts "a compromise solution by which concessions are made to subsystems rather than require them to give up essential functions or resources" (Williamson 1975, 120).

A third example is *persistence bias*, where "sunk costs in programs and facilities of ongoing projects insulate existing projects from displacement by alternatives which, were the current program not already in place, might otherwise be preferred" (Williamson 1975, 121).

Internal procurement bias, internal expansion bias, and persistence bias are all examples of what is colloquially described as "an organization assuming a life of its own." A common denominator in the examples is that relationships whose features might suggest a comparatively transactional, arm's-length contracting approach, start to develop unnecessary relational characteristics simply because the contracting parties are parts of the same corporation. Much like the fundamental transformation, efficiency distortions are emergent phenomena that are difficult to prevent. The designer's task is to think of both *ex ante* and *ex post* measures for addressing them.

Ex Ante vs. Ex Post

In the governance of contractual relationships, it is useful to distinguish between the time before (*ex ante*) and the time after (*ex post*) the relationship begins. In the case of formal contracts, the signing of the contract separates the two.

In general, the designer should seek to turn as many *ex post* problems as possible into *ex ante* problems, because problems are usually more efficient to preempt than to solve after they have occurred. However, it is important to realize that many problems in relational contracting in particular cannot be addressed *ex ante*, and instead, require various *ex post* adjustments. The necessity of various *ex post* adjustments renders many complex, long-term contracts unavoidably incomplete.

Failure

In the context of contractual relationships, failure means that the requisite cooperation of the exchange parties is not secured even though there is mutual interest in the transaction. *Contractual failure* occurs when the contracting parties fail to implement the requisite safeguards to address risk to which the contracting parties would have to expose themselves. Contractual failure is a special case of the more common notion of *market failure*, where both demand and supply exist for a product or service, but the transaction fails to take place because, for one reason or another (e.g., asset specificity, asymmetric information, or externalities), supply and demand do not meet.

Feasibility (and Remediableness)

Comparative analysis of feasible alternatives stands at the foundation of all the analyses, practical implications, and recommendations found in this book. Focus on comparative analysis has a number of important implications.

The first implication is that a governance alternative should not be compared to an infeasible ideal. One sometimes encounters governance critics who play the devil's advocate by pointing to the flaws of a given alternative. But no governance alternative is perfect; therefore, a person pointing out flaws is merely stating the obvious. To merit the designer's attention, the critic should be compelled to present a feasible alternative that can be implemented with net gains. To this end, designers must remain relentlessly comparative in their approaches to governance decisions.

The idea of remaining relentlessly comparative invokes the notion of *remediableness*. A governance problem is remediable only if there is another alternative that can be implemented with projected net gains. Because governance choices tend to affect the entire organization or the entire contractual relationship instead of just one part of it, the consequences of any given choice must be analyzed *in their entirety* (Williamson 1996, 9).

A good example of the importance of projecting net gains is the make-or-buy decision. Suppose that the designer of an industrial firm worries about the high cost of producing a component internally and, consequently, turns to outsourcing as the alternative. Failing to incorporate the increased transaction costs, the designer may conclude that because the internal production cost of a component exceeds the external supplier's asking price, outsourcing is the comparatively efficient option. However, if the increases in transaction costs exceed the production cost savings, switching from internal production to outsourcing will not result in net gains. Considering the issue in its entirety by incorporating transaction costs might lead the designer to conclude that no net gains can be projected. Consequently, the uncomfortably high cost of producing the component internally is not remediable by outsourcing.

Identifying a better alternative after the fact often fails the feasibility criterion. In the outsourcing example, suppose that after failing to incorporate transaction costs, the industrial firm outsources the component and sells the facility and the equipment used to produce the component to the supplying firm. After realizing that the outsourcing option proved even more expensive, reversing the outsourcing decision and repurchasing the production facility may no longer be feasible. In general, remorsefully looking back at choices with perfect hindsight tends not to be practically useful. Organizations must live with the choices they make, which is why designers must emphasize conscious foresight in all decisions.

Fiduciary (and Fiduciary Duty)

Constituencies such as employees, suppliers, and lenders have an unambiguous contractual relationship with the organization. In the contracting process, the exchange parties negotiate the rights and the responsibilities of each, which then become embedded in formal contracts (e.g., employment contracts, buyer-supplier contracts, and loan agreements).

Building on the idea of the *fiduciary*, discussed in the context of governance by Blair and Stout (2001), we propose that whereas the relationship between the organization and its management is contractual, the relationship with those in charge of oversight—most notably, the board of directors—should be thought of as fiduciary. Blair and Stout (2001, 404) aptly described the fiduciary relationship as "other-regarding" and "mediating." Consequently, a person with a fiduciary role should neither be a stakeholder nor represent one, instead, those in a fiduciary role are "charged with the task of balancing the sometimes-conflicting claims and interests of the many different groups that bear residual risk and have residual claims on the firm" (Blair and Stout 2001, 404). This quote succinctly captures the essence of the other-regarding role of the fiduciary.

It is in our view misleading to think of the board member's relationship with the organization in contractual terms, because the essence of the fiduciary relationship is *not* about negotiable rights and responsibilities. The fiduciary role is more appropriately thought of as a duty toward the organization. Further, as Blair and Stout (2001, 406), and many others, have remarked, despite common belief, there is nothing in corporate law that compels the fiduciary to serve just one constituency, such as the shareholder:

> Despite the emphasis legal theorists have given shareholder primacy in recent years, corporate law itself does not obligate directors to do what the shareholders tell them to do. Nor does corporate law compel the board to maximize share value. To the contrary, directors of public corporations enjoy a remarkable degree of freedom from shareholder command and control. Similarly, the law grants directors wide discretion to consider the interests of other corporate participants in their decision making—even when this adversely affects the value of the stockholders' shares.

The beneficiary of the director's fiduciary duty is not any specific stakeholder group but the *entire organization*. Indeed, one of the important functions of corporate law is to *shield* directors from shareholder control (Blair and Stout 2001, 406).

Forbearance (and Quasijudicial Functions)

Consider the case of a contract dispute between a buyer and a supplier. If the two are separate firms not belonging to the same corporate parent, they can as a last resort refer to the courts to settle the dispute through a court ruling.

However, if the two are under unified ownership, reference to the courts is not an option, because an organization would be effectively suing itself. Instead, the organization must address the dispute as a matter of private ordering. Within the organization, "contract law . . . is that of *forbearance*, according to which internal organization is its own court of ultimate appeal" (Williamson 1996, 378 [emphasis added]). How an organization structures its internal principles and processes of forbearance is a foundational governance decision. To this end, the internal organization has a number of important *quasijudicial functions* (Williamson 1975, 30).

Fundamental Transformation

Consider the situation in which a firm seeks competitive bids from a large pool of candidate suppliers for a standard auditing service. As the buyer is considering its options, it need not pay attention to the identities of individual suppliers, because all suppliers are *ex ante* substitutable. Suppose the buyer then chooses one of the candidates from the pool and enters into a buyer-supplier contract, which is renegotiated and renewed every twelve months.

At contract renewal, is the buyer going to face a pool of substitutable suppliers? This may no longer be the case because in the preceding twelve months, the buyer has learned to collaborate with a specific auditor and to adapt to unforeseen circumstances. Perhaps the buyer has also discovered that the chosen auditor reliably delivers its services, thereby signaling a positive reputation effect. Instead of facing an *ex post* pool of equally attractive suppliers, one stands out from the rest. A fundamental transformation has occurred.

Williamson (1985, 13) noted that the fundamental transformation has "pervasive importance for the study of economic organization." Whereas at the outset the buyer was dependent on the pool of suppliers only in the aggregate sense (it needed someone to audit its books), it has now become dependent on a specific supplier in the sense that it is economically more efficient to continue with the same supplier. Symmetrically, the supplier now prefers the specific buyer. As a result, the contractual relationship has been infused with bilateral dependency. There is indeed something fundamental about this transformation: Bilateral dependency exposes both contracting parties to risk, and consequently, both parties should be incentivized to design the requisite safeguards to protect the relationship.

The fundamental transformation often occurs inadvertently over time as the contracting parties find more efficient ways of collaborating during contract duration. In this sense, the fundamental transformation is an emergent (as opposed to deliberately designed) property of a contractual relationship. The deliberate design decisions pertain to the kinds of safeguards that are implemented to address the risks that arise from bilateral dependency.

Governance

We define governance as the totality of the deliberate choices the designer makes about management, oversight, and risk. To this end, governance can be circumscribed by three questions:

1. Who in the organization is trusted to make the most important decisions about how activities are organized, how resources are allocated, and how performance is evaluated (*management*)?
2. What general guidelines and principles govern decision-making to ensure that decisions are made in the best interest of the organization (*oversight*)?
3. What safeguards are in place to ensure the cooperation of the organization's most important constituencies, particularly those who have voluntarily put something at stake in the organization (*risk*)?

These three questions must be addressed as a going concern, not merely at the founding of the organization. In fact, an essential aspect of governance is how management, oversight, and risk evolve over time. For example, a crucial governance question in a growing corporation heading toward an initial public offering is how and when to separate oversight from management.

Our approach to governance embraces a predominantly private-ordering perspective. However, we readily acknowledge that those who view governance from an external point of view would define it in a way that emphasizes compliance, law, regulation, and policy. An illustrative example of an externally oriented approach can be found in OECD's definition of corporate governance, which emphasizes the role of the legal, regulatory, and institutional environments. But this is not a sign of inconsistency, it merely means that OECD's definition of governance serves a different purpose than ours.

Hazard

Consider an undesirable event such as a car accident. To safeguard yourself against the risk of a total economic loss of your vehicle, you contract with an insurance company for comprehensive collision coverage. At the same time, it should be obvious that the insurance policy in and of itself does nothing to help you avoid the hazard of a collision. Acknowledging this, you choose to mitigate the hazard by always obeying the speed limits, not operating your smartphone while driving, never driving while intoxicated, and so on. The measures we take to manage risk differ from those we take to mitigate hazards.

As an example of a hazard in contracting, consider the oil refining value chain (Klein, Crawford, and Alchian 1978). Suppose an oil company owns and operates the oil fields and the refineries, both of which are subject to considerable site specificity and physical asset specificity. Suppose further that an oil pipeline is the only way of transporting the oil from the fields to the refineries. The oil company is well advised to own and operate the pipelines as well. If it did not, it would expose its (highly specific) assets to an economic *holdup problem* (Goldberg 1976) by the company that owns and operates the pipelines.

Just like texting while driving constitutes a hazard, so does exposing one's organization to the holdup problem. Klein et al. (1978, 310) elaborate:

> [The] specialized producing and refining assets are therefore "hostage" to the pipeline owner. At the "gathering end" of the pipeline, the monopsonist pipeline could and would purchase all its oil at the same well-head price

regardless of the distance of the well from the refinery. This price could be as low as the marginal cost of getting oil out of the ground (or its reservation value for future use, if higher) and might not generate a return to the oil-well owner sufficient to recoup the initial investment of exploration and drilling. At the delivery-to-refinery end of the pipeline, the pipeline owner would be able to appropriate [a significant portion of the profits] of the refineries. The pipeline owner could simply raise the price of crude oil at least to the price of alternative sources of supply to each refinery that are specialized to the pipeline.

A straightforward way to avoid the economic holdup problem is common ownership of the oil fields, the pipelines, and the refineries; in other words, vertical integration would effectively attenuate the contracting hazard. At the same time, vertical integration would not eliminate various risks due to high levels of asset specificity, which would call for additional safeguards.

The economic holdup problem is a special case of the more general notion of *contractual hazards*, which arise from inadequate safeguarding of the relationship. Inadequate safeguarding may pose a hazard to one of the contracting parties, or both, but it always poses a hazard to the relationship.

Incentive Intensity

When an employee is incentivized by an hourly rate or a fixed salary, the amount of compensation does not depend on the amount of effort exerted or the amount of output produced. A fixed salary is an example of low incentive intensity (or low-powered incentive). In piece rate, in contrast, the worker's hourly pay depends on the amount of output produced; piece rate is an example of high incentive intensity (or a high-powered incentive).

The appropriate level of incentive intensity in an exchange relationship should be determined through a comparative analysis by asking, "What level of incentive intensity makes the contractual relationship comparatively efficient?" As a general rule, high-powered incentives are preferred over low-powered ones, because higher incentive intensity tends to foster efficiency by mitigating free riding, among other positive effects. In situations in which the individual's work effort and performance are salient, high-powered incentives are preferable; employees can voluntarily exert as much effort as they choose and be compensated accordingly. A self-employed taxi driver is a good example of a high-powered incentive: The driver is incentivized to take on as many customers as possible during a work shift. High-powered incentives tend to work well also when not only effort and performance but also the way effort links to performance is salient.

However, there are contexts in which comparatively low-powered incentives may be a better alternative. The eight-hour shift of a police officer is a good example. If police officers were incentivized by the number of arrests they make or the number of speeding tickets they write during a work shift, the predictable outcome is that even the most insignificant and inconsequential infractions (such as driving just over the speed limit on a deserted highway) would be penalized. In the case of law enforcement, a sufficiently high base salary that increases with years of service is a better alternative. Linking salary increases to years of service is beneficial, because the public benefits from having more experienced law enforcement officers. However, because of the low-powered incentive, the police officer cannot make more money simply by "working harder" (however defined).

Incentive intensity can also be applied at the level of entire organizations, or organizational subunits. For example, one decision industrial firms must make regarding their production units is whether to assign them profit-and-loss (P&L) or simply cost responsibility—the former constitutes a comparatively high-powered incentive. But assigning a production unit P&L responsibility makes sense only if both the costs and the revenues of the unit are salient. Costs tend to be salient, but revenue is unambiguous only if a market price can be credibly established. This is not the case in many industrial firms where production units sell their outputs at some arbitrary transfer price to an internal sales unit. Arbitrary transfer prices make the production unit's revenue, and consequently its profit, arbitrary as well. Arbitrary profitability calculations may be useful for accounting and tax purposes, but they likely lack credibility as a basis for compensation. It is generally ill advised to hold organizational subunits or their managers responsible for something over which they have little control. Williamson (1994, 102) elaborates: "High-powered incentives obtain if a party has a clear entitlement to and can establish the magnitude of its net receipts easily. Lower-powered incentives obtain if the net receipts are pooled and/or if the magnitude is difficult to ascertain." That many industrial firms assign only cost responsibility to their production units stems precisely from the fact that operations create value jointly with other business functions.

Note that incentive intensity is not about the level of compensation but, rather, about the extent to which compensation is affected by the amount of output produced. The stronger this link, the higher the incentive intensity, and the stronger the effect of increased effort on compensation.

Institution

Colloquially, we think of institutions in terms of large, important organizations such as the University of Illinois, the United States Department of State, or the World Bank. In the context of organization design and governance, we adopt a more abstract, broader definition offered by North (1991, 97): "Institutions are the humanly devised constraints that structure political, economic and social interaction. They consist of both informal constraints (sanctions, taboos, customs, traditions, and codes of conduct), and formal rules (constitutions, laws, property rights)." North (1991, 97) further described the purpose of institutions in a useful way: "Throughout history, institutions have been devised by human beings to create order and reduce uncertainty in exchange." The enforcement of institutions can similarly occur through both formal (e.g., law enforcement) and informal (e.g., codes of conduct) means (Granovetter 1985).

The University of Illinois, the United States Department of State, and the World Bank continue to be institutions under North's definition as well; however, under the broader definition we would also classify contracts, invoices, and warranty clauses as institutions, as they "create order and reduce uncertainty" in contractual relationships.

An institution can also assume the form of an abstract principle. For example, the principle of *contra proferentem* in dispute resolution maintains that if there is an ambiguous term in the contract that can be interpreted in multiple ways, the courts should apply the principle of "construing ambiguous language against the drafter [of the contract]" (Boardman 2006, 1108). The objective of *contra proferentem* is "to give drafters an incentive to draft cleanly" (Boardman 2006, 1108). *Contra proferentem* is sometimes described as a *doctrine*, which suggests it has indeed acquired the status of an institution.

It is useful to think of institutions generally as "the rules of the game" that are enforced by some (formal or informal) authority (Alston et al. 2018, 3). In the context of organization design and governance, institutions pertain to the rules that govern how the work is done, who exercises oversight, and how risk is governed. The institutional environment of an organization is defined as the collection of all the central "rules of the game" that affect the economic actions within and across organizations.

Some institutions are a matter of law, policy, and regulation, but the ones particularly relevant to the designer are the ones associated with private ordering; that is where the designer can seek organizational efficiency by making choices among feasible alternatives.

Main Problem

Should the CEO also chair the board of directors in a limited liability company? Before this question can be addressed, the designer must formulate the problem that board composition is aimed to address. We call this formulation the *main problem*. In all organization design and governance decisions, the designer should always start by specifying the main problem. If there are multiple problems, the designer should seek to prioritize them, and the problem with top priority becomes the main problem.

In the board composition example, the main problem is often formulated as one of agency: Does the CEO (the agent) act in the best interest of the organization (the principal)? If the main problem board composition is aimed at addressing is the agency problem, then the separation of the CEO and the chairperson roles is recommended.

In contrast, if the main problem is defined as the ability to make strategic decisions quickly in a rapidly changing environment, then having the same person be in charge of the top management team and the board of directors may be comparatively efficient. However, if the CEO also chairs the board, additional safeguards may be needed to ensure one person does not acquire too much power in the organization and create a potential entrenchment hazard.

The prescription of formulating the main problem does not imply that the designer should formulate only one problem; the prescription is to have the designer think about the design problems in an analytical, prioritizing, and discriminating way. As the COVID-19 vaccine example in chapter 4 seeks to establish, the designer's task is impossible without clear definition and prioritization of problems. If all problems and all stakeholders are important, then nothing and no one is important. Overpermissive and all-inclusive

formulations of governance problems are in our view one of the most challenging obstacles to the designer, which is why specifying the main problem
is essential.

Management

For the purposes of organization design and governance, *management* refers
to all those aspects of the organization that are responsible for ensuring that
the work gets done: resource allocation, design of the central value-creating
processes, control, coordination, and reward systems.

Management may or may not involve organizational members whose
title is that of a manager. A case in point, in self-managing organizations
(SMOs), work planning and execution are allocated directly to employees.
Furthermore, one need not venture into SMOs to find situations in which
organizational members are empowered to take on managerial tasks, for example, by being included in the planning of their own work; employee em-
powerment was one of the cornerstones of the Total Quality Management
movement in the 1990s (Cole and Scott 2000).

Value-adding activities in organizations involve a combination of humans
and technology. We also include in management all those nonhuman assets that are used to coordinate activities. In our view, whereas thinking of
employer-employee and buyer-supplier relationships in contracting terms
is salient, we suggest that similar contractual thinking be extended to technology. For example, whether an industrial firm finances production equipment through debt or equity is a matter of governance, with important
contractual implications (Williamson 1988).

Myopia

In ophthalmology, myopia (or nearsightedness) refers to a condition
in which objects are seen distinctly only when they are near to the eye.
Analogously, myopia in governance decisions describes a situation in
which the contracting parties consider primarily the short-term efficiency
implications. Note that being myopic is not about the inability to predict the
future; it is about the inability, or perhaps more accurately reluctance, to address governance decisions as long-term issues.

Myopia links directly to efficiency. Although not all attempts at being efficient in the short term are myopic, focusing on the short-term implications in governance and contracting runs the risk of being myopic, particularly if the quest for short-term gains jeopardizes credibility.

Consider the example of a large buyer that purchases standard components from a smaller component supplier. There are many alternative suppliers from which the buyer can choose, and consequently, purchasing managers at the buyer firm may feel tempted to "squeeze" the supplier to improve its own productivity and profitability. This may be ultimately myopic due to the fundamental transformation. A forward-looking buyer would seek ways to design the relationship such that the supplier has a high-powered incentive to learn and develop its skills.

Organization

Universities, firms, and legislatures are organizations. Indeed, an obvious way of thinking about organization is to think about legal entities called organizations.

In this book, we adopt a broader definition. Whereas entities called organizations are relevant to our exposition, they are not the essence of organization. From the point of view of organization design and governance, the question is less about how entities called organizations are designed and more about how value-creating cooperative relationships are organized. In this book, the word *organization* refers more broadly to the principles and practices of organizing contractual relationships.

Consider the conventional buyer-supplier contract. Although the buyer and the supplier are obviously relevant contracting entities, we propose that the essence of organizing resides not in the entities but in their relationship. Therefore, it makes little sense to consider the characteristics of one entity without simultaneously incorporating both the characteristics of the other entity and the interactions the two entities have with one another. When the pioneer organization economist John R. Commons (1934) noted that the basic unit of analysis should be the transaction, he specifically instructed us to look beyond the entities into the structure of the relationship in a way that infuses order, mitigates conflict, and ultimately achieves *mutual* gain.

Emphasizing the relational aspects of organizing usefully turns attention to the ways in which contracting parties are dependent on one another and complement one another. Particularly relevant for designers are situations of bilateral dependency, that is, when both contracting parties have a vested interested in maintaining the relationship. Understanding bilateral dependency paves the way to understanding how stakeholder relationships emerge.

As a final example of thinking of organization not in terms of entities but sets of contractual relationships, consider antitakeover provisions. Most importantly, it is *not* the entity (the firm) that requires protection. Instead, the designer's attention turns to the specific stakeholder relationships that may (or may not) require protection. In contemplating antitakeover provisions, designers commonly direct attention to the relationship that shareholders have with the organization. Consequently, the analysis of antitakeover provisions focuses on their potential impact on shareholder interests, and protection is prescribed if it increases shareholder bargaining power.

Oversight

All organizations must ensure that the decisions its members make serve the best interest not of those who make the decisions but of the entire organization. One of the central tasks of *oversight* is to ensure such alignment; ensuring that the organization satisfies the demands of the institutional environment is another. We use the general label *oversight* to refer collectively to all the individuals, groups, structures, and principles that work toward these objectives.

An obvious entity contributing to oversight is a board of some kind: board of directors, board of trustees, board of regents, and so on. However, there are also many entities external to the organization that have central roles in oversight. For example, stock exchanges, government agencies, and legislatures exercise either direct or indirect oversight over publicly traded corporations. These entities are sources of various compliance requirements imposed on the organization.

Various aspects of oversight can also be embedded in the organization's founding documents, such as the articles of incorporation, corporate bylaws, and shareholders' agreements. These documents tend to focus more on how the organization is *governed* than on how it is *managed*.

Ownership

The owner of a house is the person whose name appears on the property deed. More generally, we tend to think of ownership of an asset in terms of who has title. However, in the context of governance, we propose that the notion of ownership be viewed differently. We define ownership through control rights, and in particular, residual rights of control. Ownership also includes the right to transfer an asset (e.g., Barzel 1989), but transfer is less relevant for our exposition.

In a contractual relationship, the owner of an asset has two prerogatives with relevant implications. Specifically, the owner is entitled (1) to exercise control over the decisions that are not specified in contracts (residual control), and (2) to the economic surplus the organization generates (residual claimancy). Both residual control and residual claimancy are at the heart of ownership. Since these two rights may not go hand in hand (Hart 1989, 1766), both require the designer's attention.

Private Ordering (vs. Legal Centralism)

Consider the way in which two contracting parties settle disputes. Will they try to work things out themselves or will a third party be involved? Private ordering refers to contractual arrangements whereby the contracting parties seek to settle disputes as private matters, without involving external third parties. There is no clear-cut definition for what constitutes a third party but, to be sure, one of the parties suing the other would clearly involve a third party (the courts).

Dispute resolution offers a salient example of private ordering. More generally, Williamson (1985, xii) noted that "the governance of contractual relationships is primarily effected through the institutions of private ordering rather than through legal centralism." Indeed, private ordering (relying on the contractual pillar) becomes salient as we contrast it with jurisprudence (relying on the institutional pillar). Consistent with Williamson, governance questions in this book are approached primarily from the private-ordering perspective where the focus is on the "self-created mechanisms" (Williamson 1996, 378) by which exchange parties structure and manage their relationships.

Probity (and Probity Hazard, Sovereign Transaction)

In some exchange relationships, it is imperative that all transactions be executed with utmost integrity or *probity*. Of course, one might argue that probity is important in all contractual relationships that involve any degree of risk. However, there are contexts in which its absence is particularly disconcerting. For example, it is one thing for a supplier to act in a self-serving and opportunistic way in its relationship with a buyer; a government agency or a branch of the military doing the same in its relationship with the president is quite another. In some contexts, probity must be placed at the very core of the relationship.

Because probity links directly to risk, it is often discussed in conjunction with the *probity hazard*. Probity is further relevant in contexts such as foreign policy, which belongs to the general category of *sovereign transactions*: "[T]here are certain tasks that we expect government to perform [...] because it alone embodies the public's authority. Certain tasks are sovereign tasks" (Wilson 1989, 359). But as Williamson argued, even sovereign transactions may benefit from an efficiency analysis, most notably, "a governance structure that supports a presumption of or predisposition toward cooperativeness will relieve the hazards of probity" (Williamson 1999, 324). Williamson (1999, 324) further maintained that "the potential cost savings that would accrue to high-powered incentives in foreign affairs are not great."

The concept of probity is useful in establishing important boundary conditions for efficiency. Unless the organization has not resolutely established probity, conducting efficiency analyses is both premature and misguided. This is in our view best described by political scientist James Q. Wilson, whose position is aptly summarized by Williamson (1999, 310):

> While Wilson invites the application of transaction cost economics to politics, he also cautions that 'Careful attention to transaction costs will not alone determine where [the] line should be drawn' (1989, 359). Not only is the output of government 'complex and often controversial' (Wilson 1989, 348), but agencies often have 'multiple objectives, government programs have distributional effects, and considerations of equity and accountability are often important'. (Wilson 1989, 348)

As an example of the interplay between probity and efficiency, we might ask whether it makes sense to direct attention to inferior prison food quality (indeed an efficiency-related issue, see Hart 2003) if there are more fundamental concerns, such as violation of the inmates' constitutional rights, other legal rights, and even basic human rights. Should not all attention first be directed at establishing the integrity of the prison organization, and only subsequently engage the designer in a discussion of organizational efficiency?

Profit-seeking vs. Nonprofit Organizations

The conventional definition of a for-profit organization as one that seeks an economic surplus is in our view not useful for governance. The reason is that it is common for nonprofits to produce an economic surplus and have net worth; universities and many cooperatives are good examples. What is relevant is whether the organization has a stakeholder that can claim the surplus, that is, whether there is a residual claimant. Accordingly, we make the distinction by invoking residual claimancy: A for-profit organization has a residual claimant that is entitled to the surplus, but a nonprofit organization has no other residual claimant than the organization itself (Fama and Jensen 1983a).

Whether the organization has a residual claimant or not is relevant to governance because it has fundamental implications for how a possible surplus is governed. Nonprofit organizations must ensure that the surplus is not expropriated through private benefits. In fact, a tax-exempt nonprofit organization may lose its tax-exempt status for the fiscal year if tax authorities discover its surplus has been privately expropriated.

Public vs. Private Organizations

In contrast with the for-profit/nonprofit distinction where the two categories describe actual organizations, the public/private distinction tends to define the ends of a continuum rather than describe actual organizations; many if not most public organizations are more accurately described as public-private partnerships. Consider the university as an example. The university may be considered a public organization but, at the same time, it has scores of private actors embedded within it. For example, security services, cafeteria services, and custodial services are often provided by private organizations. Similarly, many commercial airlines in Europe in particular are at least partly state owned. For example, the Republic of Finland (represented by the Finnish Prime Minister's Office) owns 56 percent of the shares in Finnair, the flag carrier and largest airline in Finland. Although some organizations are fully private and others fully public, there are numerous hybrid forms.

Because there are many hybrid forms, it is more useful to examine the public/private distinction by reference to the internal workings of the organization: Which parts of management should be populated by civil servants and which parts should be contracted out to private entities? How should compensation be structured in employment contracts? If there is a public interest in the organization, what kinds of oversight roles can be delegated to private actors? Can representatives of private interests occupy fiduciary roles in the first place? What kind of risk will the public (e.g., taxpayers) bear? How does the designer implement safeguards to protect the public interest against expropriation by private actors?

The designer's task is to make informed choices regarding the role of public and private actors in the organization. This task does not in our view involve the categorization of the organization as either public or private, which is why most discussions on the privatization of public organizations remain elusive. We must start by specifying what exactly is being privatized, why, and how.

Rationality (and Bounded Rationality, Self-Interest vs. Opportunism)

In the general sense, any goal-oriented behavior is rational: If one wants to attain x and y is a means to it, then it is rational to do y (this is known as the *practical syllogism*, see von Wright 1963). Note that this definition implies that one cannot speak about rationality without first specifying an objective. For the purposes of this book, we assume the designer seeks efficiency. However, the general objective of efficiency is too general to be actionable. For an objective to become actionable, the designer must be able to justify a direct link from the objective to alternative courses of action (March and Simon 1993, 177). This is why formulating a more specific main problem is required. In the context of efficient governance, designers are rational when their choices address the main problem in a comparatively efficient way.

Conventional economic theory assumes decision makers are rational in the sense that they choose the best option from *all* possible options; indeed, rationality implies *optimization*. In this book, we subscribe to the more realistic notion of being able to choose the comparatively efficient option from the *known* alternatives. We also acknowledge that the designer's rationality is bounded. Simon (1997, 88) aptly described human behavior as "*intendedly* rational, but only *limitedly* so."

That behavior is intendedly rational is crucial because it embraces the premise that the designer is acting in the best interest of the organization. Consequently, we offer no encouragement to designers who engage in self-serving behaviors and pursue their own agendas at the expense of organizational efficiency. In fact, curbing individual rationality that is aimed at goals inconsistent with those of the organization is one of the central tasks of oversight.

Seeking what is best for organizational efficiency is built on the general idea of self-interest. The assumption (and prescription) is that designers behave in ways that are beneficial for their organizations. However, the assumption (and prescription) is also that self-interest is sought by adhering to the constraints and expectations of the institutional environment.

There are also stronger forms of self-interest such as opportunism, described by Williamson (1996, 378) as "[s]elf-interest seeking with guile, to include calculated efforts to mislead, deceive, obfuscate, and otherwise confuse." Just like we have little to say to those engaging in self-serving behaviors, our message to those inclined to act opportunistically is that our objective is to help designers make the lives of the dishonest maximally uncomfortable. To this end, we seek to help those who act in good faith safeguard their contractual relationships.

A bounded-rationality approach toward an uncertain future maintains that although the future can never be fully or even adequately predicted, designers are capable of making decisions in a forward-looking manner that incorporates conscious foresight. Importantly, therefore, bounded rationality does not imply myopia. Throughout our exposition, we want to emphasize the premise that no matter how boundedly rational behavior is, rationality always remains the intention: "Parties to a contract who look ahead, recognize potential hazards, work out the contractual ramifications, and fold these into the *ex ante* contractual agreement obviously enjoy advantages over those who are myopic or take their chances and knock on wood" (Williamson 2000, 601).

Residual (and Residual Claimant, Residual Interest)

Let us start from the top line of a firm's income statement and work our way to the bottom line. Once all the requisite appropriations and contractual obligations—salaries, invoices, interest, taxes, depreciation—have been subtracted from revenue, there may be something left over. This economic surplus or net income is the residual. The rules that govern the management and the distribution of the residual are central to governance.

In most jurisdictions, shareholders are the only stakeholder whose rights to the residual have been secured in law. In short, shareholders "have a *legal* claim on the firm's net receipts" (Klein et al. 2012, 311 [emphasis added]). A relevant question in for-profit organizations is whether constituencies other than shareholders can *reasonably* claim residual interest.

The general position taken in this book is that shareholders may not be the only stakeholders with a justifiable residual interest. For example, suppose a group of employees in a high-technology firm commits their time and their effort to developing a set of skills that not only create considerable value for the firm but are also firm-specific in the sense that they will be less useful if the employees leave the organization. Commitment to such specificity is a form of investment risk that creates bilateral dependency between the firm and the employee group in a way that is analogous to the bilateral dependency between the firm and its shareholders. In fact, one might argue that the dependency is even stronger in the case of the employees, because they cannot sell their investments at market value the same way shareholders of public corporations can. Consequently, it would be reasonable to conclude that the employees committing to specificity are a stakeholder with a legitimate (but not legal) residual interest (Klein et al. 2012).

Economic surplus is a salient manifestation of the residual. There is, however, another type of residual that also merits attention in a contractual relationship. Since all complex contracts are unavoidably incomplete, there are many issues that remain unspecified. Insofar as these issues involve the use of assets and the allocation of resources, decisions regarding these unspecified issues are the prerogative of the owner of the asset. In the economics literature, these prerogatives are discussed under the rubric of *residual rights of control*. In the case of economic surplus, we simply speak of *rights to the residual*.

Risk (and Switching Cost)

An industrial firm that performs the final assembly of a product such as an automobile or a smartphone does not have the capability to produce many of the components needed in the final assembly—the firm needs suppliers. Similarly, the scale of many firms is not sufficiently high to justify in-house legal counsel; therefore, they must contract with external law firms. All organizations are, in one way or another, dependent on other organizations.

As long as a contracting party depends on other parties only in the aggregate sense, the risks in contracting are both negligible and remediable; a bad experience with a supplier can be remedied by switching to another. Risk enters when switching costs are no longer negligible and an organization becomes dependent on a *specific* organization. Single-sourcing is a good example. HP is dependent on Canon for laser printer cartridges and on Intel and AMD for processors. The reason HP cannot buy processors from a fully competitive market is because the market structure of processors is oligopolistic, that is, dominated by a small number of sellers.

Risk must be considered separately for unilateral and bilateral dependency. When dependency is unilateral, as in the case of a large powerful buyer and a smaller captive supplier, the exchange relationship is subject to the *holdup problem* (Goldberg 1976). To be sure, as consumers we can all think of situations in which we have become dependent on a specific supplier, but the supplier is in no appreciable way dependent on us; instead, they are only dependent on the customer base in the aggregate sense. Due to this asymmetric dependency, the supplier may be able to "hold us up" as customers. Being exposed to a holdup problem is a risk under unilateral dependency.

Under bilateral dependency, there really is no holdup problem. Instead, the relevant risk has to do with the fact that bilaterally dependent relationships tend to be more efficient because they are characterized by various forms of specificity that lead to higher switching costs. Investments in specificity are often justified due to the efficiency gains they bestow upon the relationship. In car manufacturing, for example, component suppliers sometimes physically collocate their component plants with the car manufacturer's final assembly plant. When the two plants are physically collocated, the supplier is able to deliver its components to the final assembler both "just in time" (exactly when they are needed) and "in sequence" (in the order in which they are required in the final assembly). In-sequence delivery is relevant when the components are parts of customizable configurations (e.g., seat materials and colors).

It is easy to imagine the astronomical switching costs associated with a car manufacturer terminating a contract with a seat supplier that operates a massive seat plant right next to the car manufacturer's final assembly plant. In the case of unilateral dependency, unilateral risk stems from the potential holdup problem on the side of the potential hostage; in the case of bilateral dependency, switching costs give rise to risk on both sides.

Safeguard

When contracting parties become bilaterally dependent, they expose themselves to potential exchange hazards and risk. Premature and unexpected termination of the contract would have severe economic consequences for both parties. Consequently, the parties are well advised to think of both *ex ante* and *ex post* ways to safeguard the contractual relationship. An obvious safeguard is a carefully crafted long-term contract that secures the rights and the responsibilities of both transacting parties. Or, in the case of one party supplying the other components that can only be used in the buyer's products, potential order cancellations due to unpredictable demand must be safeguarded; the supplier having to bear the full cost of demand unpredictability is unlikely to constitute a mutually credible alternative.

Here, we emphasize reciprocal acts and the mutual interest of safeguarding the relationship. In short, the unit of analysis is the relationship, not the contracting parties, let alone just one of them.

Specificity (and Temporality, Dedicated Assets)

Consider a situation in which a productive asset such as a piece of production equipment or an employee skill is being applied in a way that generates the highest amount of value. Then imagine that the asset can no longer be applied in this best use. What is the difference in the value of the asset in its best versus next-best use? The higher the difference, the higher the (asset) specificity. Highly specific assets have low redeployability.

Williamson (1996) presented five different types of specificity. First is *site specificity*, which arises from the geographic location of the asset. For example, a coal mining plant may be collocated with an electricity plant (Joskow 1988). Once sited, the coal mining and the electricity-producing assets are for all practical purposes immobile. Furthermore, in the case one was relocated, the other would likely have to relocate as well.

Second is *physical asset specificity*, in which one or several transacting parties make investments in equipment that involves design characteristics specific to the transaction. Because the technology acquires relation-specific characteristics, it may have lower economic value in alternative uses. For example, a supplier in the automobile industry may invest in customer-specific dies to stamp components (Klein, Crawford, and Alchian 1978).

Third is *human capital specificity*, in which investments in relationship-specific human capital often arise through various learning-by-doing processes (Harris and Helfat 1997). For example, software programmers may be required to commit their time to developing a company-specific proprietary programming language.

Fourth is *temporal specificity* that arises from interdependencies over time (Masten 1984). For example, because produce must be handled in a timely manner in the supply chain, it may be inefficient to run a highly fragmented supply chain that involves multiple organizations; instead, vertical integration of the different supply chain stages may be required as a safeguard (Bucheli, Mahoney, and Vaaler 2010).

Finally, *dedicated assets* are found in contexts where a supplier makes investments in production capacity with the aim of selling a substantial volume of output to a particular customer (Williamson 1985, 194). Even if these assets did not exhibit site or physical asset specificity, they would still constitute a relation-specific investment. If the contract in which the dedicated assets are involved were terminated prematurely, the supplier would be left with substantial excess capacity, which would be problematic even in the absence of physical asset specificity.

Stakeholder (and Stakeholder Analysis)

There are many constituencies that are, in one way or another, involved in the activities of an organization: employees, customers, suppliers, financiers, local communities, and the society more generally. But there is a specific category of constituencies who have, by virtue of becoming involved in the organization, made a wager of some kind on the organization's outcomes

(Orts and Strudler 2002). We reserve the label *stakeholder* to refer to these constituencies. We further define stakeholder in symmetrical terms: Two parties are *one another's stakeholders* if they have responsibilities toward one another and are interested in one another's success.

Providing equity financing to a firm by purchasing shares is a conspicuous example of a wager; therefore, shareholders are the obvious stakeholder in a limited liability company. However, there are also other, less conspicuous wagers. In general, any commitments that constituencies make to the specific organization constitute wagers that may merit the designer's attention. Employees who commit to the development of the organization's distinct *core competences* are effectively making a wager on the outcome that these core competences will be valuable in the future. If the core competences lose their value, so do employee commitments to specificity. Therefore, employees who have committed to specificity can be argued to have a legitimate residual interest comparable to that of the shareholders. Consequently, those employees who commit to specificity may require not only a salary in exchange for their time and their efforts but also a return on their investments to specificity. One governance option is to turn employees formally into residual claimants by means of an employee stock ownership program. Some corporations may go even further and offer stock options to all employees, not just executives (Oyer and Schaefer 2005).

In general, any constituency that has a legitimate residual interest in the organization should be considered a stakeholder. However, because not all wagers are the same, stakeholder status subscribes to degrees. The objective of a stakeholder analysis is to determine which constituencies have more at stake than others, and subsequently, devise the requisite governance structures that safeguard the cooperation of those with the most at stake.

The ultimate objective of a stakeholder analysis is to ensure that the wagers the organization needs are actually made. For example, if the organization's success hinges on its ability to attract equity financing, governance structures must be designed in a way that ensures that investors place their bets; if the organization depends heavily on organization-specific innovation and R&D, it must contract with its employees in a way that ensures sufficient commitments to specificity; and so on. If stakeholder governance fails and the requisite wagers are not made, the organization faces an underinvestment problem, which immediately jeopardizes the organization's viability.

Transaction Cost

Transaction costs include all *ex ante* (searching, drafting, and negotiating) and *ex post* (addressing unanticipated disturbances) costs associated with the execution of a contract. In simple transactions, transaction costs are negligible; buying a carton of milk from the grocery store is a representative example. In more complex relationships, transaction costs can be so substantial that they merit the designer's attention; a parts manufacturer that produces make- and model-specific components to the final assembler of automobiles is a representative example.

Whereas both *ex ante* and *ex post* costs are relevant, the latter tend to be more significant and merit more attention from the designer. Because complex contracts are often unavoidably incomplete, long-term relationships tend to involve the need for adaptation due to unanticipated disturbances that the *ex ante* contract did not, or simply could not, cover. Not being able to address such disturbances can be the source of significant *ex post* transaction costs. In general, the magnitude of transaction costs in exchange relationships tends to be associated with three main factors: (1) specificity, (2) frequency of transacting, and (3) uncertainty. Transaction costs tend to be higher at higher degrees of specificity, frequency, and uncertainty (Williamson 1985).

The relationship between transaction costs and governance decisions is, however, not straightforward. For example, even though increasing frequency of transacting does increase transaction costs, it also justifies the design of specialized governance structures that may in fact result in net gains even if the exchange relationship remained interorganizational.

The association between specificity and governance choice is more straightforward in that increasing specificity tends to associate with the choice of intraorganizational transacting. But even here, the designer must resist the temptation of following simple rules. One reason is that depending on the context, it may well be the case that specificity is not a given but a decision variable. For example, an industrial firm may be able to choose between using general-purpose and special-purpose technology in its production. If the firm wants to avoid carrying production equipment on its balance sheet, it may choose to contract with an external supplier that uses general-purpose equipment that can be readily modified by proper tooling to serve the buying firm. This is an important reminder that transaction costs being *associated with* specificity does not necessarily mean they are *driven by* specificity. Specificity may constitute a decision variable, not something the designer must take as a given (Riordan and Williamson 1985). As always, the designer's task is to engage in an analysis of the alternative governance options in the specific exchange context.

Value Creation vs. Value Capture (and Preappropriation vs. Postappropriation)

An automobile without defects is more valuable than one with defects; a fully recovered patient is more valuable than one who must be readmitted to the hospital; a one-time prison inmate is economically more valuable than a career criminal.

Value manifests itself in numerous ways in organizations and in the society more broadly. Some forms of value are unambiguous and can be assigned a monetary value, others are more elusive. But the idea that hospitals and prisons create value just like an automobile assembly plant does should not be too controversial. Further, the notion of *more valuable* in the context of prisons or hospitals does not require that we assess value in monetary terms. That lowering the number of readmissions in hospitals and recidivism rates in prisons are sources of value is salient without assigning monetary values to readmission and recidivism. Since we address efficiency in *comparative* terms, there is no need for *absolute* measurement of value. Instead, if there are two known, feasible alternatives one of which creates comparatively less waste than the other, then that option should be preferred no matter what absolute level of waste it generates.

A fundamental realization about efficient organization is that one can pursue efficiency without actually having to measure it in the conventional economic sense.

Who benefits from defect-free automobiles, recovered patients, and a released prisoner who never returns to prison? Who ultimately appropriates the value that is created is obviously an important question, but we propose it is in fact not central to efficient organization. The only assumption required is that value is distributed in a way that maintains the credibility of the organization in the eyes of those on whom it depends for value creation. But beyond this assumption, nothing else needs to be said or assumed about appropriation or value capture. Comparative efficiency analysis operates largely on the preappropriation, value-creation side of the organization.

A focus on value creation means that in the context of for-profit corporations, profit is less relevant than value added—profit is a residual and as such, a postappropriation measure of performance. As we proceed from the top line to the bottom line of an income statement, profit is what remains after all the appropriations have been made. Powerful stakeholders may be in a position to appropriate disproportionate amounts of value. Consequently, what remains at the end is more a reflection of the power dynamics of the appropriation process than efficient organization. Therefore, a corporation need not be profitable to be efficient, and efficiency does not ensure profitability.

Coff (1999, 120) offers two illustrative examples of value creation and appropriation not going hand in hand. After World War II,

> U.S. auto manufacturers clearly were generating [earnings] before intense foreign competition changed the nature of the game. Yet unions and management, as opposed to shareholders, appropriated a sizable portion of the [earnings]. Similarly, IBM assembled the strategic capabilities that built most of the modern personal computer industry. However, Intel and Microsoft were ultimately able to appropriate much of the associated [earnings].

These two examples aptly show that value appropriation occurs both within and across organizations. This book is *not* about how appropriation occurs.

Viability

An organization is viable when it has secured all the inputs it needs as well as the means by which the inputs are converted into outputs.

Some inputs are generic and can be purchased from input markets at negligible risk. As far as viability is concerned, the organization must secure sufficient financing to obtain these market inputs. Other inputs and, in particular, means of conversion are not readily available in the market; instead, they involve various degrees and kinds of specificity. In industrial production, for example, some parts and components required for final assembly must be engineered to customer specifications. Similarly, some parts of the production process can use off-the-shelf, general-purpose technologies, but others require the design of special-purpose equipment with low redeployability.

Any input, be it a component, conversion technology, or an employee skill designed for the specific organization, involves a wager of some kind. The organization's viability hinges on ensuring that all the requisite wagers are made.

Wagers come in many forms. Providers of equity financing make their wagers as they purchase shares in the company; inability to convince the investors to place their bets leads to underinvestment in equity, which jeopardizes viability in situations in which there are no alternatives to equity financing. Some employees make their wagers when they commit their time and their effort to organization-specific innovation and R&D; failure to convince employees to commit to such specificity leads to underinvestment in innovation and R&D, which may have devastating consequences for a growing high-technology firm. Finally, some suppliers make their wagers when they become dependent on the buyer through relation-specific investments; failure to convince the supplier to make such investments may jeopardize viability in contexts such as the automotive supply chain, where specialized suppliers are crucial for efficiency. The common denominator in all these commitments is that they are wagers on the *outcome* of the organization (Orts and Strudler 2002).

We propose that the central objective of governance is to establish the viability of the organization by ensuring that all the requisite wagers are made. To this end, the designer must analyze the type and the magnitude of all wagers made by the organization's constituencies, and subsequently, safeguard the central relationships by the appropriate governance structures. A systematic stakeholder analysis is aimed at achieving the objective of understanding all the wagers and their governance implications.

References

Adler, Paul S., and Bryan Borys. 1996. "Two Types of Bureaucracy: Enabling and Coercive." *Administrative Science Quarterly* 41, no. 1: 61–89.

Albert, Stuart, and David A. Whetten. 1985. "Organizational Identity." *Research in Organizational Behavior* 7: 263–95.

Alchian, Armen A., and Harold Demsetz. 1972. "Production, Information Costs, and Economic Organization." *American Economic Review* 62, no. 5: 777–95.

Alchian, Armen A., and Susan Woodward. 1988. "The Firm Is Dead; Long Live the Firm: A Review of Oliver E. Williamson's The Economic Institutions of Capitalism." *Journal of Economic Literature* 26, no. 1: 65–79.

Alonso, Ricardo, Wouter Dessein, and Niko Matouschek. 2008. "When Does Coordination Require Centralization?" *American Economic Review* 98, no. 1: 145–79.

Alston, Eric, Lee J. Alston, Bernardo Mueller, and Tomas Nonnenmacher. 2018. *Institutional and Organizational Analysis: Concepts and Applications.* Cambridge: Cambridge University Press.

Argyres, Nicholas, and Kyle J. Mayer. 2007. "Contract Design as a Firm Capability: An Integration of Learning and Transaction Cost Perspectives." *Academy of Management Review* 32, no. 4: 1060–77.

Argyres, Nicholas S., and Brian S. Silverman. 2004. "R&D, Organization Structure, and the Development of Corporate Technological Knowledge." *Strategic Management Journal* 25, no. 8–9: 929–58.

Balakrishnan, Srinivasan, and Birger Wernerfelt. 1986. "Technical Change, Competition and Vertical Integration." *Strategic Management Journal* 7, no. 4: 347–59.

Barnard, Chester I. 1938. *The Functions of the Executive.* Cambridge, MA: Harvard University Press.

Barney, Jay B. 1991. "Firm Resources and Sustained Competitive Advantage." *Journal of Management* 17, no. 1: 99–120.

Barzel, Yoram 1989. *Economic Analysis of Property Rights.* Cambridge: Cambridge University Press.

Bebchuk, Lucian A. 2003. "Why Firms Adopt Antitakeover Arrangements." *University of Pennsylvania Law Review* 152, no. 2: 713–53.

Bebchuk, Lucian A., John C. Coates, and Guhan Subramanian. 2002. "The Powerful Antitakeover Force of Staggered Boards: Theory, Evidence, and Policy." *Stanford Law Review* 54, no. 5: 887–951.

Bebchuk, Lucian A., and Alma Cohen. 2003. "Firm's Decisions Where to Incorporate." *Journal of Law & Economics* 46, no. 2: 383–425.

Bebchuk, Lucian A., and Roberto Tallarita. 2020. "The Illusory Promise of Stakeholder Governance." *Cornell Law Review* 106: 91–177.

Berle, Adolf A., and Gardiner C. Means. 1932. *The Modern Corporation and Private Property.* New York: Macmillan.

Bernstein, Ethan, and Nitin Nohria. 2016. *Note on Organizational Structure (9-491-083)*. Cambridge, MA: Harvard Business School.

Bhardwaj, Akhil, and Mikko Ketokivi. 2021. "Bilateral Dependency and Supplier Performance Ambiguity in Supply Chain Contracting: Evidence from the Railroad Industry." *Journal of Operations Management* 67, no. 1: 49–70.

Bhardwaj, Akhil, and Anastasia Sergeeva. Forthcoming. "Values-Based Trust as a Shift Parameter for Collective Organizing: The Case of Magnum Photos." *Journal of Management Studies*.

Blair, Margaret M., and Lynn A. Stout. 1999. "A Team Production Theory of Corporate Law." *Virginia Law Review* 85, no. 2: 247–328.

Blair, Margaret M., and Lynn A. Stout. 2001. "Director Accountability and the Mediating Role of the Corporate Board." *Washington University Law Review* 79, no. 2: 403–49.

Boardman, Michelle E. 2006. "*Contra Proferentem*: The Allure of Ambiguous Boilerplate." *Michigan Law Review* 104, no. 5: 1105–28.

Broom, Leonard, and Philip Selznick. 1955. *Sociology: A Text with Adapted Readings*. New York: Row, Peterson.

Brownlee, Hunter J. 1994. "The Shareholders' Agreement: A Contractual Alternative to Oppression as a Ground for Dissolution." *Stetson Law Review* 24, no. 2: 267–310.

Bucheli, Marcelo, Joseph T. Mahoney, and Paul M. Vaaler. 2010. "Chandler's Living History: The Visible Hand of Vertical Integration in Nineteenth Century America Viewed under a Twenty-First Century Transaction Costs Economics Lens." *Journal of Management Studies* 47, no. 5: 859–83.

Burns, Tom, and George M. Stalker. 1961. *The Management of Innovation*. London: Tavistock.

Caterpillar. 2021. *Proxy Statement*. Retrieved from investors.caterpillar.com/financials/sec-filings.

CDW Corporation. 2019. *Form 10-K Annual Report*. Retrieved from sec.gov/edgar.shtml.

Chandler, Alfred D. 1962. *Strategy and Structure: Chapters in the History of the American Industrial Enterprise*. Cambridge, MA: MIT Press.

Chandler, Alfred D. 1977. *The Visible Hand: The Managerial Revolution in American Business*. Cambridge, MA: Harvard University Press.

Chandler, Alfred D. 1990. *Scale and Scope: The Dynamics of Industrial Capitalism*. Cambridge, MA: Belknap Press.

Clark, Robert C. 1985. "Agency Costs versus Fiduciary Duties." In *Principals and Agents: The Structure of Business*, edited by John W. Pratt and Richard J. Zeckhauser, 55–80. Boston, MA: Harvard Business School Press.

Clegg, Stewart R., David Courpasson, and Nelson Phillips. 2006. *Power in Organizations*. Thousand Oaks, CA: SAGE.

Coase, Ronald H. 1937. "The Nature of the Firm." *Economica* 4, no. 16: 386–405.

Coff, Russell W. 1999. "When Competitive Advantage Doesn't Lead to Performance: The Resource-Based View and Stakeholder Bargaining Power." *Organization Science* 10, no. 2: 119–33.

Colburn, Kimberly. 2007. *The Art of Artistic Direction*. Eugene, OR: University of Oregon.

Cole, Robert E., and W. Richard Scott. 2000. *The Quality Movement & Organization Theory*. Thousand Oaks, CA: SAGE.

Commons, John R. 1934. *Institutional Economics*. Madison, WI: University of Wisconsin Press.

Cremers, K. J. Martijn, Vinay B. Nair, and Urs Peyer. 2008. "Takeover Defenses and Competition: The Role of Stakeholders." *Journal of Empirical Legal Studies* 5, no. 4: 791–818.

Cuypers, Ilya R. P., Jean-François Hennart, Brian S. Silverman, and Gokhan Ertug. 2021. "Transaction Cost Theory: Past Progress, Current Challenges, and Suggestions for the Future." *Academy of Management Annals* 15, no. 1: 111–50.

Cyert, Richard M., and James G. March. [1963] 1992. *A Behavioral Theory of the Firm.* 2nd ed. Englewood Cliffs, NJ: Prentice-Hall.

David, Paul A. 1985. "Clio and the Economics of QWERTY." *American Economic Review* 75, no. 2: 332–37.

Davidson, Carl. 1988. "Multiunit Bargaining in Oligopolistic Industries." *Journal of Labor Economics* 6, no. 3: 397–422.

DeAngelo, Harry, and Edward M. Rice. 1983. "Antitakeover Charter Amendments and Stockholder Wealth." *Journal of Financial Economics* 11, no. 1: 329–59.

Dearborn, DeWitt C., and Herbert A. Simon. 1958. "Selective Perception: A Note on the Departmental Identification of the Executive." *Sociometry* 21, no. 2: 140–44.

Dey, Aiyesha, and Joshua T. White. 2021. "Labor Mobility and Antitakeover Provisions." *Journal of Accounting and Economics* 71, no. 2: Article 101388.

DiIulio, John J. 1987. *Governing Prisons: A Comparative Study of Correctional Management.* New York: Free Press.

Dodd Jr, E. Merrick. 1932. "For Whom Are Corporate Managers Trustees?" *Harvard Law Review* 45, no. 7: 1145–63.

Drucker, Peter F. 1973. "On Managing the Public Service Institution." *The Public Interest* 33, no. 1: 43–60.

Ebrahim, Alnoor, Julie Battilana, and Johanna Mair. 2014. "The Governance of Social Enterprises: Mission Drift and Accountability Challenges in Hybrid Organizations." *Research in Organizational Behavior* 34, no. 1: 81–100.

Eccles, Robert G., and Harrison C. White. 1988. "Price and Authority in Inter-Profit Center Transactions." *American Journal of Sociology* 94, Suppl.: S17–S51.

Fama, Eugene F., and Michael C. Jensen. 1983a. "Separation of Ownership and Control." *Journal of Law and Economics* 26, no. 2: 301–25.

Fama, Eugene F., and Michael C. Jensen. 1983b. "Agency Problems and Residual Claims." *Journal of Law and Economics* 26, no. 2: 327–49.

Feyerabend, Paul. 1995. *Killing Time: The Autobiography of Paul Feyerabend.* Chicago, IL: University of Chicago Press.

Fisch, Jill E. 2018. "Governance by Contract: The Implications for Corporate Bylaws." *California Law Review* 106, no. 2: 373–409.

Fiss, Owen M. 1984. "Against Settlement." *Yale Law Journal* 93, no. 6: 1073–90.

Fuqua, Don. 1986. *Investigation of the Challenger Accident: Report of the Committee on Science and Technology, House of Representatives, Ninety-Ninth Congress, Second Session.* Washington, DC: US Government Printing Office.

Galbraith, Jay R. 1971. "Matrix Organization Designs." *Business Horizons* 14, no. 1: 29–40.

Galbraith, Jay R. 2002a. *Designing Organizations: An Executive Guide to Strategy, Structure, and Process.* Rev. ed. San Francisco, CA: Jossey-Bass.

Galbraith, Jay R. 2002b. "Organizing to Deliver Solutions." *Organizational Dynamics* 31, no. 2: 194–207.

Galbraith, Jay R. 2009. *Designing Matrix Organizations That Really Work.* San Francisco, CA: Jossey-Bass.

Galbraith, Jay R. 2014. *Designing Organizations: Strategy, Structure, and Process at the Business Unit and Enterprise Levels*. 3rd ed. San Francisco, CA: Jossey-Bass.

Galli, Jaime D. 2011. *Organizational Management in the Non-Profit Performing Arts: Exploring New Models of Structure, Management, and Leadership*. Eugene, OR: University of Oregon.

Gamble, John, Margaret Peteraf, and Arthur Thompson. 2021. *Essentials of Strategic Management: The Quest for Competitive Advantage*. 7th ed. New York: McGraw Hill.

Ghinger, John J. 1974. "Shareholders' Agreements for Closely Held Corporations: Special Tools for Special Circumstances." *University of Baltimore Law Review* 4, no. 2: 211–44.

Gioia, Dennis A., Shubha D. Patvardhan, Aimee L. Hamilton, and Kevin G. Corley. 2013. "Organizational Identity Formation and Change." *Academy of Management Annals* 7, no. 1: 123–92.

Glaeser, Edward L., and Andrei Shleifer. 2001. "Not-for-Profit Entrepreneurs." *Journal of Public Economics* 81, no. 1: 99–115.

Goldberg, Victor P. 1976. "Regulation and Administered Contracts." *Bell Journal of Economics* 7, no. 2: 426–48.

Gomery, Douglas. 2005. *The Hollywood Studio System: A History*. London: British Film Institute.

Goold, Michael, and Andrew Campbell. 2002a. *Designing Effective Organizations: How to Create Structured Networks*. San Francisco, CA: Jossey-Bass.

Goold, Michael, and Andrew Campbell. 2002b. "Do You Have a Well-Designed Organization?" *Harvard Business Review* 80, no. 2: 117–24.

Granovetter, Mark. 1985. "Economic Action and Social Structure: The Problem of Embeddedness." *American Journal of Sociology* 91, no. 3: 481–510.

Greenwood, Royston, Christine Oliver, Kerstin Sahlin, and Roy Suddaby, eds. 2008. *The SAGE Handbook of Organizational Institutionalism*. London: SAGE.

Gross, Malvern J., John H. McCarthy, and Nancy E. Shelmon. 2005. *Financial and Accounting Guide for Not-for-Profit Organizations*. New York: Wiley.

Grossman, Sanford J., and Oliver D. Hart. 1980. "Takeover Bids, the Free-Rider Problem, and the Theory of the Corporation." *Bell Journal of Economics* 11, no. 1: 42–69.

Grossman, Sanford J., and Oliver D. Hart. 1986. "The Costs and Benefits of Ownership: A Theory of Vertical and Lateral Integration." *Journal of Political Economy* 94, no. 4: 691–719.

Gulati, Ranjay. 2010. *Cisco Business Councils (2007): Unifying a Functional Enterprise with an Internal Governance System (Harvard Business School Case 9-409-062)*. Cambridge, MA: Harvard Business School.

Gulati, Ranjay, and Harbir Singh. 1998. "The Architecture of Cooperation: Managing Coordination Costs and Appropriation Concerns in Strategic Alliances." *Administrative Science Quarterly* 43, no. 4: 781–814.

Hamel, Gary. 2011. "First, Let's Fire All the Managers." *Harvard Business Review* 89, no. 12: 48–60.

Hansmann, Henry B. 1980. "The Role of Nonprofit Enterprise." *Yale Law Journal* 89, no. 5: 835–901.

Hansmann, Henry B. 1987. "The Effect of Tax Exemption and Other Factors on the Market Share of Nonprofit versus For-Profit Firms." *National Tax Journal* 40, no. 1: 71–82.

Harris, Dawn, and Constance Helfat. 1997. "Specificity in CEO Human Capital and Compensation." *Strategic Management Journal* 18, no. 11: 895–920.

Hart, Oliver. 1989. "An Economist's Perspective on the Theory of the Firm." *Columbia Law Review* 89, no. 7: 1757–74.

Hart, Oliver. 2003. "Incomplete Contracts and Public Ownership: Remarks, and an Application to Public-Private Partnerships." *Economic Journal* 113, March issue: C69–C76.

Hart, Oliver, Andrei Shleifer, and Robert W. Vishny. 1997. "The Proper Scope of Government: Theory and an Application to Prisons." *Quarterly Journal of Economics* 112, no. 4: 1127–61.

Hatch, Mary Jo, and Majken Schultz, eds. 2004. *Organizational Identity: A Reader.* Oxford: Oxford University Press.

Hayek, Friedrich A. 1945. "The Use of Knowledge in Society." *American Economic Review* 35, no. 4: 519–30.

Hirshleifer, David, and Sheridan Titman. 1992. "Share Tendering Strategies and the Success of Hostile Takeover Bids." *Journal of Political Economy* 98, no. 2: 295–324.

Holmström, Bengt R., and Jean Tirole. 1989. "The Theory of the Firm." In *Handbook of Industrial Organization*, edited by R. Schmalensee and R. D. Willig, 61–133. Amsterdam: North Holland.

HP. 2019. *Sustainable Impact Report.* Retrieved from investor.hp.com/governance/sustainability/.

HP. 2020. *Form 10-K Annual Report.* Retrieved from investor.hp.com/financials/sec-filings/.

Hughes, Everett C. 1939. "Institutions." In *An Outline of the Principles of Sociology*, edited by Robert E. Park, 283–346. New York: Barnes and Noble.

Illinois Department of Public Health. 2021. *COVID-19 Vaccination Plan.* Retrieved from https://dph.illinois.gov/covid19/vaccination-plan.html.

Jenoff, Pam. 2012. "Going Native: Incentive, Identity, and the Inherent Ethical Problem of In-House Counsel." *West Virginia Law Review* 114, no. 2: 725–57.

Jensen, Michael C. 1986. "Agency Costs of Free Cash Flow, Corporate Finance, and Takeovers." *American Economic Review* 76, no. 2: 323–29.

Jensen, Michael C. 2001. "Value Maximization, Stakeholder Theory, and the Corporate Objective Function." *Journal of Applied Corporate Finance* 14, no. 3: 8–21.

Jensen, Michael C. 2002. "Value Maximization, Stakeholder Theory, and the Corporate Objective Function." *Business Ethics Quarterly* 12, no. 2: 235–56.

Jensen, Michael C., and William H. Meckling. 1976. "Theory of the Firm: Managerial Behavior, Agency Costs and Ownership Structure." *Journal of Financial Economics* 3, no. 4: 305–60.

Jensen, Michael C., and Richard S. Ruback. 1983. "The Market for Corporate Control: The Scientific Evidence." *Journal of Financial Economics* 11, no. 1: 5–50.

Johnson, William C., Jonathan M. Karpoff, and Sangho Yi. 2015. "The Bonding Hypothesis of Takeover Defenses: Evidence from IPO Firms." *Journal of Financial Economics* 117, no. 2: 307–32.

Joskow, Paul L. 1988. "Asset Specificity and the Structure of Vertical Relationships." *Journal of Law, Economics & Organization* 4, no. 1: 95–117.

Kahneman, Daniel. 2011. *Thinking, Fast and Slow.* New York: Farrar, Straus and Giroux.

Kahneman, Daniel, Paul Slovic, and Amos Tversky. 1982. *Judgment under Uncertainty: Heuristics and Biases.* Cambridge: Cambridge University Press.

Kaplan, Robert S., and David P. Norton. 2008. *The Execution Premium: Linking Strategy to Operations for Competitive Advantage.* Cambridge, MA: Harvard Business School Press.

Keski-Valkama, Alice, Eila Sailas, Markku Eronen, Anna-Maija Koivisto, Jouko Lönnqvist, and Riittakerttu Kaltiala-Heino. 2007. "A 15-Year National Follow-Up: Legislation Is Not Enough to Reduce the Use of Seclusion and Restraint." *Social Psychiatry and Psychiatric Epidemiology* 42, no. 9: 747–52.

Kesner, Idalene F., and Roy B. Johnson. 1990. "An Investigation of the Relationship between Board Composition and Stockholder Suits." *Strategic Management Journal* 11, no. 4: 327–36.

Ketokivi, Mikko, and Xavier Castañer. 2004. "Strategic Planning as an Integrative Device." *Administrative Science Quarterly* 49, no. 3: 337–65.

Ketokivi, Mikko, and Joseph T. Mahoney. 2017. "Transaction Cost Economics as a Theory of the Firm, Management, and Governance." *Oxford Research Encyclopedia of Business and Management*, edited by Ramon J. Aldag. Oxford: Oxford University Press.

Ketokivi, Mikko, and Joseph T. Mahoney. 2020. "Transaction Cost Economics as a Theory of Supply Chain Efficiency." *Production and Operations Management* 29, no. 4: 1011–31.

Kirkpatrick, David, and Tyler Maroney. 1998. "The Second Coming of Apple." *Fortune* 138, no. 9: 86–92.

Klein, Benjamin, Robert G. Crawford, and Armen A. Alchian. 1978. "Vertical Integration, Appropriable Rents, and the Competitive Contracting Process." *Journal of Law and Economics* 21, no. 2: 297–326.

Klein, Peter G., Joseph T. Mahoney, Anita M. McGahan, and Christos N. Pitelis. 2012. "Who Is in Charge? A Property Rights Perspective on Stakeholder Governance." *Strategic Organization* 10, no. 3: 304–15.

Knight, Frank H. 1941. "Anthropology and Economics." *Journal of Political Economy* 49, no. 2: 247–68.

Larcker, David, and Brian Tayan. 2015. *Corporate Governance Matters: A Closer Look at Organizational Choices and Their Consequences.* 2nd ed. Old Tappan, NJ: Pearson Education.

Leavitt, Harold J. 2005. *Top Down: Why Hierarchies Are Here to Stay and How to Manage Them Effectively.* Boston, MA: Harvard Business School Press.

Lee, Michael Y., and Amy C. Edmondson. 2017. "Self-Managing Organizations: Exploring the Limits of Less-Hierarchical Organizing." *Research in Organizational Behavior* 37, no. 1: 35–58.

Leslie, Christopher R. 2014. "Antitrust Made (Too) Simple." *Antitrust Law Journal* 79, no. 3: 917–40.

Levitt, Barbara, and James G. March. 1988. "Organizational Learning." *Annual Review of Sociology* 14, no. 1: 319–40.

Liebowitz, Stan J., and Stephen E. Margolis. 1990. "The Fable of the Keys." *Journal of Law & Economics* 33, no. 1: 1–25.

Liu, Tingting, and J. Harold Mulherin. 2019. "How Has Takeover Competition Changed over Time?" *Journal of Applied Corporate Finance* 31, no. 1: 81–94.

Lowe, Katherine E., Joe Zein, Umur Hatipoğlu, and Amy Attaway. 2021. "Association of Smoking and Cumulative Pack-Year Exposure with COVID-19 Outcomes in the Cleveland Clinic COVID-19 Registry." *JAMA Internal Medicine* 181, no. 5: 709–11.

Mace, Myles. 1971. *Directors: Myth and Reality.* Cambridge, MA: Harvard University Press.

Macher, Jeffrey T., and Barak D. Richman. 2008. "Transaction Cost Economics: An Assessment of Empirical Research in the Social Sciences." *Business and Politics* 10, no. 1: 1–63.

Mahoney, Joseph T. 2002. "The Relevance of Chester I. Barnard's Teachings to Contemporary Management Education: Communicating the Aesthetics of Management." *International Journal of Organization Theory and Behavior* 5, no. 1: 159–72.

Manne, Henry G. 1965. "Mergers and the Market for Corporate Control." *Journal of Political Economy* 73, no. 2: 110–20.

March, James G., and Herbert A. Simon. 1993. *Organizations*. 2nd ed. New York: Wiley.

Masten, Scott E. 1984. "The Organization of Production: Evidence from the Aerospace Industry." *Journal of Law and Economics* 27, no. 2: 403–17.

Masten, Scott E., and Edward A. Snyder. 1993. "*United States versus United Shoe Machinery Corporation*: On the Merits." *Journal of Law & Economics* 36, no. 1: 33–70.

McNamara, Gerry, Paul M. Vaaler, and Cynthia Devers. 2003. "Same as It Ever Was: The Search for Evidence of Increasing Hypercompetition." *Strategic Management Journal* 24, no. 3: 261–78.

Meyer, John W., and Brian Rowan. 1977. "Institutionalized Organizations: Formal Structure as Myth and Ceremony." *American Journal of Sociology* 83, no. 2: 340–63.

Milgrom, Paul, and John Roberts. 1990. "The Economics of Modern Manufacturing: Technology, Strategy, and Organization." *American Economic Review* 80, no. 3: 511–28.

Milgrom, Paul, and John Roberts. 1992. *Economics, Organization & Management*. Upper Saddle River, NJ: Prentice-Hall.

Mulherin, J. Harold, Jeffry M. Netter, and Annette B. Poulsen. 2017. "The Evidence on Mergers and Acquisitions: A Historical and Modern Report." In *The Handbook of the Economics of Corporate Governance*, edited by Benjamin E. Hermalin and Michael S. Weisbach, 235–90. North-Holland: Elsevier.

Neste. 2020. *Annual Report*. Retrieved from neste.com/for-media/material/annual-reports.

North, Douglass C. 1991. "Institutions." *Journal of Economic Perspectives* 5, no. 1: 97–112.

Organisation for Co-operation and Economic Development. 2015. *G20/OECD Principles of Corporate Governance*. 3rd ed. Paris: OECD.

Orts, Eric W. 1992. "Beyond Shareholders: Interpreting Corporate Constituency Statutes." *George Washington Law Review* 61, no. 1: 14–135.

Orts, Eric W., and Alan Strudler. 2002. "The Ethical and Environmental Limits of Stakeholder Theory." *Business Ethics Quarterly* 12, no. 2: 215–33.

Oyer, Paul, and Scott Schaefer. 2005. "Why Do Some Firms Give Stock Options to All Employees? An Empirical Examination of Alternative Theories." *Journal of Financial Economics* 76, no. 1: 99–133.

Parmar, Bidhan, R. Edward Freeman, Jeffrey S. Harrison, Andrew C. Wicks, Lauren Purnell, and Simone de Colle. 2010. "Stakeholder Theory: The State of the Art." *Academy of Management Annals* 4, no. 1: 403–45.

Penrose, Edith T. 1959. *The Theory of the Growth of the Firm*. Oxford: Oxford University Press.

Penrose, Edith T. 1995. *The Theory of the Growth of the Firm*. 3rd ed. Oxford: Oxford University Press.

Pfeffer, Jeffrey. 1987. "A Resource Dependence Perspective on Intercorporate Relations." In *Intercorporate Relations: The Structural Analysis of Business*, edited by Mark Mizruchi and Michael Schwartz, 25–55. Cambridge: Cambridge University Press.

Pfeffer, Jeffrey, and Gerald R. Salancik. 1978. *The External Control of Organizations: A Resource Dependence Perspective*. New York: Harper & Row.

Phillips, Robert A., and Joel Reichart. 2000. "The Environment as a Stakeholder? A Fairness-Based Approach." *Journal of Business Ethics* 23, no. 2: 185–97.

Pindur, Wolfgang, Sandra E. Rogers, and Pan Suk Kim. 1995. "The History of Management: A Global Perspective." *Journal of Management History* 1, no. 1: 59–77.

Pollman, Elizabeth. 2019. "Startup Governance." *University of Pennsylvania Law Review* 168, no. 1: 155–221.

Porter, Michael E. 1985. *Competitive Advantage: Creating and Sustaining Superior Performance*. New York: Free Press.

Powell, W. W., and P. J. DiMaggio, eds. 1991. *The New Institutionalism in Organizational Analysis*. Chicago, IL: University of Chicago Press.

Prahalad, C. K., and G. Hamel. 1990. "The Core Competence of the Corporation." *Harvard Business Review* 68, no. 3: 79–91.

Pratt, Katherine. 2000. "The Debt-Equity Distinction in a Second-Best World." *Vanderbilt Law Review* 53, no. 4: 1055–158.

Pucker, Kenneth P. 2022. "The Myth of Sustainable Fashion." *Harvard Business Review*. An online essay retrieved from hbr.org/2022/01/the-myth-of-sustainable-fashion.

Rawls, John. 1999. *A Theory of Justice*. Rev. ed. Cambridge, MA: Belknap Press.

Real Madrid. 2019. *Corporate Social Responsibility and Sustainability Report*. Retrieved from realmadrid.com/media/document/corporate-social-responsibility-2019-20.pdf.

Rechner, Paula L., and Dan R. Dalton. 1991. "CEO Duality and Organizational Performance: A Longitudinal Analysis." *Strategic Management Journal* 12, no. 2: 155–60.

Rindfleisch, Aric, and Jan B. Heide. 1997. "Transaction Cost Analysis: Past, Present, and Future Applications." *Journal of Marketing* 61, no. 4: 30–54.

Riordan, Michael H., and Oliver E. Williamson. 1985. "Asset Specificity and Economic Organization." *International Journal of Industrial Organization* 3, no. 4: 365–78.

Rogers, William P., Neil A. Armstrong, David C. Acheson, Eugene E. Covert, Richard P. Feynman, Robert B. Hotz, Donald J. Kutyna, Sally K. Ride, Robert W. Rummel, Joseph F. Sutter, Arthur B. C. Walker Jr., Albert D. Wheelon, and Charles E. Yeager. 1986. *Report of the Presidential Commission on the Space Shuttle Challenger Accident*. Washington, DC: US Government Printing Office.

Ross, Stephen A. 1973. "The Economic Theory of Agency: The Principal's Problem." *American Economic Review* 63, no. 2: 134–39.

Rousseau, Denise M., and Zipi Shperling. 2003. "Pieces of the Action: Ownership and the Changing Employment Relationship." *Academy of Management Review* 28, no. 4: 553–70.

Rousseau, Denise M., and Zipi Shperling. 2004. "Ownership and the Changing Employment Relationship: Why Stylized Notions of Labor No Longer Generally Apply—A Reply to Zardkoohi and Paetzold." *Academy of Management Review* 29, no. 4: 562–69.

Rubin, Paul H. 1978. "The Theory of the Firm and the Structure of the Franchise Contract." *Journal of Law and Economics* 21, no. 1: 223–33.

Ryan, Harley E., and Roy A. Wiggins. 2004. "Who Is in Whose Pocket? Director Compensation, Board Independence, and Barriers to Effective Monitoring." *Journal of Financial Economics* 73, no. 3: 497–524.

Santos, Filipe M., and Kathleen M. Eisenhardt. 2005. "Organizational Boundaries and Theories of Organization." *Organization Science* 16, no. 5: 491–508.

Sawhney, Mohanbir, Robert C. Wolcott, and Inigo Arroniz. 2006. "The 12 Different Ways for Companies to Innovate." *MIT Sloan Management Review* 47, no. 3: 75–81.

Selznick, Philip. 1957. *Leadership in Administration.* New York: Harper & Row.

Selznick, Philip. 1996. "Institutionalism 'Old' and 'New.'" *Administrative Science Quarterly* 41, no. 2: 270–77.

Shelanski, Howard A., and Peter G. Klein. 1995. "Empirical Research in Transaction Cost Economics: A Review and Assessment." *Journal of Law, Economics, and Organization* 11, no. 2: 335–61.

Shleifer, Andrei, and Lawrence H. Summers. 1988. "Breach of Trust in Hostile Takeovers." In *Corporate Takeovers: Causes and Consequences*, edited by Alan J. Auerbach, 33–56. Chicago, IL: University of Chicago Press.

Silverman, Brian S. 2002. "Organizational economics." In *The Blackwell Companion to Organizations*, edited by Joel A. C. Baum, 467–93. Oxford: Blackwell.

Simon, Herbert A. 1997. *Administrative Behavior.* 4th ed. New York: Macmillan.

Starik, Mark. 1995. "Should Trees Have Managerial Standing? Toward Stakeholder Status for Non-Human Nature." *Journal of Business Ethics* 14, no. 3: 207–17.

Stinchcombe, Arthur. 1965. "Social Structure and Organization." In *Handbook of Organizations*, edited by James March, 142–93. Chicago, IL: Rand McNally.

Stipanowich, Thomas J. 2010. "Arbitration: The 'new litigation.'" *Illinois Law Review* 10, no. 1: 1–60.

Sumner, D. A., and J. V. Balagtas. 2002. "An Overview of U.S. Dairy Policy." In *Encyclopedia of Dairy Sciences*, edited by H. Roginski, J. W. Fuquay and P. F. Fox. London: Academic Press.

Sundaramurthy, Chamu, James M. Mahoney, and Joseph T. Mahoney. 1997. "Board Structure, Antitakeover Provisions, and Stockholder Wealth." *Strategic Management Journal* 18, no. 3: 231–45.

Swedberg, Richard. 1990. *Economics and Sociology: Redefining Their Boundaries.* Princeton, NJ: Princeton University Press.

Thompson, James D. 1967. *Organizations in Action: Social Science Bases of Administrative Theory.* New York: McGraw-Hill.

Turbide, Johanne, and Claude Laurin. 2014. "Governance in the Arts and Culture Nonprofit Sector: Vigilance or Indifference?" *Administrative Sciences* 4, no. 4: 413–31.

UAW-GM. 2015. *Agreement between the UAW and GENERAL MOTORS LLC.* Retrieved from uaw.org/uaw-auto-bargaining/generalmotors/.

University of Illinois. 2020. *Annual Financial Report.* Retrieved from obfs.uillinois.edu/about-obfs/annual-reports/.

Volkswagen Group. 2020. *Annual Report.* Retrieved from annualreport2020. volkswagenag.com.

von Wright, Georg H. 1963. "Practical Inference." *Philosophical Review* 72, no. 2: 159–79.

Wasserman, Noam. 2012. *The Founder's Dilemmas.* Princeton, NJ: Princeton University Press.

Weick, Karl E. 1995. *Sensemaking in Organizations.* Thousand Oaks, CA: SAGE.

Weingast, Barry R., and William J. Marshall. 1988. "The Industrial Organization of Congress; or, Why Legislatures, Like Firms, Are Not Organized as Markets." *Journal of Political Economy* 96, no. 1: 132–63.

Wilkins, David B. 2012. "Is the In-House Counsel Movement Going Global? A Preliminary Assessment of the Role of Internal Counsel in Emerging Economies." *Wisconsin Law Review* 2012, no. 2: 251–304.

Williamson, Oliver E. 1975. *Markets and Hierarchies: Analysis and Antitrust Implications*. New York: Free Press.

Williamson, Oliver E. 1979. "Transaction-Cost Economics: The Governance of Contractual Relations." *Journal of Law and Economics* 22, no. 2: 233–61.

Williamson, Oliver E. 1983. "Credible Commitments: Using Hostages to Support Exchange." *American Economic Review* 73, no. 4: 519–40.

Williamson, Oliver E. 1985. *The Economic Institutions of Capitalism: Firms, Markets, Relational Contracting*. New York: Free Press.

Williamson, Oliver E. 1988. "Corporate Finance and Corporate Governance." *Journal of Finance* 43, no. 3: 567–91.

Williamson, Oliver E. 1991. "Comparative Economic Organization: The Analysis of Discrete Structural Alternatives." *Administrative Science Quarterly* 36, no. 2: 269–96.

Williamson, Oliver E. 1994. "Transaction Cost Economics and Organization Theory." In *The Handbook of Economic Sociology*, edited by Neil J. Smelser and Richard Swedberg, 77–107. Princeton, NJ: Princeton University Press.

Williamson, Oliver E. 1996. *The Mechanisms of Governance*. Oxford: Oxford University Press.

Williamson, Oliver E. 1999. "Public and Private Bureaucracies: A Transaction Cost Economics Perspective." *Journal of Law, Economics & Organization* 15, no. 1: 306–42.

Williamson, Oliver E. 2000. "The New Institutional Economics: Taking Stock, Looking Ahead." *Journal of Economic Literature* 38, no. 3: 595–613.

Williamson, Oliver E. 2002a. "The Merger Guidelines of the U.S. Department of Justice: In Perspective. Talk given at the 20th anniversary of the adoption of the 1982 Merger Guidelines, June 20, 2002, The Antitrust Division of the US Department of Justice. Retrieved from http://www.justice.gov/atr/hmerger/11257.htm.

Williamson, Oliver E. 2002b. "The Theory of the Firm as Governance Structure: From Choice to Contract." *Journal of Economic Perspectives* 16, no. 3: 171–95.

Williamson, Oliver E. 2008. "Corporate Boards of Directors: In Principle and in Practice." *Journal of Law, Economics, & Organization* 24, no. 2: 247–72.

Wilson, James Q. 1989. *Bureaucracy*. New York: Basic Books.

Wolf, W. B. 1973. *Conversations with Chester I. Barnard (ILR Paperback Series No 12)*. Ithaca, NY: Cornell University.

Worley, Christopher G., and Edward E. Lawler, III. 2006. "Designing Organizations That Are Built to Change." *MIT Sloan Management Review* 48, no. 1: 19–23.

Wynn, Rolf. 2004. "Psychiatric Inpatients' Experiences with Restraint." *Journal of Forensic Psychiatry & Psychology* 15, no. 1: 124–44.

Index